legislation a decade later. Whitfield examines how the Till incident invaded the consciences of individual blacks and whites across the country — from W.E.B. DuBois and William Faulkner to Muhammad Ali, Bob Dylan, and Julius Lester. He explores the callousness of the Eisenhower administration and some legislators in Washington in the face of racial unrest, and shows how black organizations helped ignite a nation to the call for the just and humane treatment of all its citizens.

Today, when urban and racial tensions give rise to renewed confrontation and recriminations, the Emmett Till case continues to symbolize the lethal force of racism and to galvanize Americans to combat its dreadful legacy and pursue justice for all.

STEPHEN J. WHITFIELD is professor and chairperson of American studies at Brandeis University and holds the Max Richter Chair in American Civilization.

A Death in the Delta

A
DEATH
IN THE DELTA
THE STORY OF
EMMETT TILL

STEPHEN J. WHITFIELD

93-467

THE FREE PRESS
A Division of Macmillan, Inc.
NEW YORK

Collier Macmillan Publishers
LONDON

The Free Press
A Division of Macmillan, Inc.
866 Third Avenue, New York, N.Y. 10022

Collier Macmillan Canada, Inc.

Printed in the United States of America

printing number
1   2   3   4   5   6   7   8   9   10

Library of Congress Cataloging-in-Publication Data

Whitfield, Stephen J.
   A death in the Delta : the story of Emmett Till / Stephen J.
Whitfield.
     p. cm.
   Includes bibliographical references and index.
   ISBN 0-02-935121-9
   1. Southern States—Race relations. 2. Racism—Southern States—
History—20th century. 3. Milam, J. W.—Trials, litigation, etc.
4. Trials (Murder)—Mississippi—Sumner. 5. Till, Emmett,
1941–1955. 6. Afro-Americans—Mississippi. I. Title.
E185.61.W63 1988
345.73′02523—dc19
[347.3052523]   88-16328
                                                CIP

To Lee
"Ce n'est qu'un début"

Contents

Preface

In 1954 a Mississippi circuit court judge named Tom P. Brady became the intellectual godfather of the Citizens' Councils with a vitriolic speech that was later expanded into a pamphlet. Written in ten days, *Black Monday* was a denunciation of the *Brown* v. *Board of Education* decision that had been rendered that May. Brady, who was a Yale-educated native of Mississippi and later a member of its supreme court, warned in addresses in Greenwood and Indianola that the Supreme Court opinion would encourage the disruption and breach of the codes that prohibited male-female relations across the color line. In one typically lurid passage, he expressed his horror of such relations by apparently comparing blacks to chimpanzees. In another he prophesied awful racial violence: "The fulminate which will discharge the blast will be the young negro schoolboy. . . . The supercilious, glib young negro, who has sojourned in Chicago or New York, and who considers the counsel of his elders archaic, will perform an obscene act, or make an obscene remark, or a vile overture or assault upon some white girl."[1]

Judge Brady's prediction seemed to be fulfilled the following August, when the mutilated body of a black teenager was recovered from the Tallahatchie River. The national press reported that Emmett Till had been murdered for whistling at a white Mississippi woman, whose putative avengers—her husband and his half-brother—were quickly acquitted by an all-white jury. The case caused considerable national excitement and even attracted international attention. Only a year and a half after the Supreme Court had invalidated racial segregation in public schools, both the teenager's "crime" and his punishment seemed an atavism, an incongruity in the modern era, the definitive expression of Southern racism, the lethal but logical culmination of the Jim Crow system itself. If that was the extreme point to which white supremacy led, then the regional arrangement of race relations that had been consolidated after the Civil War and Reconstruction was revealed at its most palpably unjust—and hence at its most vulnerable.

The viciousness of the murder of Emmett Till spurred efforts to accelerate the tempo of civil rights advances for Southern blacks. The case therefore deserves analysis for its function in promoting the liquidation of legally enforced racial segregation after the 1950s. Scattered evidence also indicates the impact that both the murder of Till and the acquittal of the defendants exerted upon Southern Negroes, some of whom matured into activists in the struggle against Southern racism in the 1960s.

At least three thousand blacks have been lynched in the United States since Emancipation. But in addition to the terrible crime perpetrated against those whose lives were cut short by torture and terror, the victims have also suffered oblivion. The general public can perhaps identify, or at least dimly recall, only one of them. Almost nobody knows their names—except that of Emmett Till (1941–55). Why the memory of his brief life and his ugly death cannot be erased is ultimately the subject of this book.

I distinctly remember the moment when I first learned of his fate. Waiting on my piano teacher's porch, I was leafing through a copy of *Look* magazine when I came across the story of Till's death; it was searing. He had been only a year older than I when he was murdered in the region where I had been born and raised, and though he was black, it was not difficult to recoil from the horror that had befallen him. The crime was so astonishing in its malevolence, the provocation of which he was accused so harmless, the whole atmosphere of vindictive racism so unjust, the impunity that his killers enjoyed so unnatural that reading about the Till case stabbed home an early proof of the injustice that permeates human experience. This book has been written in the hope that fuller knowledge can salvage some meaning from a pointless death in the Mississippi Delta, and to discover whether any redemptive value has emerged in its aftermath. Nothing can serve as recompense for the loss of a life. But scholarship is partly based on the premise that ignorance and indifference and forgetfulness are worse than, say, the satisfaction of curiosity, if we are ever to wrest purpose and value from the annals of our species.

Since this book is devoted to a single historical incident, I take some comfort in hoping that something akin to Paul Valéry's remark about poetic composition may be applicable to writing about the past as well: precision may be more difficult to achieve than profundity. Of course these two ideals are hardly incompatible, and only with a certain depth of insight can an author know how to select the facts and arrange a satisfactory depiction of what once might have happened. Precision can yield its own profundity as well, for an author's interpretations cannot foreclose the reader's own discerning gloss on the text, the possibility that larger as well as divergent meanings can be found.

Nevertheless, though the wide ramifications of the Till case should be apparent in the text that follows, the reader may be struck by how localized it is. *A Death in the Delta* is not a general history of lynching in microcosm, nor is it an examination of the rape complex, nor is it intended as more than an illustration of the fatal operations of white supremacy. I have tried only to be faithful to the relevant facts of the case, to elucidate its impact, and then to consider its significance.

The scope of this book is not regional but is primarily confined to Mississippi, which one of its sons, David Herbert Donald, has called "such a distinctive and peculiar place, with a tenacious hold upon its natives even after they have long left the state."[2] The intensity of white racial attitudes in its Black Belt counties may have obscured for too long the diversity of the rest of the South. But such Negrophobia also did much to influence the public culture of the state and perhaps even the region, and that partly explains why the Till case has appeared to bear such symbolic weight. For, until recently, the great bulk of the white citizens of Mississippi seemed dedicated to assuming the heaviest burdens of the Southern past, to being bewitched beyond reason and common sense by what a character in a postbellum novel by George Washington Cable called "the shadow of the Ethiopian."[3] One teenager violated the crucial feature of the *code noir* in that particular locale—a state that seemed for so long to be afflicted with shivers of irrepressible guilt and with the most implacable curses. The consequences of that violation were therefore lethal, and its overtones reverberant. That is why the story of Emmett Till did not end with his death.

Acknowledgments

The research that I have conducted has not blurred the face of evil, though scholarly investigation has shown those 1955 events to have been more complicated—hence more intriguing—than I could have imagined. For me the Till case is now like those diabolical puzzle boxes with false bottoms that remain wrapped in mystery, that elude final resolution and certainty. Nevertheless I deeply appreciate the skill and courtesy of librarians and archivists at the John Davis Williams Library at the University of Mississippi and at the interlibrary loan desk of Goldfarb–Farber Library at Brandeis University. Lea Walker of the Afro-American Communities Project of the National Museum of American History was helpful in providing and Xeroxing material, as was Helen Ritter of the American Jewish Committee. The Mazer Fund for Faculty Research at Brandeis University also permitted me to spend a week in Mississippi, an opportunity for which I am thankful. Mrs. Martha Hunt Huie, whose late husband had written that article in *Look*, was a gracious hostess in Memphis and was most generous in making her personal papers available to me. Emmett Till's mother, Mrs. Mamie T. Mobley, did not respond to my requests for an interview, however, and this book was written without her cooperation.

In Joseph Boskin, Lawrence J. Friedman, James O. Horton, Lois E. Horton, Richard H. King, David M. Oshinsky, David Starr, and Michael Tierney, I have been fortunate in attaching myself to friends who also proved themselves keen and perceptive critics of earlier versions of this work. The comments of Dan T. Carter were also quite thoughtful and invaluable. Raymond O. Arsenault recalls having donated the idea for this work, a paternity claim I have no inclination to dispute; I thank him. The help of Donald Altschiller has been exceptional. It was also beneficial to present an earlier and much shorter version of this work to the graduate students in the History of American Civilization program at Brandeis.

My literary agent, Gerard F. McCauley, has been decisive in transforming a manuscript into a book. For the same reason I am grateful to Joyce Seltzer, senior editor of The Free Press. The generous interest of Sam and Marjorie Oolie and Howard and Barbara Rich in this project is also a pleasure to acknowledge; they are true patrons of learning.

Obstinately loyal support and cheerful encouragement are among the attributes of my wife. Herself a student of history, she offered valuable advice, judgment, and attentiveness. In love and appreciation, this book is dedicated to her.

O N E

The Ideology of Lynching

The seamless web of history must be broken somewhere, and I am breaking it here to relate Till's story. In a sense the Till case has its distant origins in the establishment of slavery in the American South. Carl Degler, one of the very few American scholars who actually practices comparative history, has noted that because the region was located outside the tropics, the South became the only slave society in the Western Hemisphere in which whites outnumbered blacks. The West Indies, Brazil, and other places in Latin America attracted relatively fewer European settlers and even fewer white women; and the resultant imbalance created demographic pressure toward interracial sexual relations and marriage. Without similar incentives to cushion the shocks of the predominance of so many Africans brought in bondage, whites in the American South were more free to develop an ideology that underscored their own superiority and that imposed rigid barriers separating them from blacks.[1]

The liquidation of slavery and the end of Reconstruction challenged the white South to redefine the character of race relations, and it is in the late nineteenth century that the genesis of the Till case can be most clearly discerned. For the victim as well as his murderers were participants in a more vast and portentous historical drama than they could ever have realized. They were caught up in the destiny of an image—the black rapist—that does not fully emerge in Southern white mythology much earlier than the late 1880s.[2] It was then that a frenzied ideological attack on miscegenation was inaugurated, for social Darwinism spread the fear among

1

whites that marriage or sexual intimacy with blacks would degrade and eventually extinguish Anglo-Saxon civilization itself. Blacks themselves were depicted as still scarcely more than savages, as an inferior race incapable of genuine equality—or of sexual restraint. The Virginia historian Phillip Alexander Bruce lent his authority to the view that black men found "something strangely alluring and seductive ... in the appearance of the white woman; they are aroused and stimulated by its foreignness to their experience of sexual pleasures, and it moves them to gratify their lust at any cost and in spite of every obstacle."[3]

In 1892, two years after the new Mississippi constitution had defined a Negro as anyone with at least one Negro great-grandparent, the state legislature made it a crime, punishable by up to five hundred dollars and ten years in the penitentiary, for any citizen or resident of the state to "cohabit, or be guilty of one single act of intercourse," across the color line. In 1921 further legislation prohibited anyone from even *advocating* or *suggesting* "social equality or ... intermarriage between whites and Negroes." The maximum penalty was a five-hundred-dollar fine or six months' imprisonment, or both.[4] The fear of black male sexuality seemed to compel the crystallization of a closed society, for miscegenation posed the ultimate challenge to the integrity and stability of the order that white Americans—especially Southerners—had created.

The self-contradictory ideology of white supremacy—which simultaneously defined the black male as inferior yet somehow irresistible—was partly transcended by the horror that the black male posed in the guise of an attacker. Thus all forms of social equality had to be prohibited, lest the wrong message be communicated. "To the ignorant and brutal young Negro," the novelist Thomas Nelson Page argued in 1904, social equality "signifies but one thing: the opportunity to enjoy, equally with white men, the privilege of cohabiting with white women." This presumed insight into black motives "will explain, in part, the universal and furious hostility of the South to even the least suggestion of social equality."[5]

Such fears triggered the feverish imagination of popular writers like Thomas Dixon, whose best-selling novels *The Clansman* and *The Leopard's Spots* made the danger of black sexual violation an indelible image in his native region—and elsewhere. The emotional center of such works has been aptly located in Louise Westling's recent criticism of Southern literature. She demonstrates that in

The Clansman (1905), for example, "the climactic turn in Dixon's plot comes when a mother and daughter who represent the most radiant qualities of antebellum life commit suicide to escape the shame of the daughter's rape by a black man. . . . When the white male leaders of the town learn of the event, they see it as the ultimate degradation of their culture. . . . " Professor Westling then explains that "these men dedicate themselves to revenge in a strange ritual substituting the blood of the dead women and the water of the local river for the blood of Christ. . . . This sacrifice rouses the assembled host to execute justice upon the rapist and ultimately to restore order. . . . "[6] Such fierce acts of white violence were putatively designed to secure a social order anchored in race and to affirm that the black criminal deserved whatever fiendish punishment the righteous could inflict. For the rape of a white woman went beyond the ordinary criminal propensity that was increasingly ascribed to once-docile and agreeable former slaves. And such rituals of vengeance as the North Carolina novelist described were manifestly culture-specific.

These lurid views were hardly confined to popular literature, however; they saturated the public culture of the fin-de-siècle South and were to have lethal consequences. Consider, for example, the inner demons of South Carolina governor and later United States senator "Pitchfork" Ben Tillman, whose cultivation and learning did not inhibit him during a 1892 gubernatorial campaign from specifying the "one crime that warrants lynching; and Governor as I am, I would lead a mob to lynch the negro who ravishes a white woman."[7] Indeed, Tillman *encouraged* this breach of law and order against any black for the alleged rape of a white woman. The intensity of his feelings on the subject may well have been a product of his own particular background. During his childhood, Tillman's mother had owned thirty African slaves, illegally brought on a slave ship, and he lived on a plantation with his three unmarried sisters. Forty years later Tillman still remembered with a shudder those native Africans as "the nearest form of the missing link with the monkey I have ever put my eyes on." They embodied "everything which is low and degrading."[8] But his private repugnance was neither concealed nor unique, neither delegitimated nor uninfluential.

His sense of horror was, in fact, so fresh that Tillman's chilling oratory on the floor of the United States Senate in 1907 deserves special notice. After describing the rape of a lovely young white woman, he imagined her "thus blighted and brutalized," telling her father of her "death in life. . . . Is there a man here with red blood in his veins," Tillman asked his colleagues in that distinguished deliberative body, "who doubts what impulses the father would feel? Is it any wonder that the whole countryside rises as one man and with set, stern faces, seek[s] the brute who has wrought this infamy? . . . Shall men cold-bloodedly stand up and demand for him the right to have a fair trial and be punished in the regular course of justice?" Tillman answered his own question: "So far as I am concerned, he has put himself outside the pale of the law, human and divine. He has sinned against the Holy Ghost. He has invaded the holy of holies. He has struck civilization a blow, the most deadly and cruel that the imagination can conceive. It is idle to reason about it; it is idle to preach about it. Our brains reel under the staggering blow, and hot blood surges to the heart. Civilization peels off us, any and all of us who are men; and we revert to the original savage type whose impulses under such circumstances have always been to 'kill! kill! kill!'"[9] Recoiling from the shadow of black barbarism, even a respected and articulate political leader could thus be transformed into what Lawrence J. Friedman has termed "the white savage."[10]

Despite the distinct character of the senator's immediate contact with Africans, his sense of dread was not unique, which is why the lynchings of the era cannot be categorized as aberrant but as communal acts. Even the Arkansas demagogue Jeff Davis, a governor and United States senator who was not notably Negrophobic, could warn in his 1904 campaign: "We may have a lot of dead negroes in Arkansas, but we shall never have negro equality; and I want to say that I would rather tear, screaming from her mother's arms, my little daughter and bury her alive than to see her arm in arm with the best nigger on earth."[11] The generalization of a recent writer that "the more prominent Southern leaders had always publicly opposed lynching"[12] is therefore false, because to do so might well have threatened their political popularity in an era of intense racial hatred.

Demagogic endorsements of mob action fit in snugly with an older regional cult of bravado, and with the tendency of white Southerners to engage in personal violence well in excess of national norms. Even today Southern whites commit murder more frequently than do non-Southern whites, and their flash point of homicidal anger appears to be lower.[13] Historians like Bertram

Wyatt-Brown and Edward L. Ayers have shown an early nineteenth-century stress on "honor" rather than the satisfaction of legal obligations. Not only among the planter aristocracy but among virtually all white males, Ayers notes, "the failure to respond to insult marked them as less than real men, branded them, in the most telling epithets of the time, as 'cowards' and 'liars.'" He adds that "honor and 'public opinion' came to seem synonymous, an overwhelming force that compelled men to wage fights for which they had little heart. . . . " Thus "the heart of honor was the respect of others" that the law could rarely provide. As Andrew Jackson's mother told him, "The law affords no remedy that can satisfy the feelings of a true man." Local juries were therefore very reluctant to convict any white Southerner who could claim self-defense on the basis of any threat, no matter how veiled.[14] Ayers' study of *Vengeance and Justice* contrasts the Southern exaltation of honor with the Northern ethos that made "dignity" pivotal—the belief, however much scuttled in practice, that "each individual at birth possessed an intrinsic value at least theoretically equal to that of every other person."[15] Such cultural differences persisted, especially in the isolated rural South, well into the mid-twentieth century.

Respectable women, however, were not expected to be able to defend themselves. Southern ladies were exalted in so rarefied a fashion, and were expected to be so unsullied, that any slights to their purity were inflated to sometimes lethal importance. Even the most innocent of encounters between them and black men were electrically charged with danger and anxiety, with the risks of contamination and pollution. Even the least "pure" white women had to be romantically championed like Dixie Dulcineas. (Ruby Bates and Victoria Price, involved in the Scottsboro case that erupted in 1931, were so regarded.) Avenging their occasional loss of virtue—and vindicating the honor of Southern civilization itself—was pivotal to the historical phenomenon of lynching.

This is not manifest from the statistics alone, however. According to the archives of Tuskegee Institute in Alabama, 4,743 persons were lynched between 1882—the earliest date for which reliable evidence can be gathered—and 1968. Of these victims, 3,446, or over 72 percent, were black. In the state of Mississippi alone, 534 blacks were lynched between 1882 and 1951—the highest number in the Union. Yet less than 26 percent of the black victims in the South were accused (much less convicted, of course) of rape or attempted rape.[16] In fact, as Wilbur J. Cash pointed out, the odds that a white woman would be sexually assaulted by a black man were "much less, for instance, than the chance that she would be struck by lightning."[17]

But measurement is not synonymous with meaning; and the subjective import that enmeshed the question was illuminated in *God Shakes Creation,* an account of the Mississippi Delta which one of its children of pride, David L. Cohn, published in 1935. The fear of the black rapist could not be rationalized out of the Delta white man, nor made to "seem ridiculous in his eyes with structures of smooth syllogisms. . . . His wife and daughters are not to him mere figures in tables of averages. They are flesh and blood whom he loves and cherishes," Cohn concluded, "and he cannot ever be brought to see that the ravished body of one dear to him represents merely the haphazard workings of chance."[18] A culture that gave such weight to personal relations—to family bonds and friendships as well as to feuding—could not easily be mollified by the marshaling of data.

That may be why the small proportion of lynchings that were triggered by charges of sexual aggression, as Jacquelyn Dowd Hall has asserted, "gripped the southern imagination far out of proportion to statistical reality. . . . Participants might see in 'lynch law' their ideal selves: the protectors of women, dispensers of justice, and guardians of communal values." She adds: "The ritual of lynching . . . served as a dramatization of hierarchical power relationships based both on gender and on race. . . . Masculine guilt over miscegenation, the veiled hostility toward women in patriarchal society, the myths of black sexuality—[these formed] a dense web of sexual violation and desperate rationalization."[19] That is why death was a penalty that fell disproportionately on black males who were accused—or sometimes convicted—of sexual assault. Whatever the reputation of the region for hospitality toward white visitors, lynch mobs were also most likely to strike at blacks who were considered to be outsiders, who drew suspicion as strangers or were condemned as "bad." "When a 'bad negro' did suddenly appear," Ayers has remarked, "the white community quickly closed ranks. Men of widely varying backgrounds temporarily joined in a common cause."[20]

By the early twentieth century, Mark Twain was calling his native land the United States of Lyncherdom. Though the phenomenon was widely tolerated, it had become almost exclusively Southern, and nine out of ten victims were black. Lynchings did noticeably decline beginning in the 1920s. The frenzy of posses and blood-hounds became more restrained; the rope, the torch, and the hide-ous tortures became somewhat less common; and the ritual public displays of corpses generally abated—but not because the fears of black savagery had subsided. Instead, substitutes for these expres-sions of Southern "honor" were developed. "Although twice as many threatened lynchings were prevented as were carried out dur-ing the decade of the twenties," Hall has written, "the thwarted lynch mob frequently demanded that public officials impose the death sentence in a hasty mockery of a trial. If these 'legal lynchings' were included in the statistics, the death toll would be much higher." Police methods and the judicial system had the same effect in punishing the crazed lusts of black rapists, or those believed to be such criminals.[21] Interracial assault was the one crime that seemed to arouse bestial fears and primordial passions in otherwise law-abiding Southern white citizens.

How extreme this suspicion of the aggressiveness of the black man was permitted to go was shown in an incident involving James Weldon Johnson—poet, musician, attorney, and diplomat as well as executive secretary of the National Association for the Advance-ment of Colored People (NAACP). In 1901, after a fire destroyed much of his hometown of Jacksonville, Florida, Johnson was inter-viewed by a white reporter from New York. When Johnson agreed to meet her in the park in broad daylight to go over her article, his friendly meeting with the journalist was noticed by a white streetcar conductor, who reported the conversation. Eight or ten white mili-tiamen then arrived to take Johnson into custody; he was beaten and bruised and heard shouts of "Kill the damned nigger! Kill the black son of a bitch!" Though Johnson was eventually released, the horror of that combustible hatred and of his own utter vulnerability did not leave him—or allow him to sleep undisturbed—for two dec-ades. Another example of inflamed and exaggerated white anxiety occurred in Yanceyville, North Carolina, where a black sharecrop-per named Matt Ingram was convicted of assaulting a white woman who was no closer than seventy-five feet away. Until court maneu-vers freed Ingram, he was forced to spend two and a half years in prison, because of the leering way he had allegedly looked at her.[22]

In such circumstances blacks grew up knowing to an often very fine calibration their "place" in the South, and it was a subjugation that only escape to the North might remedy. If lynchings had become rare by the time that the United Nations proclaimed its Declaration of Human Rights after the Second World War, it was largely because fear had become so effective an instrument. Just as the average number of whippings inflicted upon slaves gives no precise sense of the thoroughness of the social control that their owners exerted in the antebellum era, so too the decline in mob violence by the mid-century cannot convey the terror that permeated black communities in the South. "The threat of lynching is likely to be in the mind of the Negro child from earliest days," the social scientist John Dollard reported from Mississippi during the Great Depression. "Memories of such events came out frequently in the life histories of Negroes," some of whom had been required to watch these communal rituals. The future president of Fisk University, Charles S. Johnson, argued in 1941 that the effect of such terrorization on black children in the rural South was "profound and permanent." In the Delta, "lynching or the possibility of lynching is a part of the cultural pattern," or at least was so until World War II.[23] If Beale Street could talk, it would have revealed symptoms of repression and fear far deeper than many conventional histories have succeeded in penetrating.

Richard Wright, who was born near Natchez in 1908, had learned by the age of fifteen of the lynchings of a stepuncle and of the brother of a neighborhood friend. The testimony of this most acute of Uncle Tom's children is pertinent, for Wright recalled that "the things that influenced my conduct as a Negro did not have to happen to me directly; I needed but to hear of them to feel their full effects in the deepest layers of my consciousness. Indeed, the white brutality that I had not seen was a more effective control of my behavior than that which I knew. . . . "[24] The white-dominated communities from which some blacks fled ensured that nightmares of rope and faggot would not be completely repressed nor these signs of limitless power ignored; and even after the customary allowances are made for the exceptions and aberrations that inevitably bob to the surface in human affairs, the etiquette of caste was vigilantly maintained, especially in the smaller Southern towns, well into the mid-twentieth century.[25]

Certainly the dread of miscegenation remained powerful. Not long after Till himself was born, Gunnar Myrdal published his landmark study, *An American Dilemma*. When he and his team of social scientists asked white Southerners to choose among six categories in gauging what they believed blacks most wanted, first was "intermarriage and sex intercourse with whites." (Among blacks, incidentally, that category ranked last.)[26] Continuing nevertheless to claim keen insight into the souls of black folk, the author of *You and Segregation* (1955), Senator Herman Talmadge of Georgia, conjectured with confidence that "the ultimate aim and goal of NAACP leaders in the present segregation fight is the complete intermingling of the races in housing, schools, churches, public parks, public swimming pools and even in marriage." This particular tract, published under the imprint of the Vulcan Press in Birmingham, Alabama, also announced that "God Advocates Segregation," though Senator Talmadge cited no primary source.[27] Another leading segregationist, Judge Leander Perez of Louisiana, also claimed that the key item on the civil rights agenda was intermarriage: "You make a Negro believe he is equal to the white people[,] and the first thing he wants is a white woman. And that's why there are so many criminal assaults and rapes."[28]

Such views became more pronounced after the Supreme Court invalidated racial separation in public schools. Most of the Southern white newspaper editors whom *U.S. News & World Report* interviewed explained that Southern opposition was motivated by fear of "eventual amalgamation of the races—meaning miscegenation, intermarriage or whatever you want to call it." One editor elaborated that "Negroes are . . . generally more retarded in school than white children . . . [so that] a Negro of 14 may be in the fourth grade with a white girl of 10 or 11, and the Negro is a fully developed man, sexually." The editor of the *Jackson Daily News* was certain that "integration is merely the first step, or an opening wedge, toward mixed marriages, miscegenation, and the mongrelization of the human race." Frederick Sullens had warned soon after *Brown v. Board of Education* was handed down that "human blood may stain southern soil in many places because of this decision, but the dark red stains of that blood will be on the marble steps of the United States Supreme Court Building." He thundered that "white and Negro children in the same schools will lead to miscegenation. . . . " The front-page editorial concluded that "Mississippi cannot and will not try to abide by such a decision."[29] The attorney general of Georgia feared that the reasoning behind the unanimous opinion would permit "a constitutional attack on our laws prohibiting intermarriage of Negroes and white people."[30] Eugene Cook's logic at least was correct. But even after the Supreme Court struck down antimiscegenation statutes in a case aptly entitled *Loving* v. *Virginia* (1967), the neurotic bugaboo of massive racial "amalgamation" of course proved unjustified.[31]

But in the era after World War II, the vestiges of the myth of the savage black rapist did not completely evaporate. Judge Brady, a former professor of sociology at the University of Mississippi, was considered a towering intellectual figure within the Citizens' Council movement that was formed in Indianola, Mississippi, two months after *Brown* v. *Board of Education*. He echoed "Pitchfork" Ben Tillman's views, though without the imprimatur of the United States Senate. Deeming that Supreme Court decision equal in historical importance to the signing of the Declaration of Independence, Brady warned against the consequences of public school desegregation in the following terms: "When a law transgresses the moral and ethical sanctions and standards of the mores, invariably strife, bloodshed and revolution follow in the wake of its attempted enforcement. The loveliest and purest of God's creatures, the nearest thing to an angelic being that treads this terrestrial ball is a well-bred, cultured Southern white woman or her blue-eyed, golden-haired little girl." The Brookhaven jurist warned that *Brown* v. *Board of Education* would not be obeyed: "We have, through our forefathers, died before for our sacred principles. We can, if necessary, die again."[32] It was a sign of modernization that, in fact, white supremacists like him were whistling Dixie. Though Brady was to deliver a nominating speech for Governor Ross Barnett five years later as presidential candidate of the Democratic Party, even the leaders of the Citizens' Councils eventually displayed no resolve to die for the sake of such principles (or even be jailed for their beliefs), though some other Southern whites were still quite willing to kill for them.

The lingering dread of liaisons between black males and white females that permeated the dominant race can even be traced in the career of a respectable Upper South journalist, James J. Kilpatrick. Though his rhetoric was less inflammatory than Judge Brady's in Mississippi, the author of *The Southern Case for School Segregation* (1962) ultimately vindicated Jim Crow in identical terms. In a television debate with Martin Luther King, Jr., soon after the 1960 election, Kilpatrick articulated a right "to preserve the predominately [*sic*] racial characteristics that have contributed to Western civilization over the past two thousand years, and we do not believe that the way to preserve them lies in fostering any intimate race mixing. . . . " The editor of the *Richmond News-Leader* therefore championed the perpetuation of racial segregation in a "few essential social areas where intimate personal association, long continued, would foster a breakdown, especially among young people, of those ethnic lines that seem to us important."[33] Reverend King's assurance that he aspired to be treated as the white man's brother—not his brother-in-law—had little effect on Kilpatrick's punditry, which the *National Review* boosted. The magazine seemed to back the Virginian's case for second-class citizenship for blacks. Though ordinarily hostile to efforts to legislate morality, the *National Review* declared after the invalidation of *Plessy* v. *Ferguson* that "the White community in the South is entitled to take such measures as are necessary to prevail, politically and culturally, in areas where it does not predominate numerically. . . ." This blood-and-soil stance was too much even for editor William F. Buckley's own brother-in-law, L. Brent Bozell; the future ghostwriter of Senator Barry Goldwater's *Conscience of a Conservative* blamed the magazine for condoning Southern white lawlessness.[34]

In the immediate aftermath of *Brown* v. *Board of Education*, the Deep South exhibited the paranoia of a closed society that could not distinguish the defense of a "few essential social areas" from the entire structure of white supremacy. The preservation of white patriarchy seemed to require the suppression of even the most insignificant challenges to its authority. In Gunnar Myrdal's view, sex was "the principle around which the whole structure of segregation of the Negroes . . . [was] organized." And it was because of sex that racial segregation, which seems in retrospect so unintelligible and so kooky (if not insane), was intended to permeate every aspect of society—and generally did. Blacks and whites presumably worshiped the same God, but in courtrooms they had to take an oath on separate Bibles. In schools they were presumably taught the same version of Southern and American history, punctuated with idealization of the Old South and glorification of the Lost Cause. But according to a statute in Florida, their textbooks were stored in separate warehouses. A Montgomery, Alabama, ordinance extended the logic of racism to the leisure class by forbidding blacks and whites from playing checkers, dominoes, or cards together. Seated in separate areas the races watched the same movies; but the requirements of satisfying the Southern market ensured that, according to the Motion Picture Production Code, "miscegenation (sex relationship between the white and black races) . . . [was] forbidden" from presentation on the screen.[35]

Such rigidity and anxiety meant that black men in particular had to be unusually wary in avoiding casual contact with, or even the slightest sign of interest in, white women. Studying Indianola in the Delta in the 1930s, Dollard reported that a local black man was fearful of receiving an innocent letter from a white woman. In the 1940s the black press highlighted a car accident in Georgia, in which a desperate white woman died when a black man, who instinctively shrank from the consequences of physical contact, failed to rescue her.[36] In the 1960s a black woman in Mississippi warned the disguised journalist John Howard Griffin, who was pretending to have crossed the color line: "You know that you don't want to even look at a white woman. In fact, you look down at the ground or the other way. . . . " She tutored the white Negro down to the smallest detail: "If you pass by a picture show, and they've got women on the posters outside, don't look at them either. . . . Somebody's sure to say, 'Hey, boy—what are you looking at that white gal like *that* for?'"[37] The atmosphere could therefore be volatile; and if a black stranger did something peculiar, the small-town and rural South in particular could explode on impact. Natural amicability and generosity could be misinterpreted, and even the most innocent of gestures could be dangerous.

This was the ambience that surrounded Emmett Till when he hopped off an Illinois Central train the third week in August 1955, intending to spend a part of his summer vacation with his cousins in the Magnolia State. The Delta, in the lapidary formulation of David Cohn, "begins in the lobby of the Peabody Hotel in Memphis and ends on Catfish Row in Vicksburg"; but geographers formally defined and confined the Delta to the fertile wedge of land between the Mississippi and Yazoo rivers. It is not to be confused with the delta of the Mississippi River, which is below New Orleans; and indeed it is not to be mistaken with anywhere else in the world. One of its native sons, Willie Morris of Yazoo City, has eloquently

testified to its "pull ... its abiding mysteries and strengths—re-
trieved from the ocean and later the interminable swamp—and the
men of all colors ... who had fought it into its reluctant and tentative submission." The Delta dominated a state that has been like
no other in the Union—"so eternally wild, so savagely unpredict-
able, so fraught with contradictory deceits and nobilities," so di-
vided in "the gulf between its manners and morals, the extraordinary apposition of its violence and kindliness."[38]

About two hundred miles long and up to eighty-five miles wide,
its dark, flat, alluvial land was fashioned for large-scale agriculture,
from the era of the slave plantation to the modern mechanized do-
main of agribusiness. The politics of this northwestern quarter of
the state have characteristically been "aristocratic" and conservative, the dominion of an oligarchy; and there its black population
is concentrated. "A common belief in Negro communities outside
Mississippi," reported a sociologist who studied the Delta, "is that
it is the worst place in the entire country for Negroes. To some
extent this opinion is shared by Negroes in Mississippi."[39] And yet
they lived and worked there in huge numbers: in 1950 the county
with the smallest nonwhite proportion was Warren (51 percent),
while Tunica County had the highest (82 percent).[40]

The physical setting itself is striking. Visiting this bedeviled and
beguiling area a year after Till hopped off that train, Robert Penn
Warren noted "the sad and baleful beauty of the Delta," with "its
ruined, gaunt, classic clay hills, with the creek bottoms throttled
long since in pink sand," with Highway 61 south from Memphis—
the unofficial capital of the Delta—cutting "straight as a knife
edge" through it, a "concrete slab ... dizzily glittering in the August
sun-blaze."[41] It is so flat a landscape, recalled one native who was
born a year before Till, that "if you stand on a levee or a railroad
bed[,] you're on a high spot, and the horizon is visible in every direction. Farms and family houses and communities stand as sharply
etched against that wide sky as against history." A later black trav-
eler wrote that the Delta "stretches before you like the sea, an un-
broken monotony of land so flat as to appear unnatural. So pervasive is this low-ceilinged, almost total flatness that one loses all other
dimensions of space and vision. An endless succession of cotton and
soybean fields surround the road" that buses take, going south on
Highway 61 and then splitting off onto Highway 49 from Memphis,

which is located about eighty miles north of Tallahatchie County. The sticky, shimmering, punitive heat in the summer could seem independent of the sun itself. And since the soil was slowly losing its extravagant fecundity, a morsel of local folk wisdom announced that, with its humid dawns and long twilights, "the Delta will wear out a mule in five years, a white man in ten, and a nigger in fifteen."[42]

T W O

Chicago Boy

"Bobo" Till was born near Chicago on July 25, 1941. His father, Louis Till, had been born in Missouri, had moved to Chicago, became a soldier, and died in Europe in the summer of 1945, two years after his divorce from Bobo's mother. Mamie Till Bradley had been born in Tallahatchie County, and helped to make Chicago a city that sheltered more Mississippi-born blacks than anywhere in the United States outside Mississippi itself. In the 1940s, over 214,000 blacks migrated to Chicago. The overwhelming majority of them came from the South, and of them about half came from Mississippi. The fare from Memphis on the Illinois Central Railroad was $11.10; and the *Chicago Defender,* a newspaper familiar to many Delta blacks, encouraged sharecroppers to move north.[1] After the death of Louis Till, Bobo's mother remarried and was then divorced, and earned $3,900 a year working as a voucher examiner in the Air Force Procurement Office. When she took a vacation that August, Mrs. Bradley planned to rest by sending away her son, who had just completed the seventh grade at the all-black McCosh Elementary School on the South Side.

He was known as a prankster, a risk taker, and a smart dresser who nevertheless did well in school. To his mother Bobo was trustworthy, considerate, and industrious; and she remembered him as having attended church regularly. Cousins remembered him as "the center of attention" who "liked to be seen. He liked the spotlight." Bobo was self-assured despite a speech defect—a stutter—that was the consequence of nonparalytic polio that he had suffered at the age of three.[2] He was about five feet four or five inches tall, weighed about 160 pounds, and was muscular and stocky. Along with a cousin, also from Chicago, named Curtis Jones, Till was staying at the home of his great-uncle, Moses "Preacher" Wright, a sharecropper, and Wright's wife Elizabeth.

Bobo Till did not act like his Southern cousins. To the white gas station operators and storekeepers, he said "yeah" and "naw" instead of the customary "yassah" and "nawsah." Even more striking was the photograph he carried in his wallet of a white girl who he claimed was his girlfriend up in Chicago. He boasted of the attributes of "that white stuff" and enjoyed passing the photo around to his friends and relatives.[3] Jones, himself the grandson of Moses Wright, later remembered that there were photos of both male and female classmates.[4]

On the evening of August 24, after Bobo had been visiting for a week, he joined seven boys and a girl—all teenagers, three of whom were also visiting the Delta—in a 1946 Ford and drove to Money, a hamlet of a couple of hundred residents located in Leflore County. The two had one paved road and consisted of three stores, plus a post office, a school, a gas station, and a building for ginning cotton. One of the stores, which featured a standard large Coca-Cola sign in front, specialized in selling snuff and fatback to black field hands who lived in the nearby tar-paper shacks. It was owned and operated by Roy Bryant, a twenty-four-year-old former soldier, and his wife Carolyn Bryant. She was from Indianola, the twenty-one-year-old daughter of a plantation manager and a practical nurse. Five feet tall and weighing 103 pounds, she had won two beauty contests while in high school. When the eight adolescents pulled up to Bryant's Grocery and Meat Market about 7:30 P.M., Roy Bryant was carting shrimp to Texas, leaving his wife alone with Juanita Milam, the wife of Bryant's half-brother, J. W. Milam. About a dozen other young blacks, all but two of whom were males, were congregating outside the store at the time the Till party arrived.[5]

What happened next is a matter of continuing disagreement, a historical imponderable, though its consequences would be mortal and would resonate for years thereafter. It would become an international incident; but what transpired there remains mired in dispute and is likely to be forever clouded in uncertainty. It is said that when Sir Walter Raleigh was incarcerated in the Tower of London, he decided to write A History of the World. But when he witnessed an altercation beyond the bars of his cell and could not figure out exactly what had happened, he wondered about the validity of the project—a parable of the precariousness and even futility of the historian's task that is itself self-reflexive, because the veracity of this anecdote is dubious. Even though the episode in Bryant's store in Money happened little more than three decades ago, it has been subject to divergent accounts.

Mrs. Bryant testified under oath in late September about the incident; and other important testimony came a few months after the trial from Bryant and Milam themselves, when they were immune from prosecution for murder. According to their version of events, supplemented by a journalist's interrogation of Till's relatives, the newcomer again bragged of his Chicago girlfriend that Saturday evening. A couple of the others then began taunting him, daring the Chicago boy to go inside the store and ask Carolyn Bryant for a date. Jones recalled that one of the local black boys had told Till: "Hey, there's a [white] girl in that store there. I bet you won't go in there and talk to her."[6] Rather than slink away from the challenge that his boastfulness had provoked, he decided to enter the store alone.

While the other blacks watched through the window from outside, Mrs. Bryant came forward from the counter, with Till in front. He requested—and then got—two cents' worth of bubble gum, but then squeezed her hand firmly and asked: "How about a date, baby?" Carolyn Bryant immediately withdrew and began to move toward the back of the store, behind a partition, where her sister-in-law was staying.

Till jumped between two counters to block her path, raised his hands and held her waist, reassuring her, according to testimony that she later gave in court: "Don't be afraid of me, baby. I ain't gonna hurt you. I been with white girls before." Mrs. Bryant also testified that he used "unprintable" words. It was then that one of Bobo's cousins rushed in and pulled him away from the store. Carolyn Bryant ran to the Milam car, where she knew a pistol could be found. When she reentered the store with a gun, Till was still so eager not to lose face among his cousins and friends that he said "Bye, baby" and "wolf whistled" at her. Although Jones, who had been playing checkers with an elderly local black outside, was not an eyewitness to the incident, he later claimed that his cousin had said nothing other than "Bye, baby." In any event, after Mrs. Bryant had returned with a pistol, the group of blacks then drove away.[7]

Emmett Till's mother has displayed a natural desire to protect the sanctity of her son's character; and though she was not present, she too has offered an account of what happened. Mrs. Bradley claimed that, far from pretending to flirt, he whistled to stop his stutter. "He had particular trouble with b's and m's," she insisted. "He was trying to say 'bubble gum,' but he got stuck. So he whistled."[8] Because her son had difficulty with certain letters, "I taught him, whenever he had trouble stuttering, to blow it out. . . . I can see him trying to say 'bubble gum' and blowing or whistling in Mrs. Bryant's presence."[9] Though the *Jackson Daily News* seemed to accept that possibility, it was left to its editorial writer also to conjecture that Till was "feeble-minded,"[10] presumably according to the dictum that no black male in his right mind would behave in a manner so brazen and so sexually threatening as Till was accused of acting. The *Daily News* speculation was an eerie foreshadowing of the 1958 case of Clennon King, a black history professor whose attempt to enroll in the summer school of the University of Mississippi was met by highway patrolmen and a lunacy warrant. King was placed under observation for thirteen days in the state mental asylum, and after his release fled the state.[11]

A local news account said nothing about Till's whistle or that he had grabbed Mrs. Bryant's hand and waist—only that he made "ugly remarks" to her.[12] A recent biography of Martin Luther King, Jr., written by an award-winning black journalist, placed Till in Greenwood, where he was shopping in a department store and is supposed to have whistled at a white woman who was passing by. "None of the whites who saw the youth hauled out of town" by two white men "intervened," according to this manifestly inaccurate account. William Chafe, a historian specializing in civil rights, wrote that Till was "lynched because he allegedly had leered at a white woman."[13] But Till's sixteen-year-old cousin, Maurice Wright, initially offered two different and logically unconnected explanations for what had happened. He told newsmen on September 1 that the Chicago youth had indeed emitted the two notes of the "wolf call." After Till had emerged from the store, Wright claimed to have told him, "Boy, you know better than that." The visitor "just laughed." Till thus appeared culturally dislocated. But Wright also explained that Till "had polio when he was three and he couldn't talk plain. You could hardly understand him."[14] Another cousin visiting from Chicago, seventeen-year-old Wheeler Parker, told *Jet* magazine soon after the lynching that Till had indeed whistled.[15] Simeon Wright, a twelve-year-old son of Moses Wright, later concurred that Till "was definitely whistling at that girl"—which is all that the deputy sheriff of Leflore County initially claimed had happened.[16]

A shaken Carolyn Bryant immediately told Juanita Milam about the incident. A black male whom she had never seen before, physically larger than she was, and who was accompanied by black adolescents (most of them males), had grabbed her, held her, propositioned her, insulted her, and whistled at her. She had no way of knowing that the whole idea was probably a tasteless prank. Yet both Mrs. Bryant and her sister-in-law agreed to conceal the episode from their husbands. They said nothing about it an hour later, when J. W. Milam drove up to escort them back to his home in Glendora, Mississippi. By early Friday morning, when Roy Bryant returned from Texas, his wife had still said nothing—which was not the case with the blacks who had observed the incident.

For them it was a topic of excitement, a puncturing of the Jim Crow etiquette so brashly executed that it was worth sharing with others. By Friday afternoon a black who came into the store in Money informed its proprietor that a "Chicago boy" who was "visitin' Preacher" had breached the barrier of caste.[17] According to Elizabeth Wright's brother the informant was Maurice Wright, the eldest of the cousins who had been with Till that Wednesday night at the store. Wright embellished his tale, claiming that Till had told Carolyn Bryant how pretty she was. Maurice Wright may have acted out of jealousy ("Here was this Chicago boy, dressed in fine clothes and carrying a little money in his pocket"), as Crosby Smith, Moses Wright's brother-in-law, suspected. Or the youngster may have wanted to compound the prank that had instigated the incident. Or he may have wanted a half dollar's credit at Bryant's store (as Mamie Bradley averred). But whatever Maurice Wright's combination of motives, the husband of the woman who had been insulted felt compelled to react.[18]

For Bryant's sense of honor was threatened. Since his Negro customers already knew what had happened, he felt obliged at least to "whip the nigger's ass" (though not to bring any formal charges against Till to the sheriff). The Bryants were too poor to own an automobile, and since Saturday was the busiest day in the store, it was not until Saturday night at 10:30 that he could ask his half-brother to come later with his '55 Chevrolet pickup truck to punish the "Chicago boy."

Milam was thirty-six years old, stood six feet two inches, and weighed 235 pounds. Like his half-brother, he was the father of two sons. A much-decorated combat veteran of the European Theater in World War II, he made a living by renting Negro-driven mechanical cotton pickers for plantations in the Delta. "Big" Milam was the sort of man who prided himself on getting along with blacks, on knowing how to "handle" them. He had a ninth-grade education. Like Roy Bryant, Milam had a .45 Colt. Both men brought their automatic pistols to the home of "Preacher" Wright, which was an unpainted cabin behind a cotton field off a gravel road nearly three miles east of Money. Both white visitors were sober.[19]

Milam was the enforcer and was carrying a pistol in one hand and a flashlight in the other when they woke the household to get the boy from Chicago. Moses Wright assured Bryant and Milam that he had severely admonished his nephew, pleading that the boy "ain't got good sense. He was raised up yonder. He didn't know what he was doing. Don't take him." The sharecropper said that it was only the boy's second visit to Mississippi. Wright's wife Elizabeth promised to "pay you gentlemen for the damages," but J. W. Milam could not be mollified: "You niggers go back to sleep." Till, one of four youngsters sleeping in the cabin, got dressed, was marched outside, and was told to lie down in the bed of the pickup truck. One of the men asked Wright, "How old are you, 'Preacher'?" He answered that he was sixty-four. "If you cause any trouble," Wright was told, "you'll never live to be sixty-five." Then the pickup truck disappeared into the night.[20]

Neither Milam nor Bryant had ever seen Till before, nor did they know or ask his name. They drove across the Tallahatchie River Bridge at Money, heading for Big River near Rosedale. There, they said later, they intended to pistol-whip the lad and then frighten him by threatening to throw him off a hundred-foot bluff in what Milam later called "the god-damndest, scariest place in the Delta." But they could not find the spot in the dark, and it was five o'clock that Sunday morning when the truck returned to the Milam home in Glendora. Juanita Milam and the children were in Greenville, visiting her parents. Bryant and Milam then marched Till into the toolhouse and pistol-whipped him several times.

They claimed that to their amazement Till did not whimper or beg for mercy or show remorse. He may not have suspected how much danger he was in. To the contrary, they asserted, he continued to boast of white girls with whom he was intimate, and once again he pulled out his wallet to prove his conquests. Milam was outraged and decided to kill him. "Chicago boy," he remembered—out of the courtroom—saying, "I'm tired of 'em sending your kind down here to stir up trouble. Goddamn you—I'm gonna make an example of you—just so everybody can know how me and my folks stand."

Needing something heavy enough to keep Till's body at the bottom of the river, Milam ordered him back into the truck. They drove to a gin near Boyle, where Till was forced to lift a heavy fan onto the truck. It was already daylight. They drove back past Glendora, near where Milam hunted squirrels. Till was told to carry the fan to the riverbank, then to strip. He did not cry. Milam remembered taunting him in the basic vocabulary of white supremacy: "Nigger, you still as good as I am?" Apparently the last words Emmett Till ever heard were Milam's second question: "You still done it to white girls and you gonna keep on doin' it?" Then, according to their own account delivered after the trial, Milam fired one bullet at Till's head, joined Bryant in tying the fan to the victim's neck, and dumped the body into the Tallahatchie River.[21]

The NAACP denied that the half-brothers' crime was a "murder of passion"—it was "futile, cold, brutal."[22] On the contrary, if Bryant and Milam are accepted as credible witnesses, it was neither premeditated nor plotted, but was instigated by what they considered the abducted youth's provocative audacity. That may be a matter of interpretation, but in any event this was one cause célèbre in which no serious doubts have ever clouded the identity of the killers.

Soon after the abduction, Elizabeth Wright had asked a white neighbor to intercede, but he refused. According to one account, she and Moses Wright then drove to Sumner, the home of her brother, Crosby Smith, who went that Sunday morning to the sheriff in Greenwood, George Smith. Leaving his truck in front of the courthouse, Wright's brother-in-law accompanied the sheriff on a futile search along riverbanks and under bridges. "We went by custom when something like that happened," Crosby Smith later explained. "That's usually what they done to 'em." According to another account, Curtis Jones phoned the sheriff from a plantation owner's house to report that Till was missing. That same morning one of the other visitors at the Wright home phoned Mamie Till Bradley, who contacted the Chicago police, who in turn began phoning sheriffs in Mississippi. That noon, on the complaint of Wright and of Crosby Smith, the sheriff of Leflore County arrested Milam and Bryant, who admitted the abduction of "a little nigger boy" but not the murder that they had committed a few hours earlier. They were nevertheless jailed in Greenwood on suspicion of murder.[23]

Less than three days later, a white youth fishing in the Tallahatchie River at Pecan Point found the hideously decomposed body of a male human being. The deputy sheriff who was summoned to the scene wheeled his patrol car onto a dirt road about three miles west of Phillipp, parked at a clearing, and then slowly walked down the steep embankment. The lower half of the badly beaten corpse protruded above the surface of the Tallahatchie River. Though a fan weighing about a hundred pounds had been attached to the neck with barbed wire, only the right side of the head was intact, suggesting terrible torture. The beating, one policeman said, was the worst that he had observed in eight years of law enforcement. The protruding tongue was eight times normal size, and one eye dangled. Above the right ear was a hole the size of a bullet, and on one finger was a ring inscribed with the initials L. T. The naked body was discovered twelve miles north of Money, and only fifteen miles from the birthplace of Mamie Till Bradley. The United Press story that had been filed from Greenwood, initially reporting that two men were being charged with abducting a Negro youth, was updated: "Kidnapped Youth Found Slain Near Greenwood."[24]

So badly mangled and decomposed was the body that Wright could identify it as Till's only by the initialed ring. The sheriff of Tallahatchie County, Harold Clarence Strider, had wanted burial to be immediate. But Curtis Jones phoned Chicago, informing Mamie Till Bradley, thirty-three, of the death of her only child and reporting the sheriff's intention as well. She demanded that the corpse be sent home, despite the reluctance of the sheriff's office, which had the mortician order that the casket not be opened. That order was violated soon after it reached the Illinois Central terminal in Chicago, where Mrs. Bradley, seated in a wheelchair, went limp with grief. She was surrounded by friends and supporters whom ministers led in prayer. Mrs. Bradley wanted to be certain, however, that the body was indeed her son's. After studying the hairline and the teeth, she declared that she wanted an open-casket funeral and, after crying, "Lord, take my soul," collapsed. She later told reporters: "Have you ever sent a loved son on vacation and had him returned to you in a pine box, so horribly battered and water-logged that someone needs to tell you this sickening sight is your son—lynched?"[25]

Mrs. Bradley vowed that "the entire state of Mississippi is going to pay for this."[26] She wanted "the world [to] see what they did to my boy," and perhaps ten thousand lined the streets outside the Rainer Funeral Home on the first day that the pine casket was open for viewing. On Saturday, September 3, the McCosh Elementary School pupil was finally buried, as an estimated two thousand mourners gathered outside the Roberts Temple Church of God on State Street. Though Mrs. Bradley received over $4,000 from the mourners and in the mail, a minister urged the congregation from the pulpit to contribute to a fund for the NAACP, "so that this will not happen again." According to the *Nation,* the black community of Chicago "is aroused as it has not been over any similar act in recent history," and *Newsweek* agreed.[27] The *Cleveland Call and Post,* a black newspaper, discovered through polling leading black radio preachers throughout the United States that five out of six were commenting on Till's murder; and half were demanding that "something be done in Mississippi" immediately.[28]

Because the corpse had been recovered in Tallahatchie County, one of the eighteen counties in the Delta, the homicide was presumed to have occurred there. The half-brothers were therefore indicted in its county seat of Sumner on two counts of kidnapping and murder. That part of the Delta deserved to rank as one of the most economically and culturally impoverished corners of the United States. The median per capita income of Tallahatchie County was $607 per year, which made it the sixth poorest of the eighty-two counties in the most impoverished state in the union. In Mississippi itself the per capita income in 1950 had been $703 per year. Four-fifths of the residents of Tallahatchie County annually earned under $2,000, with blacks mostly working as sharecroppers or tenant farmers on vast plantations, and the white hill people generally owning small farms of up to a hundred acres on barely cultivable land. The education levels of Tallahatchie County were the third worst in the state. The average adult had completed only 5.7

years of school, the average black only 3.9 years. The base of the county was so rural that its largest town, Charleston, had a population of only 2,629; and it was so unaffected by the Industrial Revolution that there was only one factory, which manufactured automobile seat covers.[29]

Prosecuting attorney Hamilton Caldwell later acknowledged that he had opposed the indictment of Bryant and Milam, because he doubted that a jury would convict any white man found to have murdered a black who was accused of such insults to a white woman. Such homicides could presumably be committed with impunity in Mississippi. But eighteen white men, mostly planters, were nevertheless persuaded to give Bryant and Milam their day in court, facing a murder charge for which maximum penalty was death and the minimum penalty life imprisonment. It appears that the indictments were so exceptional that the black newspaper in Jackson felt obliged to praise "white men [who] took this step against other white men for a crime against a Negro," and a black Baptist convention that was meeting in Memphis went out of its way to commend the grand jury for its "speedy handling of the case." So did an editorial in the New York Times. But when the case came to court, one of the counts was dropped, since Till was presumably taken away not in Tallahatchie County but in Leflore, where his great-uncle's cabin was located.[30] Since Bryant and Milam in fact acknowledged abducting Till in that county, its grand jury considered an indictment for kidnapping, which carried a maximum ten-year penalty upon conviction, after their murder trial in Tallahatchie County.

Despite the trigger-happy reputation of the Magnolia State, some initial reactions showed considerable effort to establish distance from the depravity of which Bryant and Milam were accused. Governor Hugh White championed a "vigorous prosecution" of those responsible for the crime, and claimed that "Mississippi deplores such conduct on the part of its citizens and certainly cannot condone it." He even sent a telegram to the headquarters of the NAACP in New York, assuring the organization that "parties charged with the murder are in jail. I have every reason to believe that the court will do their [sic] duty in prosecution." Governor White explicitly denied that Emmett Till had been the victim of a lynching: "It is a straight-out murder."[31]

The question was not only semantic. Categorized as an ordinary homicide, the case would discourage outside interest and intervention. A "lynching," by contrast, might stimulate inquiries into race relations when national attitudes were growing less tolerant of "the Southern way of life," and when such barbarism would affect the decisions of Northern corporations to locate or remain in so turbulent a climate. By the end of the decade, Mississippi politicians were still so eager to absolve their state of the charge of atavistic violence that they continued to deny that the Till case was a lynching.[32]

The authority in such questions was generally recognized to be the Tuskegee Institute, which had recorded no lynchings anywhere in the United States in the previous three years. In fact, 1952 was the first year in the twentieth century in which no such atrocity had been reported. But in 1955 the institute classified Till as the victim of a lynching. The slaying that August did fit the definition that Daniel T. Williams of Tuskegee proposed: "There is no process for establishing the guilt of the accused; the punishment is death, often accompanied by torture and other sadistic acts, applied in many instances to persons charged with offenses which according to the ordinary standards of civilization are of a minor character."[33] On the other hand, it differed from most of the lynchings that the institute had recorded. Missing in the circumstances of the Till slaying were the mob violence, the active community participation, the rites of violence and exorcism, and the ritual tortures that so foully besmirched American and especially Southern justice earlier in the century. Nevertheless, as a racial killing, it was intelligible only in the light of Southern mores and manners; and therefore Governor White was wrong to dismiss it as a "mere" homicide. For though it seemed an act of private vengeance, its perpetrators could have stepped from the pages of *The Mind of the South.* "When confronted with a crime that aroused his anger," W. J. Cash had written over a decade earlier with an insider's perspicacity, the Southerner demanded "immediate satisfaction for itself—catharsis for personal passion . . . now, within the hour—and not some ponderous abstract justice in a problematic tomorrow."[34]

At first many white Mississippians nevertheless echoed the governor's denunciation of the murder, depriving the culprits of any community sympathy. The deputy sheriff of Leflore County, John Ed Cothran, claimed that most citizens in the vicinity were "decent" and would not sanction such deeds. "The white people around here feel pretty mad about the way that poor little boy was treated," he told *Newsweek*, "and they won't stand for this."[35] In Money itself, a white merchant named Ben Roy asserted that "nobody here, Negro or white, approves of things like that." The local gas station operator, Ruben Neal, added: "I hate that this happened in our neighborhood."[36]

The two dailies in the state capital could scarcely have been more forthright. The *Jackson Daily News* called the slaying "a brutal, senseless crime and[,] just incidentally, one which merits not one iota of sympathy for the killers. The people of Mississippi deplored this evil act." The newspaper reported that Till's "death has appalled Mississippi." The *Jackson Clarion-Ledger* agreed that it was a "stupid, horrible crime. Intelligent Mississippians can only suppose it came about in the sick mind[s] of men who should be removed from society by due course of law."[37] In a town about twenty miles from Sumner, the *Clarksdale Press-Register* warned that "if conviction with maximum penalty of the law cannot be secured in this heinous crime, then Mississippi may as well burn all its law books and close its courts, for we cannot then stand before the nation and world as a self-governing state capable of making and enforcing its own laws and punishing [those] who most grievously offend those laws." A front-page editorial in the *Greenwood Commonwealth* asserted that "the citizens of this area are determined that the guilty parties shall be punished to the full extent of the law." Its editor, Tom Shepherd, called the "nauseating" killing "way, way beyond the bounds of human decency." Four days after the corpse was recovered from the river, the front page of the *Memphis Commercial Appeal* reprinted a host of editorials from other Mississippi newspapers, unanimously condemning the "savage crime" and the "senseless brutality."[38]

Even the general secretary of the Citizens' Councils of Mississippi, Robert Patterson, called the murder "very regrettable." Judge Brady himself, whose speech about "Black Monday" had inspired Patterson to organize the councils, later recalled: "The Emmett Till case upset me very much." The man who had predicted just such an incident—and its consequences—stressed that neither Bryant nor Milam was a member of the Citizens' Councils, so far as anyone knew. The councils, both Brady and Patterson claimed, were designed precisely to offer an effective option to white men who would otherwise combat desegregation with acts of reckless violence. At first Bryant and Milam were unable to find an attorney who was willing to represent them.[39]

John Popham, a Virginian whom the managing editor of the *New York Times*, Mississippi-born Turner Catledge, appointed as the newspaper's first full-time correspondent in the South, covered the trial. Primarily assigned to describe the racial crisis throughout the region, Popham reported that "the white community of Mississippi reacted to Till's slaying with sincere and vehement expressions of outrage. From one end of the state to the other, newspaper editorials denounced the killing, demanded swift retributive justice and warned that Mississippians could defend their theories of separation of the races only if the law enforcement machinery was geared to equal justice for both races." Popham claimed that, perhaps to a degree unprecedented in Mississippi, blacks "heard on every side a strong and vigorous condemnation by white people, friend and stranger alike, of brutality in race relations. Many of the state's Negro leaders paid tribute to this development." And, though the sample is not representative, every member of one Deep South congregation favored conviction in the Till case, its minister informed Robert Penn Warren a year later.[40]

Soon the wagons began forming a circle, however. In September 1955, as outrage outside the South mounted, as the protests filtering into the state held it accountable for the crime that two of its citizens were accused of committing, many white Mississippians hunkered down with the half-brothers. The denunciations came to dwarf in significance the venomous character of the deed that had provoked criticism from elsewhere. Even as late as 1966, a whopping 86 percent of Southern Protestants professed belief in the Devil;[41] and such habits of mind may well have inclined them to project onto vivid external evil the moral turbulence within. Local pride and self-sufficiency were imperiled, and the capacity of Mississippi whites to govern themselves—and to live with blacks toward whom they professed no hostility—came to be the central issue in the Till case. The primacy of states' rights became so urgent, the feelings of defensiveness so raw and exposed, that the murder of an adolescent declined in moral magnitude.

Such attitudes are familiar to students of the South and need hardly be traced in any detail here. The syndrome has even been labeled an "oppression psychosis."[42] But fragmentary evidence for the power of such localism can be found in the only history of Tallahatchie County, first published over two decades earlier under the auspices of the D.A.R. chapter. In that booklet, the rule of the Carpetbaggers in Tallahatchie County for a decade after the Civil War was defined as the most terrible episode in its history. The Redeemers after 1875 bequeathed "the blessings of civilization" to future residents of Tallahatchie County, even though "they labored under circumstances more adverse than we in the so-called depression . . . can imagine."[43]

The persistence of such feelings of resentment at outside intervention made it easy to shift blame in the Till case. The targets ceased to be the immediate sources of shame, the half-brothers. Instead hostility was focused on "outside agitators," especially the NAACP, which condemned "the state of jungle fury" in Mississippi and urged the federal government to halt it. Its monthly magazine, *The Crisis*, responded: "Mississippi whines that she is misunderstood, that she is slandered . . . that there are good people in the State who condemn the lynching-crime of Money. But where are they?" The magazine concluded: "No responsible, highly-placed Mississippian denounces the crime and his State's preachers of violence and hate."[44] Roy Wilkins, the executive secretary of the NAACP, continued to call Till's murder a "lynching." Wilkins, whose own parents had taken him as a child from Holly Springs, Mississippi, concluded: "It would appear that the state of Mississippi has decided to maintain white supremacy by murdering children."[45]

Strictly speaking, the charges he and *The Crisis* leveled were false and misrepresented the local political situation. No responsible state official was dedicated to infanticide; and, on the contrary, the desire to see the law take its course in the Till case was unanimously voiced. "Good people" did express outrage at the crime; it would be difficult to find an editorialist who did not recoil from its horror, however implacable the ongoing commitment to black subjugation. *Newsweek* indeed suspected that the official promise of "swift justice" was so firm precisely so that the cause of segregated public schools would not be weakened.[46] In any event, it would have been far more accurate for Wilkins and his organization to have interpreted the Till slaying as deeply embedded in a social context, in the *system* of Jim Crow that had long been fully compatible with racial murders.

Gerald Chatham, who directed the prosecution of Bryant and

Milam, warned that such Northern and black recriminations were producing resentment that would endanger the chances for a guilty verdict. The highly experienced district attorney admonished against "constant agitation" and interference: "We can handle the case without outside help."[47] Though in retrospect no black protest organization could have been less volatile and incendiary than the NAACP, the anger of Chatham and other whites was directed in particular at that organization. These "rabble-rousers" were accused of filling their coffers by exploiting a death that many whites continued to deny could be labeled a lynching and, even more important, were suspected of a Communist-influenced ambition to promote "mongrelization." Such hostility was reinforced by the dyspeptic journalist Westbrook Pegler, writing from Rome. He warned that the strategists of the NAACP were "masters of the tricks of propaganda," preventing the defendants from getting a fair trial. The columnist therefore hoped for a postponement "until this passion has died down" and "the methods of the NAACP" could be exposed. Had he been in the United States, Pegler claimed, he would have been able to present "the details of many horrible criminal assaults by negro [sic] beasts on white women in New York and Chicago." Demands emanating from the state of Illinois for federal intervention also aroused fears that states' rights would be violated, even though, the *Greenwood Commonwealth* insisted, "the people of Mississippi are no more responsible for this tragic murder and no more condone it than the people of New York."[48] White moderates were not able to claim, however, that, in the absence of publicity or "outside interference" in the past, their state had managed to abide by due process of law and the ideals of equal justice.

The xenophobia that permeated the Delta was not seriously challenged by the Greenville *Delta Democrat-Times*, which was by national standards temperate on the race question. Such moderation meant that when editor Hodding Carter, a Bowdoin College graduate, won a Pulitzer Prize for editorial writing in 1946, Senator Theodore G. Bilbo (D., Miss.), declared that "no self-respecting Southern white man would accept a prize given by a bunch of nigger-loving, Yankeefied Communists for editorials advocating the mongrelization of the race." But nine years later the Till case proved so unsettling that even the *Delta Democrat-Times* wished that a plague be inflicted on both houses. The newspaper accused the NAACP of "macabre exhibitionism" that was ultimately intended to provoke

an acquittal—then to be used as further evidence of the shameful-
ness of the Southern way of life.[49] Florence Mars, a white native of
Philadelphia, Mississippi, later recalled that the Till case "aroused
greater emotion in Mississippi than the 1954 school desegregation
decision," which seemed an abstraction, a remote danger far over
the horizon. But the peril to white female flesh seemed immediate;
and Mars, who was then thirty-two years old, noted that "the white
population as a whole believed that the defendants were justified
in whatever they did to protect their women from the lust of Negro
men."[50]

Because of the outside agitation, the local elite united behind the
defendants, a shift that occurred on the weekend of September 3–
4. Bryant had been too destitute to own either a car or a television
set, but he and Milam faced no difficulties ensuring an adequate
legal defense. Indeed all five lawyers practicing in Sumner volun-
teered to represent the defendants *pro bono,* an offer that was accepted. The shock of the Northern and Negro condemnations of
the state's racism began to overshadow the peculiar evil of the crime
itself. The outrage that was heard from "up No'f" was driving Delta
whites to rally round in defense of two of their own.[51]

In this reversal Sheriff Strider probably played a decisive role. He
had earlier trumpeted his discovery of blood on the bridge over the
Tallahatchie River on which the pickup truck had driven, and promised speedy justice. The sheriff had initially been quoted as saying
that the corpse had been dumped into the river about two days
before it was discovered—a theory consistent with the identification of the body as Emmett Till's. But Strider mysteriously changed
his mind soon thereafter. Announcing that the corpse resembled an
adult's and was too decomposed to have been in the river only a
couple of days, Strider instead spread the mischievous rumor that
Till was probably still alive. The sheriff therefore refused to do any
investigative work in behalf of the prosecution. Though he assured
reporters that the "racial element . . . does not enter into the picture," he expressed deep resentment at the "interference" of Cook
County, Illinois, and the NAACP in the affairs of Tallahatchie
County.[52]

Because of Strider's unwillingness to comply with the effort to
gather evidence against the accused men, the state attorney general
felt compelled to step into the breach. James P. Coleman had been
victorious in a field of five candidates in the Democratic gubernato-

rial primary five days before Till was murdered. Though a relatively sensible moderate, Coleman was nevertheless among the "racist rabble-rousers" whom the *Chicago Defender* "accuse[d of] . . . contributing directly to the murder of 'Bo Till," since the attorney general and the other gubernatorial aspirants "charged the atmosphere of the state for [sic] acts of violence."[53] Whatever the fairness of that characterization of so temperate a devotee of white supremacy, Coleman assigned his own special agent, Robert B. Smith III of Ripley, to assist with the prosecution. The attorney general did not give Smith a budget or personnel to engage in a probe of the circumstances of the murder, however, though two state highway patrolmen aided the former FBI man.[54] It was their task to uphold the rule of law in a setting already embroiled in bigotry, bemusement, and xenophobia—to honor a Constitution that not only forbade racial segregation but also guaranteed that criminal defendants would face a jury of their peers. In this effort the prosecution would have to confront and puncture the skepticism of, among other voices, *Jet,* the Chicago-based black magazine that wondered whether "Mississippi will whitewash its latest and most fiendish atrocity."[55]

T H R E E

Trial by Jury

That September between fifty and seventy reporters descended on the drowsy hamlet of Sumner, whose population was barely ten times larger. Though the town boasted a sign that proclaimed, A Good Place to Raise a Boy, it was not an easy place to reach. Some of the visitors arrived on Greyhound buses—the only form of public transportation—that approached Highway 49 no closer than two miles from Sumner. The court proceedings provoked front-page coverage throughout the nation. Probably not since the trial of Bruno Richard Hauptmann in the death of the Lindbergh baby two decades earlier had a kidnap-murder case generated so much publicity. Adding novelty to the journalistic corps were radio and television reporters. "For the first time," the *Delta Democrat-Times* observed, "a number of small local stations [in Mississippi and Louisiana] are staffing a news event." The response from their audiences was generally very favorable. "This is the biggest thing we've ever done," a radio reporter from New Orleans claimed. "We've got more phone calls from our listeners thanking us for having a man on the scene than anything we've done."[1]

And though "the usual court house loiterers, retired farmers and politicians" tended to "stare in apparent amazement" at the journalists swarming around the blacks closely associated with the trial, local voices seemed to raise few objections to such attention, at least initially. "What started out as just another trial has turned into a sensation in our nearby county town of Sumner," the Charleston weekly newspaper reported. "Never in the history of our state has so much out-of-state interest been taken in a case involving white and negro." The *New York Times* added its imprimatur to the local impression of widespread exposure: "A sordid murder case has focussed the glare of national attention on the intricate system of race relations which the dominant white group enforces in the name of stability."[2] And *Newsweek* added: "To the dismay of its own [white] people, Sumner . . . became the most talked about town in the country." During the trial itself, the three major television networks flew planes daily to a field in Tutwiler (seven miles away) to pick up film for editing and showing in New York.[3]

The white journalists stayed in Sumner's only "hotel," a boardinghouse run by a widow who stared at the visitors with "nervous curiosity" while fanning herself. A visitor from a New York daily newspaper, surveying the unshaven local whites in their crumpled straw hats seated on the lawn in front of the courthouse, and the segregated blacks distributing themselves beneath the Confederate statue, was heard to mutter: "Faulkner was just a reporter." Among the journalists was not only Rob Hall of the *Daily Worker* but the *Nation*'s Dan Wakefield, who found "the scenery itself . . . heavy and oppressive, like the moss that hangs from the cypress trees. . . . The air is heavy, dusty, and hot, and even the silence has a thickness about it—like a kind of taut skin—that is suddenly broken with a shock by the crack and fizz of a Coke being opened."[4]

Some local whites seemed puzzled as well as "outraged—not at the murderers of the boy, but at the widespread attention and headlines the murder had caused." One unselfconscious Delta white whom Wakefield met in Sumner "nodded his head in the direction of the Tallahatchie [and pointed out]: 'That river's full of niggers.'" The national and even international attention that Till's death attracted therefore left such citizens "angry and confused. The feeling that it was all a plot against the South was the most accepted explanation," the correspondent for the *Nation* added. "The question of 'nigger-killing' was coupled with the threat to the racial traditions of the South, and storekeepers set out jars on their counters for contributions to aid the defense of the accused murderers. Donations to the fund eventually totalled an estimated $10,000, and disqualified several prospective jurors. . . ."[5] An eight-foot cross was burned near the depot of the Yazoo and Mississippi Valley Railroad, but its implications seem to have gone unnoticed in the hubbub of the courtroom proceedings.[6]

For this trial the largest venire panel in the history of Tallahatchie

County was arranged, but the selection of the jury was not quite so arduous or complicated as it can be elsewhere in the United States. Though blacks constituted 63 percent of the slightly more than 30,000 residents of Tallahatchie County, it occasioned no surprise that none was selected to serve on the jury. Eligibility to perform that function depended upon the suffrage, and no blacks were registered to vote in the county. Indeed none of the residents could remember *any* blacks registered to vote there since the turn of the century; and the sole campaign promise of the registrar of voters and circuit clerk, Charlie Cox, was "to keep vigilance over your registration books." He was to serve in that sensitive position and to fulfill that winking promise for twenty-eight years.[7]

Since jury service was restricted to white males over the age of twenty-one, unless exempted because of old age, illiteracy, residency requirements, or compelling business reasons, perhaps only 5 percent of the population of Tallahatchie County was eligible to perform the civic duty that Alexis de Tocqueville had deemed one of the essential adornments of American democracy. Posing such questions as "Would you be prejudiced because of race?" and "Did you contribute to the fund for the defense, or would you contribute if asked to?" the prosecution successsfully challenged thirty men on the voir dire; the state also had to use eleven of its twelve peremptory challenges. The result was a jury that consisted of nine farmers, two carpenters, and an insurance man[8]—that is, the sorts of sturdy yeomen who had been hailed from the dawn of the republic as its social and moral foundation.

Xenophobia and hostility toward outsiders were rampant not only in Sumner but throughout the Delta. Only two weeks before the incident at the Bryant store, Senator James O. Eastland had informed members of the Citizens' Councils of Senatobia, Mississippi: "On May 17 the Constitution of the United States was destroyed. . . . You are not required to obey any court which passes out such a ruling. In fact, you are obligated to defy it."[9] The *Yazoo City Herald* seemed to echo the truculence of the Sunflower County plantation owner, who would become chairman of the Senate Judiciary Committee a few months later: "Through the furor over the Emmett Till case[,] we hope someone gets this over to the nine ninnies who comprise the present United States Supreme Court. Some of the young Negro's blood is on their hands also." The newspaper was so determined to dismiss the Court as merely a political institution that the editorial conveyed the impression that those nine jurists (three of them Southerners, incidentally) had been elected: "For the Negro vote in such places as Harlem, these Men of Expendiency have been willing to put into serious jeopardy the peace of the Southland." Though a direct link would be impossible to prove, the editor of a Washington, D.C., black newspaper argued that Till's death "is rooted in the stiffening resistance of unyielding Southerners" to *Brown v. Board of Education*.[10]

Even as some cars bore license plates with the inscription, "Mississippi—The Most Lied About State in the Union," Tom Ethridge of the *Jackson Clarion-Ledger* was claiming that the Northern denunciations of Mississippi constituted a "Communist plot" designed to undermine the white South. Whatever the general reputation of the region for amiable hospitality, Milam himself fully partook of the spirit of hostility during a recess in the trial session. When a reporter tried to be genial by remarking to him, "Pretty hot today, huh, J. W.?" the defendant responded with very measured words: "Hot enough to make a man feel mean."[11]

No wonder, then, that several of the reporters took to putting on Southern accents in order to try to blend into the setting, though one of them did not have to fake it. Born in Pascagoula, Mississippi, Rob Hall of the *Daily Worker* was an object of special curiosity—a real, live Communist who, the *Jackson Daily News* reported, "moves and talks as a Southerner. Actually, he is a Southerner, complete with all its [sic] customs, and actions." Under the headline "Reporter for Commies Relates How He Shifted to 'Left,'" the newspaper traced the career of the banker's son (and Hattiesburg Baptist minister's grandson) from observing at firsthand rural poverty in his native state to improving conditions in textile mills. The soft-spoken, pipe-smoking, forty-nine-year-old newsman himself became an exotic specimen for the locals to examine—not at all what they expected, though Hall denied that he carried a membership card.[12]

Wakefield found covering a murder trial in a Delta hamlet to be so eerie that "you lie in bed at night listening to the hounds baying, and during the day you see more men wearing guns than you ordinarily do outside of your television screen. I am not ashamed to confess that I was afraid." The racism was as casual as it was pervasive. Among the several gun-toting figures who ambled in and out of the courtroom, Wakefield met "a red-necked deputy whose pearl-handled pistol showed beneath the tail of his sport shirt[. He] explained that the 'dressed-up' Negroes were strangers. 'Ninety-five percent of them's not ours,' he said. 'Ours is out picking cotton and tending to their own business.'"[13] Perhaps as a jarring reminder to a few of the "dressed-up" blacks of which state they had chosen to visit, the sheriff greeted the black reporters one day after lunch with a cheerful, "Hello, niggers."[14]

Among them was James Hicks of the *Amsterdam News* and the National Negro Press Association, who recalled that "the Till case was unbelievable. I mean, I just didn't get the sense of being in a courtroom. The courtroom was segregated. . . . The black press sat at a bridge table far off from the bench. The white press sat right under the judge and jury, but we sat at a bridge table," as did Mrs. Bradley. Since a Mississippi criminal court had been the scene two decades earlier of the shooting of a black defendant accused of raping a white woman, at least some of the black journalists had devised a plan of self-defense and escape should they themselves become targets of attack.[15] Instead, they were mostly objects of curiosity and astonishment among the local whites. One of the defense attorneys had privately tried to persuade Sheriff Strider to integrate the press table, because of the threatening impact such an arrangement would have on the jury; but the sheriff rigidly insisted on the preservation of Southern custom.[16]

It was Hicks who had the delicate assignment of securing seating for another Northern observer, Representative Charles C. Diggs, Jr. (D., Mich.). One of three blacks serving in the Eighty-fourth Congress, Diggs hoped that his presence would help provide breathing space for whatever impulses toward justice and due process of law might course within the courtroom. The son and grandson of Mississippians, Diggs had wired Judge Curtis L. Swango of the Seventeenth Judicial District to ask whether he might attend the trial. The judge, a tall, informal forty-seven-year-old, a graduate of Millsaps College in Jackson and of the law school at "Ole Miss," invited him down. But by the time the representative got inside the courtroom, the whites and then the blacks had already taken all the seats. Diggs gave his card to Hicks, who started to walk up to the judge's bench but was accosted by a deputy who inquired: "Where you going, nigger?" When Hicks explained his mission and showed the deputy the card, another deputy was called over and told: "This nigger said there's a nigger outside who says he's a Congressman. . . . " "A nigger Congressman?" "That's what this nigger said," and then the first deputy laughed at so blatant a contradiction in terms. But the sheriff was summoned and then told Hicks: "I'll bring him in here, but I'm going to sit him at you niggers' table." And that is where the representative sat.[17]

At least some whites did not welcome his presence. The *Jackson Clarion-Ledger* labeled him "an impudent, South-hating Negro Congressman" who, along with three northern black attorneys, "squatted themselves" in a place where they clearly did not belong. The newspaper's editorialist suspected that "the NAACP atmosphere" that the "spectators" provided might have "an adverse effect on the state's case," since "Mississippi's courts do not like covert attempts at intimidation." The rival *Jackson Daily News* counted only two attorneys with Diggs, but concurred that he was "an insolent, arrogant South-hater," and "just another medlesome [sic] Negro politician," whose presence "must be intensely repulsive for the jurors." The newspaper hoped that "the good people of Sumner are able to stomach this blatant display of bad taste and phony sympathy; for if they react as they have just cause to do, it will make banner copy throughout the North." But with admirable restraint, local whites did not attempt to harm him, as both newspapers suspected the Congressman had expected.[18]

The *Times* reported the atmosphere within the gray brick courthouse as "controlled hostility." But on the surface, the mood was informal: the judge was in shirt-sleeves, smoking was permitted at all times, and bailiffs walked in and out carrying pitchers of ice water. The sweltering courtroom seemed to bulge with the 280 racially segregated spectators who packed it each day.[19] Crosby Smith, who had first reported to the sheriff in Greenwood that Till was missing, was not among them. He was too frightened even to go into town, and recalled: "I was mighty scared during the time that trial was going on, and for a long time afterwards."[20]

The first witness for the state was his brother-in-law, the sixty-four-year-old Moses Wright, who, along with his wife, had not slept in his own home since the night of the kidnapping. In their hiding place Wright had been warned that he himself would be killed if he were to testify in the case. But he did not leave Mississippi and instead took the stand, where he was addressed as "Uncle Mose" by the prosecution and as "Mose" by the defense. He recalled how "two white men came to his house and asked for 'the boy from Chicago—the one that did the talking at Money.'" When one of the prosecutors, District Attorney Gerald Chatham, asked Wright to identify the two abductors of Emmett Till, Wright pointed first to Milam and said, "Thar he," and then pointed to Bryant.[21]

A reporter, Murray Kempton of the *New York Post*, watched Milam's reaction. The defendant "leaned forward, crooking a cigaret in a hand that seemed as large as Mose Wright's whole chest, and his eyes were coals of hatred." But the witness "took all their blast straight in his face"; and after saying "And there's Mr. Bryant," Wright sat down "with a lurch which told better than anything else the cost in strength to him of the thing he had done." From the bridge table further away, Hicks could sense "a terrific tension in the courtroom"; but nothing happened, probably because Judge Swango pounded his gavel and said, "Order, order!" Under withering cross-examination, Wright stuck to his story, even dropping "Sir" and substituting an undeferential, "That's right," instead. It was, Kempton asserted, "the hardest half hour in the hardest life possible for a human being in these United States." Wright could feel, he later reminisced, "the blood boil in hundreds of white people as they sat glaring in the courtroom. It was the first time in my life I had the courage to accuse a white man of a crime, let alone something [as] terrible as killing a boy. I wasn't exactly brave and I wasn't scared. I just wanted to see justice done."[22]

Writing from Washington, I. F. Stone saluted Wright's bravery in testifying against the two defendants; and Congressman Diggs in retrospect considered that unflinching "Thar he" inside a steamy, segregated courtroom to be "historic." Wakefield, whose father was a Southerner, put such valor and civic responsibility in perspective. For Jim Crow was a "system in which a Negro citizen doesn't call the police if a boy is dragged from his bed in the night by white men[,] because the police are white too, and therefore the enemy. It is not really strange or remarkable that the people who are victims of such a system have begun to fight it with so little fear. They have, after all, nothing to lose." By compelling the state of Mississippi to put the half-brothers on trial, Wright had raised not only his own stature but elevated that of other subjugated Negroes as well. "The county in which he toiled and which he is now resigned to leaving," Kempton concluded, "will never be the same for what he has done."[23]

The meaning of the social system that Wright had so majestically defied during almost half an hour of testimony was further clarified when Till's mother took the stand. Mrs. Bradley "caused a sensation" when she entered the courtroom, the *Memphis Commercial Appeal* reported; and the attention she received "swept an expression of almost painful dislike across the faces of the local spectators." In the witness chair Mrs. Bradley recalled warning her son "to be very careful how he spoke, and to say 'yes, sir' and 'no, ma'am,' and not to hesitate to humble yourself if you had to get down on your knees." Because her son had been born and raised in Chicago, she explained with composure, "he didn't know" how to "be humble to white people."[24]

Willie Reed, a nineteen-year-old sharecropper's son from Sunflower County, testified in a voice so low that Judge Swango was repeatedly forced to urge him to speak louder. Reed had never seen Till before the morning of the slaying but recognized him afterward from a newspaper photograph. The ninth-grader claimed that he had seen Till in the back of the 1955 Chevrolet pickup truck, which had stopped at the barn, and had heard someone being beaten inside. There were cries, wails, and then Reed heard, "Mama, Lord have mercy, Lord have mercy." Reed had then run to the home of his aunt, Amanda Bradley, and asked her: "Who are they beating to death down at the barn, Aunt Mandy?" Reed then saw Milam, with a gun in his holster, emerge from the shed. Amanda Bradley also testified to hearing the beating from the shed.[25] After Reed's testimony, his family sent him to Chicago.[26] The mother of Curtis Jones did not permit him to leave Chicago to testify at the trial, he later reminisced, because she "was afraid something would happen to me like something happened to Emmett Till."[27]

Though neither Bryant nor Milam could be compelled under the Constitution to incriminate himself, the defense called as its first witness Carolyn Bryant, whom the reporter for the *New York Times* described as "a pretty brunette." Judge Swango ruled most of her account inadmissible, however, because the incident in the store had occurred "too long before the abduction." Over the objections of the defense, the judge declared that, according to his interpretation of the rules of evidence, testimony relating to an incident prior to the main crime in a capital case could be heard by the jury only if it affected the question of whether the deceased or defendant was the aggressor, or whether it involved an overt act. That was not the issue in this case, Swango ruled. Such decisions contributed to his reputation for integrity and probity.

With the jury absent, Mrs. Bryant claimed that a Negro with "a Northern brogue" had come into the store, paid for some bubble gun, and then grabbed her and propositioned her lewdly before she could free herself, and that he still had not stifled his "wolf whistle" after he left the store.[28] One of the defense attorneys then played the part of Till to demonstrate how she had been embraced, and also imitated the whistle itself. Such theatrics did not bear directly on the culpability of the witness's husband and brother-in-law, who claimed that they had let the teenager go before he disappeared. But at the very least, the reenactment of the taboo that was violated would hardly have diminished the jurors' sympathies for the defendants.

Strider, the sheriff of Tallahatchie County, testified for the *defense*. Taking advantage of the fact that no witness had seen Till actually being murdered, Strider claimed that all he knew about the body dredged up from the Tallahatchie River was that it was human. He speculated grotesquely that the notorious NAACP had plotted Till's so-called killing, and that Till himself was living happily in Detroit. One of the five defense attorneys, John Whitten, the chairman of the Democratic Party in Tallahatchie County as well as a first cousin of Mississippi Congressman Jamie Whitten, was then faced with the inconvenient fact of Emmett Till's ring. It sufficed for Whitten to conjecture that some sinister group had planted it on the body, and in his summation he denounced such "rabble-rousers." The attorney told the jurors that he was "sure that every last Anglo-Saxon one of you has the courage to free these men in the face of that pressure."

In a vigorous rebuttal to the defense, Robert Smith confused the Declaration of Independence with a later document when he proclaimed that "we can only keep our way of life when we support the constitutional guarantees of life, liberty and the pursuit of happiness for every citizen regardless of race; and Emmett Till was entitled to his life." Smith conceded that the deceased had acted wrongly, however. "I was born and bred in the South," the special prosecutor assured the jurors, "and the very worst punishment that should have occurred was to take a razor strap, turn him over a barrel and whip him. "I've spanked my child and you have spanked yours," Smith added. Responding to the allegations of Strider and of defense counsel, he insisted that Mamie Bradley's certainty that the corpse was indeed that of her son was decisive testimony. For "the last thing in God's creation a mother wants is to believe that her son is dead." Chatham struck the same note: "Mamie Bradley brought that child into the world. . . . Who else could identify that child? Who else could say 'that's my boy'?"

C. Sidney Carlton, another attorney for the defense and a future president of the Mississippi Bar Association (1962–63), found "nothing reasonable" in the state's account of what had happened. It was too convoluted for the defendants to have kidnapped Till in Leflore County, driven him to a plantation in Sunflower County, and then doubled back into Tallahatchie County "to dump the body into a river." Carlton warned the jurors in his summation that their forefathers would turn over in their graves if a guilty verdict were to be rendered. If Milam and Bryant were convicted, Carlton asked, "where under the shining sun is the land of the free and the home of the brave?"[29]

He need not have worried, for the jurors chose to ignore the district attorney's plea to punish the perpetrators of a "cowardly act . . . a brutal, unnecessary killing of a human being." The framework of Mississippi law did not permit any distinctions in degrees of homicide, so the jury faced three options: capital punishment, life imprisonment, or acquittal. On September 23, the jurors needed an hour and seven minutes to decide that their peers, both of whom had been born and reared in Tallahatchie County, were not guilty of murder. "If we hadn't stopped to drink pop," one juror later explained, "it wouldn't have taken that long."[30] According to one account, three ballots had in fact been cast. The first tabulation had nine for acquittal, three abstaining, the second ten for acquittal, two abstaining.[31] But one scholar who interviewed several of the jurors seven years later learned that all the ballots had been for acquittal. The jurors had "deliberated" so long because the sheriff-elect, Harry Dogan, sent word to wait a while, to make it "look good."[32]

After Clerk Charlie Cox read out the verdict, Bryant and Milam became free men who embraced their wives, accepted the congratulations of well-wishers, lit up cigars, and walked out of the courtroom. With their wives and children, the acquitted defendants then posed for the photographers and cameramen, who had set up their equipment each day of the trial at the rear entrance of the courthouse. Mrs. Bradley heard the news in the nearby all-black town of Mound Bayou. Professing no surprise at the verdict, she did not want to be in the courtroom when it was announced.[33] That day was also the 166th anniversary of the signing of the Bill of Rights.

The foreman, J. A. Shaw, Jr., a farmer from Webb, later attributed the verdict to the failure of the state to identify the body positively as that of Emmett Till. The doubts that Strider had maliciously planted about the corpse apparently had their effect, though the state did not bother to summon expert medical examiners who could have erased such doubts. Mississippi itself had been without a medical school until after World War II, and the institute located in Jackson did not graduate its first class until a year after the trial in Sumner. But a physician and an embalmer, testifying for the defense, both claimed that the body had decomposed too long for it to have been Till's.[34]

If the corpse dredged up from the Tallahatchie River was not Till's, then whose was it? From the lack of official or unofficial curiosity can be inferred the phoniness of the jury's rationale for acquittal, and the far more plausible reason that the jurors deemed the probable motives for such a homicide justifiable.[35] In a prescient editorial in the *Delta Democrat-Times,* Hodding Carter demolished the doubts that the defense had tried to implant:

> The body was identified by relatives, was accepted by the boy's mother. . . . Had such a murder been planned to replace another body for Till's, the ring engraved 1943 L. T. (for the boy's father Louis Till), someone would have had to have been killed before the boy was abducted, the ring stolen from young Till and placed on the dead person's finger. Without the prior knowledge that Roy Bryant and his half-brother would kidnap Till, as they admittedly did, such a conspiracy defies even the most fantastic reality.[36]

When journalists asked about the response of the gentlemen of the jury to the credibility and force of the testimony that the grieving Mamie Bradley had given to the court, the foreman replied: "If she tried a little harder, she might have got out a tear."[37] In fact, though otherwise composed on the witness stand, Mrs. Bradley removed her glasses and did wipe her eyes when shown a photograph of her son. "If I thought it wasn't my boy," she insisted, "I would be here looking for him now."[38] State law had prevented women from serving on the jury, an exclusion that was not formally eliminated until 1968. White women may not have been any more sympathetic to the plight and loss of Mrs. Bradley in 1955; in any event, sisterhood may not be quite powerful enough to surmount the barrier of racism. But it still may be permissible to speculate that female jurors might have found more persuasive than men the terrible force of a mother's certainty, which torpedoed the hope that Bobo could still be alive.

Strider himself inadvertently invalidated his own spooky and cynical theory when he was quizzed afterward about hate mail that he had received. Pointing a finger right at the television camera, the sheriff responded: "I'm glad you asked me this. I just want to tell all of those people who've been sending me those threatening letters that if they ever come down here, the same thing's gonna happen to them that happened to Emmett Till."[39] Since Strider had speculated that Till was alive and well up north, the 270-pound sheriff's threat was presumably rather meaningless. He did feel compelled, after the acquittal, to add: "Well, I hope the Chicago niggers and the NAACP are satisfied."[40]

They were not, but the verdict did match the pattern of crimes of violence in the South, which were scaled according to caste. The dictates of regional justice held crimes of blacks against whites to be the most serious offenses of all; the crimes of blacks against blacks, worthy of little attention; and the violence of whites against blacks, usually justified.[41] It would therefore be unwise to overinterpret the reasoning behind the verdict of the Sumner jury, which was stocked with the sort of citizens whom the defense had needed in the face of overwhelmingly incriminating evidence. The attorneys for the half-brothers had used the selection process to identify jurors who would automatically vote for acquittal—who would, in such cases, impose a test even more stringent than "beyond all reasonable doubt." The state was expected to erase all doubts whatsoever about the defendants' guilt, no matter how farfetched the elements of uncertainty. Since ten of the jurors came from the poor-white, even more Negrophobic hill section of Tallahatchie County, rather than the more paternalistic side of the Delta, the chief of the defense team was right to deprecate the forensic brilliance of counsel for the half-brothers. "After the jury had been chosen," J. J. Breland quipped, "any first-year law student could have won the case."[42]

On the other hand, even reporters who were astonished or indignant after the jury's verdict praised the conduct of Judge Swango; even Hall of the *Daily Worker* was among them.[43] Congressman

Diggs was also laudatory, asserting in Detroit that "the lone antiseptic which helped clean the bad taste of the verdict from my mouth was the fairness of Judge Curtis M. Swango."[44] The correspondent for the *Nation* singled out Swango and Chatham as "native Mississippians whose devotion throughout this occasion was to justice above states' rights and local customs. . . . The two of them seemed proof enough that their country's great historian had told us the truth when he gave us Gavin Stevens and Colonel Sartoris as well as Clem Snopes." Dan Wakefield could not have known that Judge Swango's father had come down from eastern Kentucky to boss a lumber camp in Panola County, and had asserted his authority with a standing offer to fight anyone—black or white—who challenged it, just as Faulkner's Thomas Sutpen had done in lawless Yoknapatawpha County little more than half a century earlier. A few journalists also discovered that even a valorous prosecution could share the moral myopia of the area. In an informal discussion out of court, a member of Chatham's team who had seemed on the side of the angels told the visiting reporters: "Yes suh, it's really bad down here in the Delta. . . . I'm from up in the hill country, and it's very different; we don't have a bit of trouble with our niggers up there."[45]

But such complications and melancholy ambiguities were not typical of reactions in the national press. The report of *The Crisis* was hyperbolic, but conveyed something of the shock of exoneration in its November issue: "Not since Pearl Harbor has the country been so outraged as by the brutal, insensate lynching . . . and the unconscionable verdict of the Sumner, Mississippi jury."[46] The editorial in the *Christian Century* commented that the "brevity of the trial and its incredible verdict piled shock upon shock." The magazine added that "what offends common humanity was the spirit of the defense, the atmosphere of the community, and the swift certainty of the jury's decision." Those for whom the *Christian Century* claimed to speak were "bewildered, outraged, ashamed . . . but most of all, Christians are sick." The *Pittsburgh Courier,* a leading Negro newspaper, ran a half-inch black border around its front page, as well as a headline that proclaimed "Sept. 23, 1955—BLACK FRIDAY!"[47] *Commonweal* was rather unusual in combining outrage against Mississippi with an awareness that the "moral disease" that killed Emmett Till was not confined to that state: "It is the same disease that created the Northern ghetto in which he lived, [and] the Southern shack from which he was taken to his death." The

Roman Catholic journal reminded its readers that "the illness that ultimately killed him condemns Negroes to inferior homes, schools and jobs" in Chicago and other Northern communities as well. Till's death, *Commonweal* concluded, "took racism out of the textbooks and editorials and showed it to the world in its true dimensions."[48]

Both the wolf whistle and the resounding "not guilty" were heard around the world. "All over," observed *Commonweal*, "people of every race and color read with shame and revulsion what had happened."[49] *Le Figaro* asserted that "the scandalous verdict . . . in acquitting Roy Bryant and John Milam . . . when everything pointed to their shameful guilt, will arouse worldwide indignation." The moderate Parisian newspaper had sent daily dispatches about the trial from its New York bureau, and inferred that the Sumner jury "followed the tradition that no white man in the South must ever be found guilty for killing a Negro!"[50] A liberal weekly, *France Observateur*, even noted that *l'affaire* Till exceeded even the Rosenberg trial in provoking unanimous opinions of outrage in the French press. In Rome the Vatican's *L'Osservatore Romano* noted in a strong editorial against racism that its American manifestations had, "unfortunately, caused many crimes," citing the trial in Sumner involving "a crime against an adolescent victim [that] has remained unpunished."[51]

In a survey of European opinion and press reactions, the American Jewish Committee reported that the Sumner verdict had "seriously damaged" American prestige. Western European condemnations were characterized as "swift, violent and universal. There was total and unqualified condemnation of the court proceedings, of the weakness of prosecution, the behavior of the jury and the judge, and at the verdict of acquittal." Hundreds of newspaper editorials across a spectrum of opinion from conservative and liberal as well as Communist denounced the exoneration. It demonstrated, in the summation of *Das Freie Volk* in Düsseldorf, that "the life of a Negro in Mississippi is not worth a whistle."[52] The *Christian Century* was therefore warranted in its conclusion that "the horror and indignation that are rolling in from what have been the friendliest foreign journals indicate that the townspeople [of Sumner] have engineered a local tragedy into an international calamity."[53]

By contrast the newspapers closest to the scene could not have cared less about the international uproar. The *Memphis Commercial Appeal* considered the jurors' verdict sound and "the processes of the law followed in full[,] in spite of agitation, [and] inflammation of the public." Since the evidence was so circumstantial, conviction for murder, the editorialist was certain, "would have been reversed by any appeals court in the land, including Mississippi, Illinois and New York."[54] Virtually all of Mississippi's white-run newspapers concurred, praising in their editorials the "fairness and integrity" with which the ideal of due process of law was observed and realized in Sumner. The editorial in the *Greenwood Commonwealth*, for example, emphasized "the fairness and impartial manner in which Judge Swango directed the court." For such newspapers the probity of the jurist was a godsend, allowing them to evade such questions as the identity of the body, if it was not Till's. Omitting entirely from consideration the unwarranted, if unsurprising, verdict of the jury, the Leflore County newspaper concluded: "Mississippi can handle its affairs without any outside meddling[,] and its long history of proper court procedure can never be questioned by any group."[55] The *Jackson Clarion-Ledger* recorded the "vigor" of the prosecution but insisted that the state had "failed to prove its case" because "practically all the evidence against the defendants was circumstantial."[56]

Even the Greenville *Delta Democrat-Times* failed to criticize the weird verdict of the jurors. The dominant newspaper in the vicinity managed instead to shift the blame to the inadequate presentation of a "flimsy" case, and was especially critical of Sheriff Strider for his lack of zeal in locating evidence and witnesses. But editor Hodding Carter also complained that such officials were put on the defensive by the NAACP. The organization's "blanket accusations of decent people," "studied needling" of responsible officials, and "indifference to truth in favor of propaganda-making" set back the cause of the prosecution—and of justice. The editorial predicted that, because of the international exposure, "Mississippi must now suffer for it for at least another generation."[57] These local journalists were thus implicated in the charge leveled in the pages of *Commonweal*: "The world waits for the outraged voices of Southern decency protesting the sin that has been committed against the honor of the South—and of mankind."[58]

In Greenwood in November, a second grand jury of twenty members heard Moses Wright and Willie Reed testify again on the kidnapping charges that had been dropped at the outset of the trial in Sumner. Bryant and Milam had of course admitted to the abduction when they were first in custody, but claimed that they had released

Till unharmed when they realized that he was not the one that had been "talking dirty" in Money. This was the confession that Leflore County Sheriff George Smith described under oath during the trial in Sumner and repeated, along with his deputy, John Ed Cothran, in Greenwood. The evidence of abduction could not have been more incontrovertible. But the half-brothers were not indicted.[59] It was left unexplained why, after allegedly releasing Till, Bryant and Milam seemed to lose all interest in finding the actual youth who had presumably insulted Carolyn Bryant, a dishonor so blatant that it propelled them to Wright's shanty at 2 o'clock on a Sunday morning. Yet the half-brothers were never asked to explain why they were so strangely and erratically willing to drop their pressing quest for an insubordinate stranger after they mistakenly took out "the wrong boy." With the inaction of the grand jury, they were no longer at risk, however. Bryant announced that he was reopening his store; and Milam returned to his home near Glendora, where "there's some cotton-picking I've got to do."[60]

Less than a month later, a homicide occurred in Glendora that offered further proof of what happened when Mississippians were permitted to handle their own affairs without the glare of publicity or the hint of outside interference. An inebriated cotton-gin manager named Elmer Kimbell, whose best friend was J. W. Milam, pulled up to a gas station on the night of December 3 in Milam's car and asked for a full tank of gas. A black employee, Clinton Melton, complied until Kimbell changed his mind, insisting instead that he wanted only two dollars' worth. Kimbell became surly, drove off to get a gun, and returned ten minutes later, murdering Melton with two shots to the head.

The trial was again held in Sumner. But probably because Melton was a native Mississippi black, newspaper interest in the case was meager. Only one wire service sent a staffer, and the *Delta Democrat-Times* was the only newspaper in the state to send a reporter. No press table was set up, and cameras were barred from the entire property of the courthouse. The NAACP stayed away; no black congressman showed up to observe the proceedings. Hamilton Caldwell was again the prosecutor. The state had three unimpeachable witnesses, including the white employer of the late Clinton Melton, who had worked for ten years at the Glendora gas station without provoking complaints. Nor had the father of five been accused of any sexual improprieties. Kimbell pleaded self-defense, though Melton's own weapon was never found. Even the testimony of his own wife contradicted the recollections of the defendant. Sheriff Strider again testified for the defense, and Milam visited the courthouse the first day. It took the all-white jury, consisting of ten farmers, an insurance man, and an employee of a seed-manufacturing company, four hours and nineteen minutes of deliberations before it voted for acquittal. "There's open season on the Negroes now," a Tallahatchie County man told David Halberstam, one of the very few reporters to cover the trial. "They've got no protection, and any peckerwood who wants to can go shoot himself one, and we'll free him. Our situation will get worse and worse."[61]

With Negro life held in such contempt, no wonder, then, that Moses Wright felt compelled to leave Mississippi. The sharecropper whom the prosecution had addressed as "Uncle Mose" had received stacks of mail after his testimony, and the envelopes had contained offers of jobs as well as cash. After testifying before the grand jury, however, Wright himself did not return to the state again. He surrendered his old hunting dog and abandoned his car at the train depot even before the cotton crop had been harvested.[62]

Good riddance was the response of columnist W. S. Fairchild in the *Jackson Daily News.* "The people of the state certainly have no regrets over the departure of Mose," Fairchild intoned. "To live in the South and share in its bountiful wealth[,] one must be a part of its way of life." Having covered the trial itself, the newsman had concluded that "Mose is weak and we wonder what anguished dreams will disturb his sleep after the celebrity-like newness wears off. Too bad he came under NAACP influence," an organization described as "an emotional Communistic front" whose "only aim is to raise money from simple-minded and weak-minded people, who throughout their history in America have caused bloodshed." Adopting Sheriff Strider's thesis that Till's disappearance should not be equated with his death ("very few in Mississippi . . . know the real facts of the Emmett Till case"), the *Daily News* columnist urged the NAACP to stay out of the state, since only violence would result; and "the South and its people simply refuse to shed more blood on a race that has been parasites since the birth of our country." Instead of fulfilling the calling of "preacher" by preaching "tolerance," Wright had yielded to alien and unwholesome influences; and therefore his "exile" from the state was welcome: "Mose is now out of place [but] . . . this does not mean we want him back."[63]

After moving with his wife to Chicago, the former sharecropper spoke several times under NAACP auspices about the Till case and became a farmer in Argo, Illinois. Elizabeth Wright died in 1971. Her husband, the man who had fired that monosyllabic missile against a system of repression—"Thar he"—died two years later.[64]

F O U R

The Shock of Exoneration

The vagaries of justice and the pursuit of truth are not symmetrical; and the chief account of Till's murder remains the article that William Bradford Huie published in *Look* magazine on January 24, 1956. The article is the only widely accepted source to elucidate the assassins' motives. It was excerpted in the April 1956 edition of *Reader's Digest* and was later enlarged and published as a chapter in *Wolf Whistle* (1959), a short paperback that was destined for the drugstore racks and has long been out of print. No historian of this case can therefore help but incur—or fail to acknowledge—an enormous debt to Huie (1910–86), an eighth-generation white Alabamian. After graduating from the University of Alabama, he began his professional writing career by selling a "true confession" article to *True Story,* and eventually wrote twenty-one books that sold about thirty million copies. Huie was perhaps best known for his novels, *The Americanization of Emily* (1959) and *The Revolt of Mamie Stover* (1951), but he specialized in insider accounts of racial atrocities. He was an instinctive conservative who nevertheless became a vocal opponent of the racism of Governor George Wallace, as well as an unwavering champion of the civil rights movement.[1]

Huie's research on the Till case, conducted so soon after the acquittal, led the Southern publicist John Temple Graves to denounce the resident of Hartselle (in the hills of northern Alabama) as a "masterly and dastardly imaginist [sic]."[2] But Graves, a columnist for the *Birmingham Post-Herald,* did not specify what falsifications had been perpetrated in Huie's work; and he later apologized to Huie. Nor have any other journalistic or scholarly sources yet contradicted—or confirmed either—the oral testimony initially reported in *Look* magazine. And because the evidence presented in the Sumner courtroom against Bryant and Milam was essentially circumstantial, because no witness to the actual murder has ever been located or identified, the composition of *Wolf Whistle* merits attention as much as its revelations have warranted extensive quotation.

Huie was a practitioner of what later came to be derided as "checkbook journalism." A decade after the case itself, he wrote: "It is well known in Mississippi that in order to publish the truth about the Emmett Till murder, I paid those murderers with the assistance of reputable alumni of the Ole Miss Law School."[3] Two months after the trial, Huie went to Sumner to speak to one of the attorneys, hoping to ferret out the facts in the wake of the acquittals. In his first meeting there, Huie spent five hours at the office of Breland & Whitten, for "I am as 'Southern' as they are," he reported to a *Look* editor. "We can close the door, tilt the bourbon jug, and we can 'talk turkey.'"[4] To the journalist's initial inquiry in Sumner, John Whitten responded: "Well, I'd like to know what happened. I defended them, but I never asked 'em whether they killed the boy or not. I didn't wanna know," despite the opportunities to satisfy curiosity that the attorney-client privilege afforded. Huie convinced Whitten and Breland—those "two reputable alumni"—to allow him to speak to the acquitted defendants, who were exempted under the Fifth Amendment from any further jeopardy. The Alabamian promised the half-brothers money for his right to make a film of the case, and offered in effect "to pay them for the right to libel them," since he was accusing Bryant and Milam of killing young Till.

Huie remembered: "They were called in, and they agreed for the reasons I've said. They didn't think they were guilty. They didn't think they'd done anything wrong." According to Huie, "The man who had done the killing" did not therefore offer a confession in the sense of hankering to purge his soul of its anguish. There, in the office of Breland & Whitten and in a Holiday Inn in Greenwood, the murderer simply "told [him] the truth." The former defendants had never really felt in any further legal peril, and in Huie's presence they did not seem psychologically on the defensive. Huie assured them that he would never divulge them as his source in a court of law—even, say, if Mrs. Bradley and the NAACP were to sue the state of Mississippi for damages, and if he were subpoenaed as a witness.[5]

Huie handed over somewhere between $3,600 and $4,000, and later reflected that "other people find this sort of thing distasteful; and I have not found it particularly *pleasing*" (italics in original). He was "denounced by people for paying the murderers of Emmett Till," but the journalist "could never have told their story of how they murdered him without doing it." Thus he elicited the information he sought—"where they got the weight, the gin fan they put around the victim's neck, all this sort of thing." The investigator learned that Till was murdered "for no other reason than he had a white girl's picture in his wallet. . . . They didn't take him out to kill him . . . [but Till] told 'em that she was his girl. It was at the time that they thought that this sorta thing had to be stopped in order to defend the 'Southern way of life'. . . . "[6] Huie later described the visitor from Chicago as "boastful [and] brash." Because "he had a white girl's picture in his pocket and boasted of having screwed her . . . they took him out and killed him."[7]

This striking claim should be juxtaposed against the recollection of Till's mother, who was not certain which photos Bobo had in his wallet, "other than family." But she did recall having bought him a wallet shortly before his summer vacation. "Back in the '50's" she said, "when you buy a wallet, a picture of a movie star was always in it. That was Hedy Lamarr." It is rather doubtful, however, that the half-brothers would have mistaken in the morning light the actress's likeness for that of a teenager's girlfriend, and even less likely that Bobo's Mississippi cousins—no matter how provincial—could have been fooled by his boasts of carnal knowledge of Miss Lamarr. The Huie account does more generally tend to confirm, however, what the black writer Calvin Hernton was to assert a decade later: "I know for a fact that it is dangerous in the South for a Negro to be caught (arrested, for instance) with a photograph of a white female in his possession."[8]

On four separate nights that fall, Milam and Roy and Carolyn Bryant described what happened. They seemed willing to trust Huie because, as he explained to his editor, "I am not a 'liberal'; I only write about the human race, [but] I don't try to reform it." He also boasted that "I am capable of drinking out of the same jug with Milam and letting him drink first." In *Wolf Whistle* itself, however, only Milam spoke on the record, though the Bryants apparently did not contradict him. During the days of the interview period, Huie checked their accounts and seems to have confirmed their accuracy.[9] He then secured what he remembered as record prices abroad for the translation rights for the account published in *Look*; and though he also wrote a movie script under contract for RKO, its producer cancelled the film. When Representative Diggs inserted the Huie article into the *Congressioal Record*, Governor Coleman blasted Diggs and the NAACP for the sort of interference in "the Southern way of life" that had inflamed the Sumner jury four months earlier. "I assumed the NAACP wanted an acquittal for propaganda purposes," the governor charged. "Unfortunately, the jury, being stirred up as they were, proceeded to give them that propaganda."[10] But Coleman was careful *not* to assert that the *Look* article was false.

Why were the confessions uttered and sanctioned? The motives varied. Bryant was broke and needed the money; exempt from further criminal charges, Milam was proud of the vengeance and violence that he had perpetrated. Neither was ashamed of the abduction, the torture, and the murder; nor were the half-brothers so financially secure that the temptation to profit from their crime could be resisted. But Breland, a Princeton graduate who had been practicing law in Sumner for four decades, was more subtle. According to Huie, the attorney *wanted* such violence to be publicized, as a warning. "There ain't gonna be no integration," he told Huie. "There ain't gonna be no nigger votin'. *And the sooner everybody in this country realizes it, the better* [italics in original]. If any more pressure is put on us," he ominously added, "the Tallahatchie River won't hold all the niggers that'll be thrown into it." The sixty-five-year-old Breland nevertheless dismissed the half-brothers as "rednecks." Bryant was "a scrappin' pine-knot with nuthin'," while the law firm had been compelled to sue Milam "a couple of times for debt; he's bootlegged all his life. . . . Got a chip on his shoulder. That's how he got that battlefield promotion in Europe; he likes to kill folks." Then Breland explained the usefulness of the lower-class whites whom he called "peckerwoods": "Hell, we've got to have our Milams and Bryants to fight our wars and keep the niggahs in line."[11] The defendants' proclivity for violence was therefore worth advertising in a national magazine, *pour encourager les autres*. As

Breland assured Huie, publication of the story of an "approved kill-ing" would "put the North and the NAACP and the niggers *on notice* [italics in original]"—and might even force the repeal of inte-gration, "just like Prohibition."[12]

Huie's was the most widely disseminated and authoritative ac-count of the case, and it has been uncontroverted and indeed some-what amplified in Hugh Stephen Whitaker's unpublished master's thesis at Florida State University. In 1962, Whitaker, a white native of Tallahatchie County, interviewed not only Huie (in Alabama) but three of the defense attorneys (Breland, Kellum, and Whitten), pros-ecutors Hamilton Caldwell and Robert B. Smith, and Sheriff Strider and others involved in the case. Though Whitaker did not talk to Bryant or Milam, the resulting 1963 academic thesis, "A Case Study in Southern Justice: The Emmett Till Case," nonetheless ranks as a primary source as well, especially since the author utilized the transcript of the court trial itself, a document that has apparently disappeared.

Especially because the defendants never testified in open court, the primacy of the Huie account has been unchallenged. Unfortu-nately *Wolf Whistle* has also tended to obscure evidence presented at the trial that the half-brothers did not act by themselves. Testify-ing under oath, Moses Wright and Willie Reed asserted that others were involved in the abduction and execution of Emmett Till. Bo-bo's great-uncle had told Leflore County authorities, and then the grand jury and the criminal court itself, that three white men had come to his cabin around two o'clock on the morning of August 28. When they took Till outside to an automobile, Wright saw a fourth person, a woman (presumably Carolyn Bryant); and all the visitors sped away from Wright's home with Till. Wheeler Parker, the Chi-cago cousin who was sleeping in the room next to Till, also con-firmed that three white men had come into his grandfather's cabin, and that a white woman who remained in the car identified Till as "the one."[13] Reed claimed that, soon after daybreak that Sunday, he had observed a pickup truck drive up to a barn on a plantation near Drew, where Milam's brother Leslie served as the manager. In the truck, Reed asserted, were four white men and three blacks. After the beating and the screams had subsided, they had put some-thing wrapped in a tarpaulin into the back of the vehicle, and Reed later saw the blacks washing out blood from the truck. During cross-

examination he conceded that distance prevented him from identifying any of the men from the truck—except J. W. Milam, whom
Reed saw leave the barn and then reenter it, carrying a pistol.[14]

The two other white men whom Reed claimed to have seen were
never identified, much less apprehended. Of the three blacks, two
were apparently field hands named LeRoy Collins and Henry Loggins, whom the defendants knew. After the trial both Mrs. Bradley
and James Hicks of the *Amsterdam News* charged that Collins and
Loggins had been detained in jail elsewhere to prevent the presentation of their eyewitness testimony. Whitaker, the author of the 1963
master's thesis on the murder trial, claimed that the chief counsel
for the half-brothers confirmed such charges. According to Breland,
Collins and Loggins were incarcerated under false names in
Charleston, the county seat of East Tallahatchie.[15] It is not clear
whether District Attorney Chatham and Special Prosecutor Smith
made much of an effort, if any, to find and interrogate Collins and
Loggins, whose testimony might have strengthened—and indeed
widened—the state's case. But in any event, the white accomplices
of Bryant and Milam have remained anonymous. They, too, it
seems, got away with murder.

The charges of Wright and Reed thus deviate from the account
presented in *Wolf Whistle* of two half-brothers who acted by themselves in defense of their own honor as well as Carolyn Bryant's
reputation. Both Wright and Reed testified under circumstances of
extraordinary danger to them. Neither of these witnesses had any
discernible motive to invent an expanded roster of abductors and
killers and, indeed, must have felt every incentive to discourage
speculation that other whites were implicated in the sensational
crime. When Milam and Bryant gave their version of the events
to Huie, they remained immune from further prosecution; but any
possible accomplices would not have been exempted, however remote the likelihood that an all-white jury would convict them. Huie's informants therefore had a motive in disguising the existence
and identity of accomplices. It is also intriguing that, in the initial
news report of the *Greenwood Commonwealth*, Sheriff Smith was
said to be looking for a third white man as well. Two days later the
newspaper claimed that three white men and a white woman were
in the car that picked Till up at his great-uncle's shanty and drove
off with the Chicago youth into the night.[16] Whitaker, the author
of the only other account based on interviews with some of the

principals in the case, nevertheless doubted that the half-brothers had accomplices. Without having interrogated the defendants or Carolyn Bryant, Whitaker concluded: "Few, if any[,] who know J. W. Milam would expect him to solicit or accept help for this occasion."[17]

But the testimony that Wright and Reed presented in open court is simply too compelling to be discounted; and on this point, then, Huie's *Wolf Whistle* is seriously misleading. Perhaps the strongest evidence, however, comes from Huie's own correspondence with *Look* in arranging for the interviews with Bryant and Milam and for what the Alabama journalist frankly labeled the "payoff." In three private letters within a month after the trial, Huie claimed that there were four murderers, and that he knew all four of them. Their identities were never disclosed, however, presumably for legal reasons.[18]

Doubling the number of actual killers does not necessarily demolish the account that the two acquitted defendants provided; it may mean only that their account was, to avoid further indictments, too narrowly rendered. The *Look* story was only partially true, which means at worst that it was partially false and at best that it was quite misleading. The article and subsequent chapter in *Wolf Whistle* may not have transcribed any actual prevarications, but the omissions that pockmarked Huie's account were highly significant. The number of murderers affects not only the issue of legal culpability, but also the extent of communal guilt and the character of the crime itself. Thus, what happened that morning of August 28 was probably not a updated, midcentury version of a conventional lynching, in the sense that there is no warrant for considering the crime communally organized. But it is also extremely likely that in this act of private vengeance designed to frighten "a strange niggah," the defendants had company.

Another aspect of Huie's account is problematic as well. It strains credulity that Till could have been so impervious to the danger he faced, once Milam and Bryant—and probably their accomplices—had taken him out into the dark. They had suddenly awakened him at a disorienting hour of the night and had removed him from his family despite the entreaties of his great-uncle and aunt. They were physically imposing, they were armed and hostile and coercive, and they outnumbered him. However different the ways of the Delta might have seemed to the visitor, he knew that he had violated a code. Perhaps Till had not fully grasped the visceral, primordial importance attached to the ideal of white female sanctity, as Milam himself phrased it: "When a niggah even gets close to mentionin' sex with a white woman, he's tired o' livin'." But Bobo must surely have realized that a transgression had been committed—for otherwise the dare outside the grocery store, the challenge to his boastfulness would have had no point. Shortly after the incident in the store, he himself had felt uneasy and was ready to go home; the lone female adolescent among the blacks had predicted: "They'll kill him."[19] It is therefore possible that, in talking to Huie, the half-brothers fabricated—or at least exaggerated—Till's resistance to their intimidation as a way of accounting for their own terrible urge to murder him. There are no other living witnesses—or at least none willing to confess. But the description in *Wolf Whistle* of Till's cool defiance, of his numbness to the immediate threat to his life, invites skepticism if not incredulity.

William Bradford Huie's reconstruction of the motives is otherwise not likely to be rebutted. Thanks to his intrepid interviewing, the identity of at least two of the culprits is incontrovertible. Surrounding this affair are no claims of a frame-up (like "forgery by typewriter" in the Hiss case, or the rampant political and nativist prejudice that affected the Sacco and Vanzetti trial) and no wild conspiracy theories (like the "second Oswald" in the Kennedy assassination), even though no "smoking gun" (the Watergate cover-up) has been found either. But in investigating the crime itself, others got there ahead of Huie. Ruby Hurley had moved to Birmingham in 1951 to establish the first permanent office of the NAACP in the Deep South; and for the organization's magazine, *The Crisis*, she checked into the Till disappearance and murder. Joining her effort were Medgar Evers, the NAACP leader in Jackson, and Amzie Moore, who represented the organization in Cleveland, Mississippi. When the corpse was recovered from the river, the three of them dressed in overalls and worn-out shoes; and Mrs. Hurley put a red bandanna over her head. Moore completed their disguise by borrowing a car with license tags from a Delta county.

"Those were weeks of frenzied activity, weeks of special danger," Evers's wife Myrlie recalled over a decade later. He "made many trips to the Delta, investigating, questioning, searching out witnesses before they could be frightened into silence. . . . And, more than once, there were chases along the long, straight, unlighted

highways that led from the Delta back to Jackson. . . . Frequently
he was followed throughout his trips around the Delta. . . . " He
attended the trial in Sumner, and hustled one of the black witnesses
out of town and to safety in Tennessee and then north by hiding
the witness in a casket. Myrlie Evers realized "from that time on
[that] I never lost the fear that Medgar himself would be killed. . . .
I could feel my stomach contract in cold fear that I would never see
him again."[20] Eight years after Till was murdered, a sniper indeed
ambushed her husband in front of their home in Jackson. He was
thirty-seven years old, and some of his friends and admirers were
amazed that he had managed to live that long. The presumed assassin, Byron Beckwith of Greenwood, was tried but never convicted
of Medgar Evers's death.

Having spoken to Till's cousin who had watched him inside the
store, Ruby Hurley concluded that the visitor from Chicago had not
wolf whistled at all. For if Bobo Till had once suffered from infantile
paralysis, the disease might have impaired his pronunciation, she
concluded. "He whistled when he tried to enunciate words," Hurley
learned. "This was the charge that was made against him."[21] Even
if that were so, it was not of course the only violation of racial and
sexual etiquette that was supposed to have been committed. For
Bryant and Milam themselves told Huie that they came to the
Wright home to beat up "the boy who did the talking" in Money;
and they murdered the customer who had paid two cents for bubble
gum not because of a suggestive whistle but because of the picture
in his wallet.

Mrs. Hurley's account has itself recently been complemented by
that of Endesha Ida Mae Holland, who was born in Greenville and
who later taught American Studies at the State University of New
York at Buffalo. Though not in any sense a witness or observer,
Holland wrote that Till had been "standing on the corner with a
couple of his friends. A White woman passed and claimed that
young Till had whistled at her. Later that night, a mob of White
men took the Black Chicago youth back to the river," where they
mutilated and killed him. Though Holland began in the late 1960s
"using memory as a weapon to rescue and reconstruct . . . my Mississippi Delta's community of Black people," she showed unusual
carelessness in this particular effort at retrieval.[22] She got wrong the
locale, the sequence of the events, and the number of participants;
Holland also made no attempt to challenge the reliabiilty of Huie's

own account that Till did in fact whistle at Mrs. Bryant. At best, her essay, which appeared in a journal devoted to the theme of "Women and Memory," is indebted to folk tradition and to the fabrication of myth. At worst, such procedures would make the recording of memory into a surrogate for the quest for the truth and an antonym of history.

But whether the provocation was more the picture in the wallet than the wolf whistle itself, Till's aggressively erotic challenge to the niceties of Jim Crow was undoubtedly without precedent in the Delta. In that same year, white Mississippians killed three other blacks, one in broad daylight on the lawn of the Lincoln County courthouse. Two of the victims, the Reverend George Lee and Lamar Smith, were developing into political activists and had been attempting to assert their civil rights, including suffrage. There were no convictions; indeed, a grand jury failed even to bring an indictment in the Smith case, despite the commission of the crime in full view of bystanders in Brookhaven. It was a summer in which racist passions were boiling, largely because the Supreme Court's implementation decree in May stimulated NAACP chapters in cities and towns like Jackson, Vicksburg, Yazoo City, Clarksdale, and Natchez to file school desegregation petitions.[23] Although such political and legal pressure intensified the anxieties and truculence of white supremacists, the specific influence of this heightened tension on the Till case is impossible to ascertain.

Yet Till's death, Myrlie Evers recalled, was like no other, shaking "the foundations of Mississippi, both black and white—with the white community because it had become nationally publicized, with us blacks, because it said even a child was not safe from racism and bigotry and death." This case, she added, "somehow struck a spark of indignation that ignited protests around the world. . . . It was the murder of this 14-year-old out-of-state visitor that touched off the world-wide clamor and cast the glare of a world spotlight on Mississippi's racism." Much of that enormous publicity had been due to her husband's energy and tenacity: "Angry and frustrated over this particular vicious killing, Medgar made it his mission to see that word of it was spread as widely and accurately as possible. Publicizing the crime and the subsequent defeat of justice became a major NAACP effort."[24]

Immediately after the verdict of acquittal, one of the attorneys for the half-brothers wrote privately that Tallahatchie County was "the place where the NAACP selected in Mississippi to try to drive in an entering wdge in furtherance of their scheme for integration and equalization. . . . But we did not hesitate to assume our full responsibility and stopped them cold." If the Magnolia State had become a state of siege, it was not because the assaults of the leading civil rights organization were entirely misplaced. Medgar Evers's superior, Roy Wilkins, repeated during a Harlem rally shortly after the jurors' verdict that "Mississippi has decided to maintain white supremacy by murdering children." The executive secretary of the civil rights organization could not detect in the entire state any "restraining influence of decency, not in the state capital, among the daily newspapers, the clergy, not among any segment of the so-called lettered citizens." Among the most reputable voices was Greenville's *Delta Democrat-Times*, which editorialized that "to blame two million Mississippians for the irresponsible act of two is about as illogical as one can become." Ignoring the sworn testimony of both Wright and Reed, the newspaper concluded that the prosecution's case was too weak to be beyond reasonable doubt, and that a guilty verdict would have been overturned in an appeals court anywhere in the country. Nor did the editorial acknowledge the larger political horror that the slaying and acquittal revealed, which Atlanta's *New South* explained to its readers that month: "When those in positions of authority hold cheap the dignity and rights of Negroes, what could be more natural than the assumption that Negroes' lives are equally cheap? The simple-minded . . . people in our society take their cues from above."[25]

To highlight and deter the violence that segregationist politics and policies seemed to sanction, in November 1955 the NAACP released an eight-page booklet, *M is for Mississippi and Murder*. The civil rights organization also filed a formal petition with the Department of Justice, urging the federal government to stop immediately the condition of "jungle fury" that, under the impetus of the Citizens' Councils, had flared into racist murders.[26] By the end of that summer, branch offices of the NAACP had filed about sixty petitions throughout the South in accordance with recommendations from headquarters, in response to the May 31 *Brown* implementation decision of the United States Supreme Court. But the outgoing governor of Mississippi, Hugh White, had proposed the abolition of mandatory public education rather than permit the desegregation of the schools.[27]

His successor, James P. Coleman, had organized a successful, or-
thodox segregationist campaign in 1955, in which he managed to
distance himself somewhat from the Citizens' Councils.[28] His putative goal, according to one historian, was "restoring stability within
Mississippi following the Emmett Till murder in the summer of
1955." Coleman's inaugural address in January 1956 alluded to the
notorious affair, informing "our friends outside Mississippi . . . that
the great overwhelming majority of the white people of Mississippi
are not now guilty and never intend to be guilty of any murder,
violence, or any other wrongdoing toward anyone." He assured outsiders: "We do not any more approve of violence and lawlessness
than you do." But he was of course committed to the preservation
of racial segregation, telling a group of Northern newsmen that it
would be maintained for at least another half-century;[29] and it might
have been difficult for those outsiders to envision the maintenance
of such a system without recourse to violence.

Blacks constituted 41 percent of the population of Mississippi,
but only 4 percent could vote—and their numbers were actually
declining in the mid-1950s. Before the *Brown* decision, 265 blacks
had been registered to vote in three Delta counties. By late summer
of 1955, only ninety were still registered. Between 1952 and 1956,
the number of Mississippi Negroes exercising the right of suffrage
dropped from 22,000 to 8,000—and they were almost all urban. By
the end of 1955—almost nine decades after the ratification of the
Fifteenth Amendment, fourteen counties listed no black voters.[30] A
fierce sense of embattlement nevertheless still gripped the white
elite. One jurist warned in particular against "the reformers who
would make us over, according to the mess they have made for
themselves, and, yes, The Board of Sociology setting [*sic*] in Washington, garbed in Judicial Robes, and 'dishing out' the 'legal prece-
dents' of Gunnar Myrdal."[31]

Though legalisms were supposed to reflect only the sterile ingenuity of the Yankee mind, the state legislature managed to fashion
a repertory of statutes designed to restore racial order. The NAACP
was a favorite target of the solons deliberating in Jackson. It became
a crime, for example, for any organization to bring desegregation
suits in the state of Mississippi. The legislature also banned "barratry," or the encouragement of legal quarrels, even through the entire span of English common law had revealed only one indictment
for barratry since 1750.[32] For good measure, the Citizens' Councils

urged Attorney General Herbert Brownell to put the NAACP on his list of subversive organizations. Nevertheless, the civil rights group held its state convention in Jackson without harassment and, among other items on the agenda, condemned the injustice of the verdict in Sumner.[33] Despite the stillness of military defeat that still lingered from Appomattox and the Reconstruction Amendments that had been inserted into the Constitution, "interposition" became part of the lingua franca of the South. This crusty doctrine affirmed the right of sovereign states to interpose themselves between federal agencies and, say, local school boards, since the contract of 1787 strictly limited and enumerated the powers of the central government. Governor Coleman also considered posing a "challenge [to] the validity and dubious origin of the Fourteenth Amendment"; for by proving the historical contention that two-thirds of the states had not adopted it, the Constitutional authority of the *Brown* v. *Board of Education* decision would be instantly erased.[34]

Early in 1956 he established the Mississippi State Sovereignty Commission to smash the NAACP and to promote a more favorable image of the state elsewhere, by showing that racial friction and injustice were vastly overstated. The commission received an initial subsidy of a quarter of a million dollars, endowed itself with virtually unlimited investigatory powers, and cooperated with privately run states' rights organizations. By the early 1960s, under Ross Barnett, the commission was furnishing monthly contributions directly to the Citizens' Councils.[35]

Despite the state's unsurpassed poverty, with a per capita income only half that of the rest of the United States, Mississippi's black and white taxpayers were soon thereafter subsidizing its Citizens' Councils, for the purpose of intimidating and terrorizing the largest minority of blacks of any state in the Union.[36] From a black perspective, the allocations of the state government provided a transparent case study of the consequences of taxation without representation.

Four unpunished murders in Mississippi in 1955 undoubtedly kept blacks reluctant to assert their rights. Threats of violence and other forms of intimidation were used in an effort at hermetically sealing the state from alien influences. The Citizens' Councils formed its second chapter in Holmes County, adjoining Leflore County; and the first item on its agenda was an investigation of a cooperative farm, credit union, summer camp, and medical clinic named Providence Farm. There Dr. David R. Minter, a Presbyterian missionary's son, treated mostly black patients, charging them whatever they could afford. Suspicions of race mixing led to a meeting of the Citizens' Councils three days after Bryant and Milam were acquitted. The cochairman was a state representative who warned that such integrated activities as swimming parties might result in "another Till killing."

Especially worrisome was the arrest on September 23 of four young blacks who lived near Providence Farm, one of whom had allegedly called out to a white girl waiting for a bus in Tchula: "Hi, Sugar, you look good to me." The girl had screamed, and though the black youngster protested his innocence, he received a six-month jail term for the seven words he may or may not have uttered. The volatile influence of the blacks' neighbors was very much on the minds of the organizers of the meeting, who played a two-hour tape recording of the blacks' "confessions" to the county sheriff. Though Dr. Minter and the director of Providence Farm, A. Eugene Cox, courageously attended the meeting to deny any subversiveness, they and their families were "invited" by voice vote to leave Holmes County. Another state representative predicted that the continuation of Providence Farm would "lead to violence." State patrolmen blockaded the road leading to the property, and death threats were then sufficient to pull the plug on the cooperative; the Coxes and Minters left the state.[37]

On the surface, the great majority of Mississippi's blacks did not seem dissatisfied with their subjugation. Race relations appeared to be so free of turbulence that in February 1957, the monthly newspaper called *The Citizens' Council* could gloat: "It may be remembered that less than two years ago[,] all was not peaceful in Mississippi as it now is. Then our state was in the midst of an infamous and highly exploited case. . . . With patient organization and education, peace and good order were finally restored in our state. . . . " Claiming that the Citizens' Councils were formed to *prevent* violence, the executive secretary of the Mississippi chapters, Robert B. Patterson of Greenwood, warned that any outbreaks would be the sole responsibility of the Supreme Court. Such lawlessness was not on the horizon, however, from either side of the racial divide; and the organization could feel itself, in the Southern phrase, "in the high cotton." The councils defined orthodoxy on the race question in the Magnolia State, and they constituted by far the most active and vibrant segregationist organization in the former Confederacy, which was inundated with propaganda from Patterson's office. In 1957 his newspaper could accurately report that the auguries were favorable: Mississippi had "not had one single school suit, or bus suit; and all is peaceful and serene with regard to race relations."[38]

But at least one white Mississippian took no comfort in such smug placidity, and found appalling the murder of Till and the acquittal of his presumptive killers. It was freakish and implausible— it would have violated verisimilitude had it featured in a novel—but living only an hour's drive away from Sumner was one of the world's most admired writers.

William Faulkner had long intertwined the issues of race and sex within some of the most powerful passages in his fiction (and therefore in modern American literature). From the terrible castration and lynching of Joe Christmas, the mulatto who had enjoyed the favors of a white woman in *Light in August* (1932), to the dread of miscegenation that ignites the tragedy of the house of Sutpen in *Absalom, Absalom!* (1936); from the despoliation and curse of "The Bear" (1942), to the shame of lynching that punctuates what Edmund Wilson had termed the novelist's civil rights speech, *Intruder in the Dust* (1948); Faulkner had been confronting the Southern white obsession with an immediacy and urgency that suggested an inside job.[39] In a June 1955 letter to his former hostess in Stockholm, Faulkner commented on "the tragic trouble in Mississippi now about Negroes. The Supreme Court has said that there shall be no segregation . . . and there are many people in Mississippi who will go to any length, even violence, to prevent that, I am afraid. I am doing what I can," he added, " . . . but human beings are terrible. One must believe well in man to endure him, wait out his folly and savagery and inhumanity."[40] Such misanthropy collided rather obviously with the sense conveyed in his famous Nobel Prize address that "man's inexhaustible voice" and nobility would somehow prevail. But warrant for Faulkner's pessimism struck close to home a little over two months after that letter, when he was not in residence in Oxford, fifty-five miles from Sumner, but in Rome.

In a statement delivered to the United Press, the 1949 Nobel laureate issued his strongest nonfictional denunciation yet of racial injustice. In the wake of a State Department tour that had enlarged his awareness of the Third World, he managed to blend apocalyptic moral outrage with a plea for political caution. Faulkner warned the segregationists in Mississippi that "the whole white race is only one-fourth of the earth's population of white and brown and yellow and black." Therefore the provincials among whom he lived were obliged to learn that "the white man can no longer afford, he simply does not dare, to commit acts which the other three-fourths of the human race can challenge him for . . . "[41] He reminded his compatriots of the disaster of Pearl Harbor and warned them that even other whites who were Communists were aligned against them. Faulkner pleaded for American unity in so hostile an environment, and his geopolitical advice clumsily expressed his fears for national survival itself.

The statistical part of Faulkner's statement lacked the force and passion of his concluding vision, which anticipated with dread that America would be judged according to its race relations: "Perhaps the purpose of this sorry and tragic error committed in my native Mississippi by two white adults on an afflicted Negro child is to prove to us whether or not we deserve to survive. Because if we in America have reached that point in our desperate culture when we must murder children, no matter for what reason or what color, we don't deserve to survive, and probably won't."[42] The statement was issued before the Tallahatchie County jury had reached its verdict, even before a date for the trial had been set, as though Faulkner already knew upon whom responsibility for the crime rested, as though the denouement and its implications were clear.[43]

He was not the first in a line of apocalyptic writers who were to wonder whether racial violence and tragedy might not doom the American experiment itself. The turmoil that resulted in the Missouri Compromise had certainly registered that effect upon Jefferson: "This momentous question, like a fire-bell in the night, awakened and filled me with terror. I considered it at once as the knell of the Union. It is hushed, indeed, for the moment. But this is a reprive only. . . . " The slaveholder who drafted the Declaration of Independence continued to "tremble for my country when I reflect that God is just, that his justice cannot sleep forever." Tocqueville was equally premonitory in the final section of Volume I of *Democracy in America*, observing that an "inevitable" race war "perpetually haunts the imagination of the Americans, like a painful dream." From Melville's *Benito Cereno* to Robert Lowell's, from Nat Turner's confessions to William Styron's, from the lurid revulsion at black power in *The Birth of Nation* to the final *frisson* of white defeat in the speeches of Malcolm X and the writings of Imamu Amiri Baraka, from John Brown's body to James Baldwin's *The Fire Next Time* and to the Kerner Commission report (1968), two races are depicted as locked in deadly embrace, in a society spliced by hatred. In such pivotal texts, which are American editions of the Book of Revelations, the vision of brotherhood in a New World is disturbed by the reminder that the very first murder (Genesis 4:8) was fratricidal. Even when Max Weber visited the Tuskegee Institute, he felt compelled to sound the apocalyptic note in the very headquarters of accommodationism, for even there "*the* great national problem of all American life, the showdown between the white race and former slaves, could be grasped at its roots" (italics in original).[44]

Faulkner's statement on the Till case was published in the *New York Herald Tribune* on September 9, 1955. It was much more forthright and impassioned than his unsuccessful plea, published on March 27, 1951, that the state of Mississippi spare the life of Willie McGee, who had been convicted of raping a white woman.[45] Perhaps the adult McGee's innocence was more ambiguous. Perhaps the very brevity of Till's life was so striking. Perhaps the intervening four years had made the novelist more willing to acknowledge the velocity of racial change. In any event Faulkner discussed the Till case again in his essay "On Fear," published in *Harper's* in 1956; and this particular crime may well have significantly pushed the Nobel laureate toward open advocacy of the repeal of segregation. For the annual meeting of the Southern Historical Association in Memphis in November 1955, he agreed to deliver a paper on race relations. James Silver, chairman of the History Department at Ole Miss, and John Hope Franklin helped arrange the session. The distinguished author of the standard text in black history, *From Slavery to Freedom*, refused to attend the conference, however, because the convention site, the Peabody Hotel, did not permit Professor Franklin to stay there overnight. Though Faulkner made no direct allusion to Money or Sumner, the president of the Association, Bell I. Wiley, recalled the atmosphere as "a critical time in Dixie. The eyes of the South, and of the nation, were focused on a Mississippi Delta community, where Emmett Till, a visiting colored boy from Chicago, had alledgedly [*sic*] been killed." The novelist and two other panelists spoke even as "emphatic advocates of white supremacy were still exchanging congratulations on the outcome of the Till case." It was on that occasion that Faulkner proclaimed that, as late as 1955, to "be against equality because of race or color, is like living in Alaska and being against snow."[46]

He repeated his views in an interview with Jean Stein vanden Heuvel for the *Paris Review*, in which he added, making specific mention of "the Milams and the Bryants," that young adults (between twenty and forty) generally cause "the world's anguish." In accounting for how such a crime could have been committed, Faulkner made no explicit mention of racism, however, nor for that matter did he put the blame on Reconstruction. But in his meditation on the fate of man, the novelist observed: "Since his capacity to do is forced into channels of evil through environment and pressures, man is strong before he is moral." But he was well aware of how the obsession with "purity of white blood" had led to shameful crimes.[47]

Faulkner recognized the paranoia that had afflicted the white South in "On Fear": "If the facts as stated in the *Look* magazine account of the Till affair are correct, this remains: two adults, armed, in the dark, kidnap a fourteen-year-old boy and take him away to frighten him. Instead of which, the fourteen-year-old boy not only refuses to be frightened, but, unarmed, alone, in the dark, so frightens the two armed adults that they must destroy him.

"What are we Mississippians afraid of?" Faulkner asked, in noting the political, legal, and economic vulnerability of blacks. He wondered what had befallen the heirs of those who had fought so courageously at Chickamauga and Chancellorsville and the Wilderness, and then pierced the wacky logic of white supremacy: "Why do we have so low an opinion of our blood and tradition as to fear that, as soon as the Negro enters our home by the front door, he will propose marriage to our daughter and she will immediately accept him?" Faulkner was also perhaps the first to perceive that the scales of valor had tipped against the custodians of caste. For the behavior of Emmett Till had revealed that the intimidation, to which the teenager's own mother had urged him to submit, could no longer be imposed as effectively as it had been in the past.[48]

It was also possible for Faulkner to wonder what had happened to the sense of decency as well. One of the Southern ladies whose presumably superior moral instincts had placed her on a pedestal wrote a letter to the novelist, ostensibly in the name of her pastor and congregation. She asserted, according to Faulkner's paraphrase in an article published in *Life* (March 5, 1956), that "the Till boy got exactly what he asked for, coming down there with his Chicago ideas, and that all his mother wanted was to make money out of the role of her bereavement."[49] The recipient of this letter did not quote his own reply, if any; and it may well be that, against such perverse incomprehension, such closure of empathy, such ethical stupidity, no rejoinder can be effective.

At least the most authoritative voice in Southern culture did not evade the moral anguish posed by the Till case, even though Faulkner did not act with the selfless energy for social justice that, over half a century earlier, Emile Zola displayed in challenging the guilty verdict in the Dreyfus affair. But *J'accuse* was, after all, an exceptional episode in the annals of conscience, for which Zola paid the price of exile. In daring the French authorities to reopen the case, the novelist was driven by the knowledge that the actual victim of injustice and prejudice was still alive and that restitution was possible as well as necessary. Nor was the role of public spokesman congenial to so shy a figure as Faulkner. He probably had no way of knowing whether his neighbors were listening, nor does the historian in retrospect know how to calibrate the effect of Faulkner's act of social responsibility. What is certain, however, is that his willingness to articulate his opposition to racist violence contrasted most favorably with the silence or complicity of other white Mississippians.

F I V E

Washington, D.C.

The shock of the Till murder even reverberated to the inner sanctum of the executive branch in Washington, and that sort of federal attention was rather unprecedented for a Southern crime of racial violence. It was nevertheless "a misfortune for blacks in America," the historian William E. Leuchtenburg has observed, "that in the year the Supreme Court handed down the *Brown* decision, Dwight Eisenhower was president of the United States."[1] Despite the publicity provoked by the trial in Sumner, the federal government showed itself to be quite indifferent to the "jungle fury" that the NAACP charged was prevailing in the state of Mississippi. Three main factors impeded any federal attempt to satisfy black demands for the security of life and liberty there.

The president himself was hostile to black aspirations for first-class citizenship. He had opposed the desegregation of the armed services as well as the establishment of the Fair Employment Practices Commission in the 1940s. Nor did Eisenhower see the necessity for the enforcement or passage of laws designed to protect the civil rights of blacks in the South or elsewhere. Unlike Faulkner, the president failed to speak out against white racist violence—a problem that he evaded so fully that reporters discovered his ignorance that such incidents had even occurred.

Eisenhower believed that the racial question in the United States was emotional rather than rational, that "arbitrary law" could not be strong enough to solve it. However inadvertently, he was a disciple of the leading fin-de-siècle social Darwinist, William Graham Sumner, who doubted that "stateways" could make much headway

71

against "folkways." Sensitivity to the deep feelings of white South-erners therefore required that change be gradual. Although his memoirs recognize the correctness of *Brown* v. *Board of Education,* not once in his tenure of office did Eisenhower express publicly his actual approval of that decision—either the ruling itself or the principles behind it. Indeed, he told Chief Justice Earl Warren that the segregationists were "not bad people. All they are concerned about is to see that their sweet little girls are not required to sit in schools alongside some big overgrown Negroes."[2]

Indeed Arthur Larson, his under secretary of labor, claimed that Eisenhower privately opposed the Court's repudiation of the 1896 separate-but-equal ruling. The president told a campaign aide in 1956 that *Brown* had set back racial progress in the South by fifteen years. He realized too late that the appointment of Earl Warren, who orchestrated and wrote the decision overturning *Plessy* v. *Ferguson,* was "the biggest damfool mistake I ever made."[3] Nor did the president express his support for citizens who sought to implement the Supreme Court's desegregation requirement. Although William McKinley's first inaugural address had warned that "lynchings must not be tolerated in a great and civilized country like the United States. . . . Equality of rights must prevail," such sentiments were more forthright than one of his most popular Republican successors could muster.[4] No wonder then that the NAACP's temperate Roy Wilkins was provoked to jibe that "Eisenhower was a fine general and a good, decent man; but if he had fought World War II the way he fought for civil rights, we would all be speaking German today."[5]

But even if the chief executive had been more sympathetic toward black equality, even if he had managed to define civil rights as a moral imperative, partisan considerations dictated caution and inaction. In the 1952 elections Eisenhower carried four Southern states and barely missed winning two others. He did well not only among voters ensconced in the urban and suburban middle class, not only in the traditionally GOP hill country, but also in the Black Belt South, which was an unprecedented Republican boon. In two-thirds of the Black Belt counties, Ike ran ahead of the state average. It was the best performance of a Republican presidential candidate in the South since 1928. The areas that the Dixiecrats found most congenial in 1948 were the same in which Eisenhower was con-spicuously popular in 1952. The GOP candidate carried nine of twenty Mississippi counties whose population was more than 60 percent black (disenfranchised, of course) and ran ahead of the state average in nine of the remaining eleven. In the previous two decades, the highest percentage that a Republican presidential candidate had ever received in Mississippi was a meager 6.4. In 1952, Eisenhower won an astonishing 39.6 percent of the vote in that state.[6] That increased proportion threatened to falsify the Magnolia State maxim that local Republicans were being preserved from extinction only by the game laws.

It would therefore have been asking much of Eisenhower to risk jeopardizing his party's electoral chances in the 1956 election and thereafter. It was easier to counsel patience with the white South's tumultuous effort to reconcile itself with the Supreme Court's invalidation of *Plessy* v. *Ferguson*. Indeed, sympathy for white Southerners so pervaded his administration that, after the expiration of James P. Coleman's term as governor of Mississippi, this unabashed segregationist was invited to serve on the Civil Rights Commission. To be sure, some white Mississippians suspected Coleman of moderation, in part because the governor had vetoed a bill that would have jailed for five years any federal official who was convicted of attempting to desegregate schools, buses, or public facilities. Yet appearing at a Citizens' Council rally (though not at its state convention) hardly made Coleman a devotee of the brotherhood of man. Such a nomination to the Civil Rights Commission would have been like naming Attila the Hun to the board of the Carnegie Endowment for International Peace. In any event, Coleman declined the offer, preferring to combat civil rights by remaining in the trenches of Jackson.[7] On March 14, 1956, Eisenhower pleaded for "understanding of other people's deep emotions as well as our own. . . . We are not talking here about coercing, using force in a general way; we are simply going to uphold the Constitution of the United States."[8] In Eisenhower's mandate for change under the rule of law, an equivalent respect for the "deep emotions" of black Southerners, or empathy for their frustration with their plight, was not expressed.

How that constitutional responsibility was defined makes up the third explanation for the blank wall that the NAACP faced when it urged intervention to protect black lives and rights in the South. To borrow a phrase from Friedrich Engels, Eisenhower seemed to be a believer in "the withering away of the state." To demands from the NAACP and the Americans for Democratic Action for FBI investigations into the Till and other Mississippi murders, spokesmen for the Department of Justice claimed that it was the duty of states to protect their own citizens. In the context of the 1940s, in which the Deep South was actively suppressing elemental civil rights for blacks, the sanction of states' rights permitted injustices like the Till slaying to remain unremedied.[9] Presumably no federal law had been violated, either when Till was murdered nor when Bryant and Milam were acquitted. Indeed there had been no federal civil rights act since the wake of Reconstruction. Fred Graham remarked as late as 1965: "The one existing U. S. law against jury discriminaion is so puny that the Justice Department has yet to prosecute any official under it in this century. . . . Since the [1875 criminal] law punishes only past offenses, and allows only fines and not jail penalties, and since the official himself would get a trial by a Southern jury, the criminal statute is considered almost worthless."[10] The president apparently never considered giving that law any teeth.

Therefore, when ABC asked the deputy attorney general about the verdict in Sumner, William P. Rogers could decry it as "a black mark" on the American reputation for justice; in a stirring address before the Urban League in New York, he went even further, calling it "a serious black mark." But when pressed whether he meant that the trial had been unfair, Rogers disclaimed close knowledge of the details of the case.[11] That was as far as any official in the Eisenhower administration was willing to go in public. The Till murder and the absolution of his killers nevertheless strained the "policy of silence" that the executive branch had adopted. The dilemma that the administration faced, however, was how to placate the recent GOP converts from Dixiecrat status without alienating swing voters among Northern blacks, who might well share the disgust of Roy Wilkins with an administration that "said nothing and did nothing."

Urging the president to speak out on the Till case was Frederic Morrow, an attorney and former NAACP field secretary whom Eisenhower had appointed as a White House staffer two months before the murder. Morrow was the first black ever to serve in an executive capacity on a presidential staff—which meant that at first other staffers would not take meals with him, nor would any of the secretaries in the White House pool work for him. But even more frustrating perhaps was Morrow's abject failure to persuade a president courting the once-solid South to voice outrage at a death in the Delta.[12] Eisenhower had not even bothered to respond to a telegram from Mrs. Bradley, who urged him to intervene in Mississippi to halt the kind of violence that had taken her son's life. The case troubled Maxwell Rabb, a White House aide who, by default, handled minority affairs; and on December 19 he chaired a meeting of concerned administration officials, including a handful of blacks, to discuss the violence in Mississippi. But no obvious change in policy resulted.[13]

The dilemma of reconciling politics and morality came to a head on December 2, 1955, during a Cabinet meeting over which, because the president was recuperating from a heart attack, Vice President Nixon presided. Attorney General Herbert Brownell reported that the Department of Justice was under considerable pressure to investigate the rising violence in the South, especially since the Till case. When the grand jury declined to bring a true bill on kidnapping the previous month, the governor of Illinois, William Stratton, had urged federal involvement. But Brownell could find no federal offense that would trigger intervention,[14] and at the Cabinet meeting he suggested a *weakening* of the draft of the civil rights portion of the president's forthcoming State of the Union message to the Congress. The attorney general recommended that, instead of threatening to investigate the Citizens' Councils, Eisenhower simply express his support of the Court's unanimous decision in *Brown v. Board of Education* of over a year and a half earlier.

Secretary of State John Foster Dulles conceded the tragic character of the murder of Till but argued that political and constitutional reasons ought to limit the administration's involvement in civil rights. Vice President Nixon countered with a suggestion that, to avoid revealing the passivity of the executive branch, the problem should be inflicted on Congress. He acknowledged that any legislation that might get out of committee would then face a Southern Democratic filibuster, which could block any such bill. Both Dulles and Brownell endorsed Nixon's proposal, since it would also spotlight the disarray within the Democratic Party on the subject of civil rights.[15]

This Cabinet meeting illustrated not only the callousness of the Eisenhower administration to the plight of black victims of racist brutality, as epitomized in the case of Emmett Till; these officials also personified the impotence of the federal government when deadly private force and state governmental inaction were combined to protect the "Southern way of life." If new, tougher legislation could not be expected to survive the Southern Democrats in

Congress, then perhaps the executive branch might have tried to exercise some ingenuity in the enforcement of existing statutes. Brownell himself was apparently quite shocked to learn of the tenacity with which the Mississippi Citizens' Councils were working to block black voter registration and, sensitive to the prospect that the Northern black vote might be decisive in a close election if Eisenhower were too ill to try to succeed himself, the attorney general favored a civil rights bill. But the Department of Justice, under Brownell as well as William Rogers, who was his successor, had no taste for making such laws effective.[16]

Indeed, when the thirty-five-year-old Robert Kennedy became attorney general in January 1961, Senator Eastland reminded him— no doubt a little nervously—"Did you know that your predecessor never brought a civil rights case in Mississippi?"[17] The failure of the Department of Justice to intervene in the South can be attributed to considerable—if not insuperable—legal impediments. Till had not been kidnapped across state lines. Nor had he been killed by any federal officer, by any policeman, or by anyone who was acting "under color of law" or who was conspiring to deprive the teenager of "due process." But the department was also *unwilling* to intervene, as demonstrated by the inconsistent policy of the executive branch. The journalist Carl Rowan pointed out at the time that, "in Minneapolis, when a labor hoodlum placed a bomb in the car of someone he didn't like, the FBI found a way to step into the case." After extraordinary efforts, struggle, and pressure from civil rights activists, the bureau got involved in the early 1960s, arresting, for example, the Citizens' Council member from Greenville who was eventually prosecuted for assassinating Medgar Evers. Yet in the 1950s, when racist murders scarred the South, the Department of Justice, invariably insisted that new laws were needed from Congress.[18]

J. Edgar Hoover himself refused to involve the FBI, though a tentative investigation was conducted into the Till slaying.[19] The bureau advised against prosecution; and the Criminal Division of the Department of Justice concurred, because the director could perceive no violation of federal law. Even if Bryant and Milam had been tried under it, there was little reason to believe that a jury of their peers would have found them guilty. Such involvement would therefore have produced no "success," and it might have generated friction with at least some of the local law enforcement officials whose cooperation the FBI regularly needed. That is why, unlike in earlier cases involving, say, Marcus Garvey or John Dillinger, Hoover was not imaginative enough to discover an angle that would permit the intervention of his agency; and white Southerners were right to conclude that in Washington, D.C., such crimes were not being given a high priority of concern. A popular history of the bureau, which bore the imprimatur of the director himself, reflected such attitudes, concluding that "the clamor for Federal intervention in civil rights cases such as the Till case was like an echo from the 1930s. [Then] the cry rang out for a Federalized police force to stamp out gangsterism. But the real answer to the problem," Don Whitehead suggested one year after Till's assassins were sprung free, "is stronger local law enforcement backed by intelligent public opinion."[20]

In the specific instance of the Till murder, the chief legal strategist of the NAACP shared this view. "Often the sole available protection for minorities is vigorous enforcement of ordinary state laws forbidding violence against the person," Jack Greenberg wrote. So long as "juries will not convict, there is usually no other remedy than the exercise of political power and general community awakening." And at least in the period between 1955 and 1957, juries were not inclined to convict: in fourteen cases involving white defendants charged with violating the rights of blacks, Southern jurors sprang their peers loose in all but one trial.[21]

Hoover's inattentiveness to the "jungle jury" in Mississippi may also have stemmed from his own racism, which was so blatant that one scholarly analysis of the FBI considers "extended comment" on Hoover's bigotry unnecessary. The documentation is irrefutable. "Much of the Bureau was hostile to blacks and . . . very, very few blacks worked as FBI agents until the early 1970s," David Garrow added.[22] Such racial prejudice would by itself account for the absence of any indignant action from the executive branch when the corpse of a Negro was discovered floating in the Tallahatchie River. When Hoover presented a report to the Cabinet in March 1956 on "Racial Tensions and Civil Rights," he flung the weight of his own authority behind the barricades of the Southern supremacists, agreeing with them that behind the furor over "mixed education . . . stalks the specter of racial intermarriages." Advocates of integration were promoting "racial hatred," utilizing "techniques of mobilization, pressure and propaganda"; it was therefore no accident that

Communist infiltration of the NAACP deserved to be monitored. By contrast, Hoover assured the Cabinet, the Citizens' Councils were composed of "bankers, lawyers, doctors, state legislators and industrialists"—in other words, "some of the leading citizens in the South."[23] It was therefore wildly misleading for one best-selling history of the United States in the middle third of the twentieth century to claim that "federal agents" investigated the Till case and "had painstakingly assembled irrefutable evidence." It was only after a grand jury failed to indict the half-brothers for kidnapping, William Manchester added, that the FBI "reluctantly closed its file."[24]

Hoover's bureaucratic imperturbability and moral indifference were clearly reflected in his response to Mayor Richard J. Daley's protests against federal inaction in the Till case. "Hizzoner" had indeed issued an early statement denouncing the "brutal, terrible crime," and hoped that "both state and Federal" agencies would ensure that justice be done.[25] The FBI director generalized that such protests were typically Communist-inspired but then ludicrously had to explain to the Cabinet that Mayor Daley himself was not a party comrade. "To illustrate the potency of Communist pressure," Hoover reported, "I need only to cite the sequence of events in Chicago. In September, 1955, the Illinois-Indiana District Communist Party started agitation with a one-page leaflet on the Till case calling upon President Eisenhower to dismiss the Attorney General. This was followed by an agitation campaign by the Civil Rights Congress calling for pressure on the President and the State Subcommittee on Constitutional Rights. Mayor Richard J. Daley of Chicago on September 2, 1955, wired the President urging intervention. I hasten to say that Mayor Daley is not a Communist, but pressures engineered by the Communists were brought to bear on him. . . ."[26]

Such exaggerated fear of the domestic threat of Communist influence was manifestly inhibiting even the semblance of any effort to guarantee the constitutional rights of Southern blacks—or even their physical safety. The FBI director found it difficult to credit the possibility that patriotic Americans as well as Communists might wish to exert political pressure to eradicate racial injustice. Locked into a woolly obsession with Moscow-sponsored subversion, at a time when Forrest County officials were mocking the Fifteenth Amendment by demanding of prospective black voters, "How many bubbles are in a bar of soap?", Hoover could cite no evidence of a Communist threat even within so volatile a state as Mississippi, where the FBI could locate exactly one Red—and that particular backwoods Bolshevik was white.[27]

But even if the desirability of blunting the power of Communism were conceded, Hoover's assumption that the civil rights movement posed too great a threat to social and political stability was open to skepticism. Even though John Foster Dulles noted the tragedy of the Till murder, the secretary of state did not draw the conclusion that the United States government had a stake in maintaining a reputation for opposing racial injustice. Such an interest would not have been incompatible with a decent respect for the opinions of mankind, however. For the Bandung Conference was also held in 1955, a symbol of the immense political power that the Third World was projecting. The conference was covered by Richard Wright, a resident of France since 1947; his book about Bandung represented another of the Mississippian's effort to make the white man listen.

Decolonization was changing the political coloration of the planet the United States hoped to shape. Only two years after the Till case (and six months before passage of the first Civil Rights Act since Reconstruction), Ghana became an independent nation; and its diplomats in Washington were to have some impact on American politics and racial practices. "The downfall of the white-supremacy system in the rest of the world made its survival in the United States suddenly and painfully conspicuous," a scholarly analyst of the Third World observed. Segregation and the violence that enforced it "became our most exposed feature and[,] in the swift unfolding of the world's affairs, our most vulnerable weakness."[28] Such moral incongruities and political disabilities were not yet suddenly and painfully transparent in Washington, though warnings had been issued as early as the founding meeting of Association of Southern Women for the Prevention of Lynching in November 1930 in Atlanta. There Will Alexander had denounced lynching as an international embarrassment for the United States. In the mid-1930s, a pamphlet of the Association charged that lynching created "a fertile field for . . . communistic doctrines subversive of American democracy at home." This progressive organization had long since perceived such crimes as discrediting the claims of Christianity and American democracy,[29] a point apparently lost on Dulles and Hoover a generation later.

The Till case also illustrated the peculiarly timid political culture of the 1950s. For the two-time presidential candidate of the Democratic Party was not an impassioned civil rights crusader either. Adlai Stevenson also saw federalism as too impervious an obstacle to allow for executive intervention in such obviously distressing instances as the Till case. "We have to look to the states to enforce the law," the former Illinois governor announced. "In the case of the murder and kidnapping [of Till], it was committed wholly within the state of Mississippi." Before a black audience in 1956, Stevenson labeled himself a "gradualist," which provoked Roy Wilkins to write an angry letter. "In the minds of every Negro in that audience," the executive secretary of the NAACP wrote Stevenson, "were the murder of Emmett Till and the bloody suppression of the Negro vote in Mississippi . . . [and] the open defiance of the government and the U.S. Supreme Court."[30] But at least the Democratic presidential nominee did not adopt the stance of Eisenhower and Hoover, who cast a plague on both the Citizens' Councils and the NAACP. The leading civil rights organization was feared as the more dangerous of these "extremist" groups because of Communist penetration and flair for social turmoil.[31]

Though the murderers were free and at large, general remedies were proposed to break the pattern of such injustices. Some blacks urged that Eisenhower intervene, either by urging congressional passage of an antilynching bill or by publicly condemning the depravity swirling around the Till slaying. A delegation of about fifty blacks from Chicago visited the Department of Justice, in the hope of persuading it to apply federal antikidnapping statutes. The delegation was told that Washington lacked jurisdiction in the Till case. Nor was Attorney General Brownell more responsive when a Democratic representative from Brooklyn, Victor L. Anfuso, urged him to investigate this particular "miscarriage of justice."[32] Historian Harry Barnard reminded readers of the *Nation* that, when President Rutherford B. Hayes ended the military occupation of the South in 1877, the region's leaders had pledged to grant the same legal security to the freedmen as to whites. "Unless the state of Mississippi acts forthrightly to avenge the . . . murder of Emmett Lewis [*sic*] Till and also to guarantee protection to all Americans who happen to be in that state regardless of color," Barnard concluded with a flourish, "the United States government is morally and legally justified in occupying the state with Federal troops."[33] But no one in Washington had acquired the taste for a second Reconstruction.

The fullest constructive response came from the American Jewish Committee, which asserted that "in some European quarters, the Till case has temporarily offset the favorable impact created by the U.S. Supreme Court's desegregation decision and by previous reports of steady U.S. progress in civil rights during the past decade." In a report signed by its president, Irving M. Engel, and by former federal judge Simon H. Rifkind, the committee recommended three steps: (1) strengthening current federal law to make individual assaults motivated by racial and religious prejudice punishable under United States civil rights statutes; (2) reorganizing the Department of Justice so that the Civil Rights Section would become a division, under an assistant attorney general who would be given powers of investigation and prosecution when such violations occurred; and (3) increasing the personnel of the FBI to deal more effectively with such violations, and to train agents to deal specifically with such crimes.

These recommendations drew the praise of Senator Paul H. Douglas of Illinois and Representative Emmanuel Celler of Brooklyn, who headed the House Judiciary Committee. Douglas also asserted that "erasing the ugly stain created by the Till case—and similar incidents elsewhere—is one of America's major moral issues." Celler wanted to go beyond the American Jewish Committee proposals, advocating an amendment that would abrogate federal aid to any "state that has manifested a disregard of civil rights and civil liberties." (Had that amendment passed, one interesting consequence would have been a devastating drop in the income of Senator Eastland, an ardent Washington-basher whose 5,800-acre plantation in Sunflower County was heavily dependent on the generosity of cotton acreage allotments.) Both Douglas and Celler hoped that this report would give extra impetus to the drive to pass the first civil rights bill since the aftermath of Reconstruction, a hope that was not realized until two years later.[34] When Attorney General Brownell declined to testify before Celler's civil rights subcommittee, the Brooklyn representative noted the discrepancy between the administration's reluctance to cooperate with Congress and the excuse that the Department of Justice inactivity in civil rights enforcement was due to ineffective laws.[35]

Congressman Jamie L. Whitten in particular was aware of the impact of the Till case in intensifying the push for civil rights legislation, especially since Gerald Chatham had succeeded him as district attorney, and since Strider served as sheriff in Whitten's own home county. Immediately after the verdict in Sumner, Whitten had privately praised his cousin for the "fine job" that he and the other defense attorneys performed, and claimed that "the county [had] earned the respect of the thinking people of the nation."[36] The congressman was far less certain of such national support when he testified almost a year and a half later before a subcommittee of the House Judiciary Committee, Representative Celler presiding. The Mississippian conceded that, had he been on the jury, he might have voted differently. And he acknowledged that the article in *Look* magazine "would lend some weight to a belief that they might have been guilty"—as though their voluntary confession were not convincing enough! But the cousin of one of the defendants' attorneys insisted that the prosecution and judge had done all that they could, that the right of the defendants not to testify against themselves "is a principle that has existed in the English law back to Magna Carta days," and that in any event it was reasonable that jurors take the trouble to have registered and paid a poll tax of two dollars by February 1. Representative Whitten strenuously objected to "back-home pressures from the Northern areas" that were forcing his colleagues "to correct what we know needs no correction."[37]

In the testimony before the Senate Subcommittee on Civil Rights that eventually led to the Civil Rights Act of 1957, six witnesses referred to the Till case. Its reverberations were especially relevant to Part II of the act, which authorized an extra assistant attorney general in the Department of Justice to handle civil rights; and to Part V of the original bill, which set standards for federal jurors, rendering inapplicable state laws concerning jury selection, and which permitted a judge to fine or jail a person for criminal contempt without a jury trial. In the floor debate, when a challenge to the bill came in the form of a jury-trial requirement, Senator Douglas tried to defeat it, noting that in Tallahatchie County, "where Roy Bryant and J. W. Milam were found innocent of murdering 14-year-old Till," none of the 19,000 Negroes was allowed to vote and, hence, was ineligible to serve on juries. Others who mentioned or discussed the Till case were Representatives Diggs,

Whitten, Marguerite S. Church of Illinois, L. Mendel Rivers of South Carolina, and Senator Sam Ervin of North Carolina.[38]

The bill that finally passed included an amendment permitting a jury trial for anyone who faced a fine over $300 or more than forty-five days in jail on conviction. That compromise provoked the Republican national comittee director of minority affairs to complain to the Senate majority leader, Lyndon Johnson: "If a Southern jury would not convict confessed kidnappers of Emmett Till after he was found murdered, why would they convict an election official for refusing to give a Negro his right of suffrage?"[39] That, of course, was precisely why Southern senators insisted on the amendment. But overall, the 1957 act was considered at least a mild victory for the forces of civil rights.

In an era when publicists, politicians, and intellectuals were fond of sharp contrasts between American democracy and Communist tyranny, the experience of television scriptwriter Rod Serling suggested limits on American liberty of expresssion, at least in that relatively new medium. The *U.S. Steel Hour* was scheduled to present Serling's play *Noon on Doomsday*, inspired by the Till case and produced by the Theater Guild. Serling had been struck by the eagerness of the white community in Mississippi to close ranks behind the two killers, even though their neighbors seemed afterwards to feel at least some remorse. Serling nevertheless feared that his idea to draw directly on the facts of the case would torpedo the play, so he changed the victim from a black to an old pawnbroker. The number of murderers was cut in half; and the criminal became, according to television historian Erik Barnouw, "a neurotic malcontent lashing out at a scapegoat for his own shortcomings." Many readers and critics of *Crime and Punishment* had long concluded that Dostoevsky had already handled that particular topic quite adequately, if not definitively. But Serling seemed willing to risk the comparison, and the play was approved and scheduled.

Then a journalist, after a conversation with the playwright, reported that Till's murder had inspired the forthcoming television drama. Serling recalled that "all Hell broke loose." Thirty high-level executives of U. S. Steel, the Theater Guild, and the advertising agency involved then conducted negotiations over script revisions. The threat of a boycott that the Citizens' Councils might launch against U. S. Steel terrified the bastion of the *Fortune* 500. Serling asked, "Does that mean from now on, everybody below the Mason-Dixon Line is going to build from aluminum?" His sarcasm left the executives unmoved. One alternative was to change the locale so drastically that no member of the audience could even *begin* to suspect that it might have something to do with an area below the Mason-Dixon Line. So the setting was switched to New England, a region where no lynching has ever been reported in the twentieth century; and the show opened with a shot of the spire of a white village church. Even a visible Coca-Cola bottle, that essential artifact of the South, was carefully removed. One executive was responsible for ensuring that all traces of Southern accents and even those telltale contractions endemic to the speech patterns of the region had been expunged. It also became necessary to restore the missin' *g's* in present participles. The result was a play that Serling realized "bore no relationship to any existing social problem," though he was labeled "a controversial writer" whom television critics in the South identified as "the guy who wrote the Till story." Yet *Noon on Doomsday* took place nowhere—"an absurdity," Professor Barnouw mordantly concluded, "in a total vacuum."[40]

S I X

Revolution

J. Edgar Hoover's Cabinet report might have given the impression that the only whites who objected to the state of race relations in communities like Money and Sumner were Communists and their dupes (like Mayor Daley). Red-baiting, which Hoover and others perpetrated, had undoubtedly helped to reduce the numbers of whites outside the South who had been aroused by earlier episodes of racial injustice in the region. But after many thousands of blacks filed past Emmett Till's casket in Chicago, protest meetings were held in Northern black communities such as New York, Chicago, Detroit, Cleveland, and Youngstown, as well as Baltimore and Los Angeles.[1] In New York, for example, where the estimated attendance was at least 10,000, the chairman of the board of the NAACP utilized the rhetoric of the Cold War to condemn the decision in Sumner: "The jurors who returned this shameful verdict," Channing Tobias announced, "deserve a medal from the Kremlin for meritorious service in communism's war against democracy. They have done their best to discredit our judicial system, to hold us up as a nation of hypocrites, and to undermine faith in American democracy."

Roy Wilkins denounced the trial in Tallahatchie County as "a travesty, a farce, a joke as far as it demonstrated the American principle of trial by jury to secure a just verdict." Under the sponsorship of the Brotherhood of Sleeping Car Porters, three clergymen also condemned the acquittal; Reverend Donald Harrington of Community Church, for example, called it "a dagger struck in the back of America."[2] Fifty-one faculty members and a hundred undergraduates at Princeton submitted a petition denouncing "the standards of justice and attitude toward humanity" exhibited in Tallahatchie County, but their protest proposed no specific remedies.[3]

At the Harlem rally at which Mrs. Bradley also appeared, Eisenhower was asked to convene a special session of Congress to pass an antilynching bill. "We all sympathize with President Eisenhower," Representative Adam Clayton Powell, Jr., told a second New York City meeting, alluding to Ike's recent heart attack. "But certainly the President's illness cannot be used as an excuse for not calling a special session of Congress." With 20,000 in attendance in the garment center, Representative Powell then called for a national boycott of products made in Mississippi and asserted that "the lynch murder of Emmett Till" was regarded in Europe as "a lynching of the Statue of Liberty." The Harlem representative also recommended that Northerners replace Southerners as FBI agents when investigating such crimes as the Till slaying.[4]

Powell also promised that, in the next session of Congress, he would introduce a resolution that would prohibit the seating of representatives of states that prevent blacks from trying to vote "without fear of lynching or coercion of any kind." At a Detroit rally of over 4,000 persons sponsored by the NAACP, Representative Diggs condemned "the shameful and primitive disregard for the dignity of all persons" indicated by the verdict in Sumner. He, too, vowed to challenge the seating of any representatives elected from Mississippi, an idea that the Jackson *Daily News* considered so perverse that the newspaper ascribed it to "the lack of intelligence and a weakness that comes from a person of mixed blood."[5]

None of the mass rallies in the North, however, could replicate the protest meetings that had been generated over two decades earlier, for example, when the Scottsboro boys were put on trial. Perhaps the difference is explained by the problem of action: in the Scottsboro case, the aim of the NAACP and the Communists and their allies was to prevent the state of Alabama from executing nine young black defendants. In 1955 the black youth had already been killed, and the constitutional prohibition against double jeopardy deprived protestors of an insistence that Bryant and Milam be retried for homicide. There was no palpable way this particular grievance could be redressed.

Among the blacks who expressed outrage over the Till case was W. E. B. Du Bois, the radical intellectual who had been condemning lynchings—too often in vain—for half a century. By the mid-1950s Du Bois had firmly positioned himself within the orbit of Communism, convinced that the "problem of the color line," which he had predicted would be the central issue of the twentieth century, would only be solved through the abolition of the capitalism and imperialism associated with American hegemony. The abject failure of the American legal and political systems to remedy the blatant injustice in the Till case was therefore worth highlighting, though one form Du Bois selected was perhaps a little eccentric. Faulkner had been the lone white Mississippian of prominence to express outrage, but the counselor of the "go slow" approach in *Life* was picked out as a target and was challenged to a debate on racial integration. Du Bois proposed that they debate the subject on the courthouse steps in Sumner itself. Faulkner did not accept the invitation. But Du Bois continued to push for the suffrage as the best memorial to Till, and helped form a Provisional Committee for Justice in Mississippi that claimed to have sent a ton of clothes and food parcels to blacks in that state.[6]

More might have been done, Du Bois believed, had the black middle class not exploited its social advantages by promoting an ideology of "aping American acquisitive society." In his view, the black press in particular consisted, with rare exceptions, of "mouthpieces of this bourgeoisie[,] and [it] bow[s] to the dictates of big business." Few members of the black middle class wished to take risks for racial justice in the South; the physical dangers were far too palpable. Nor could it yet conceive of a dramatic acceleration in the progress toward a more tolerant, if not egalitarian, society. Du Bois quoted the leading sociologist of this class, E. Franklin Frazier, as claiming that only an occasional cause célèbre like the Till case seemed to disturb the dream of acceptance and progress.[7] It was nevertheless only among blacks (in the North) that public meetings were held to protest the travesty of justice in Sumner, and this withdrawal from the ideal of interracial solidarity troubled another radical who felt isolated during the Cold War, the editor–publisher–sole contributor to *I. F. Stone's Weekly*. The various stripes of progressives, that is, "whites in the South and in the North who would normally have been moved to act," I. F. Stone added, "have been hounded out of public life and into inactivity."

But then, in an amazingly prescient passage that anticipated the mass movement that was organized in Montgomery two months later, the independent journalist wrote: "The American Negro needs a Gandhi to lead him, and we need the American Negro to lead us. If he does not provide leadership against the sickness of the South, the time will come when we will all pay a terrible price for allowing a psychopathic racist brutality to flourish unchecked."[8] Here was a striking prophecy of the implications of the crime of the half-brothers and their exoneration by their peers.

Till's life ended a little over three months before the inauguration, early in December, of the Montgomery bus boycott—the first major Southern black declaration of war against racial injustice in the era after Reconstruction. Indeed, History cracked the South wide open on the very day that Senator Eastland was denouncing the "monstrous crime" of *Brown* v. *Board of Education* before the Citizens' Councils convention in Jackson, accusing the judges of having "violated their oaths of office," and asserting that the Citizens' Councils were defending "the racial integrity, the culture, the creative genius, and the advanced civilization of the white race." On that same day a seamstress named Rosa Parks was refusing to surrender her seat on a public bus to a white man.[9] The *Montgomery Advertiser* buried the story the next day on a back page under the headline, "Negro Jailed Here for 'Overlooking' Bus Segregation."

Although that newspaper had given prominent display to the Till case,[10] it is difficult to ascertain any direct relation between the sensational murder and acquittal and the bus boycott one state to the east. But a connection is not inherently implausible, even though perhaps the most that can be argued is that the news of yet another terrible death and miscarriage of justice added to the mounting frustration with racial oppression. It was one of many brutalities. Mrs. Parks herself never claimed that the case directly motivated her to challenge segregated seating, and indeed she had already been ejected from the front of a Montgomery bus in the early 1940s—by the same driver who challenged her in 1955. But she acknowledged the impact of the Till case in arousing blacks to indignation. "It was a very tragic incident," the longtime NAACP chapter secretary recalled. "Many such incidents had gone unnoticed in the past."[11]

When William Bradford Huie sent Martin Luther King, Jr., a copy of *Wolf Whistle*, the author explained: "I deliberately published it as a paperback original in order to assure a mass circulation this year. The first printing is one million copies—a record." King thanked him less than two weeks later, calling the first printing figure "fantastic," and adding, "This will certainly make a tremendous impact on the literary world." But the pivotal figure of the bus boycott did not seize that occasion to indicate what impact, if any, the incident Huie investigated had exerted on his own commitment to opposing such injustices.[12] Nor is there any evidence to suggest that King had read I. F. Stone's call for a Gandhi to emerge among American blacks to combat the evil of racism. Nevertheless, such dramatic events must have had their effect.

Yet Harvard Sitkoff is one of the very few historians who has conjectured that the murder of Emmett Till and its courtroom aftermath might have had something to do with the emerging force of civil rights. And even he does so exclusively within the context of the Montgomery black community, speculating that other blacks besides Dr. King had come to realize by 1955 that (in Sitkoff's words) "the continued passive acceptance of evil could only perpetuate its existence." For some Montgomery blacks, "who believed in the steady improvement in race relations, the moment of decision came with the August 1955 lynching of . . . Till and the brazen appearance of the White Citizens' Councils throughout the South. The absurdity of the fact that the days of the cotton South had ended while its racial practices continued aroused many."[13] An early but unscholarly biography of King, Lerone Bennett's *What Manner of Man*, also records the shock of the Till case on the consciousness of the young Baptist minister. This particular atrocity, the *Ebony* editor wrote, "cauterized almost all Negroes and prepared them for more radical departures. . . . The effect of all this [evidence of vulnerability] on King, as on some any other Negroes, was explosive." But no source is cited, and indeed Bennett concedes that King did nothing except "make an agonizing reappraisal of the Negro situation." In January 1956 seven white men were indicted for a series of bombings of black institutions in Montgomery, and King recalled that, "with the Emmett Till case in Mississippi still fresh in our memories, the Negroes held little hope of conviction." (That despair proved justified.)[14] This passage from *Stride Toward Freedom* is the closest King came to certifying the response in his own community to one death in the Delta, and it was a secondary effect at best. Unless the publication of the multivolume King papers now underway in Atlanta happens to uncover such testimony, documentation to prove the influence of a murder in Alabama's neighboring state is simply not extant.

Whatever specific role the case may have played in the black community of the capital of Alabama, Till's death certainly exerted a considerable psychological impact on young Southern blacks, demonstrating to them the shocking vulnerability they faced under Jim Crow. They had come to understand the lesson that Bobo Till's own mother had learned, even if they had never heard or read her version of the ineluctable imperative of human solidarity. "Two months ago I had a nice apartment in Chicago," she told a Cleveland audience that autumn of 1955. "I had a good job. I had a son. When something happened to the Negroes in the South, I said: 'That's their business, not mine.'" But, she concluded: "Now I know how wrong I was. The murder of my son has shown me that what happens to any of us, anywhere in the world, had better be the business of us all." The success of the boycott in Montgomery triggered other antisegregation protests soon thereafter, in Tallahassee; in Tuskegee; in Orangeburg, South Carolina; and elsewhere.[15]

When Representative Diggs spoke in Memphis in 1959 and was identified as an observer of the trial in Tallahatchie County, he traced one continuous line of oppression and protest: "From the Dred Scott decision of 1854 [sic] through the Emancipation Proclamation ... over the bodies of the Emmett Tills and Mack Parkers and under the determination of the Martin Luther Kings, Negroes have stalked their objectives.... " Diggs added that "our nostrils are filled with the stench of a lynch victim being pulled from a river. All these experiences, like a cancer, eat away at the core of our dignity, create frustrations and pressures and bitterness."[16] Such a burden was becoming too heavy—and too pointless—to bear, heightening the urgency of change. The sense of collective responsibility to which Mamie Bradley referred was a feeling that some Southern teenagers, granted the maturity that Till was unnaturally denied, determined to realize through action.[17]

By the end of the 1950s, such a sense was perceptible on a few campuses of the black colleges and universities of the South. Their students were usually the products of abysmal segregated public schools, though in Mississippi the legislature had spent handsomely throughout the decade to support black education, in a weird, illogical effort to make real the pretense of "separate but equal" facilities that *Brown* v. *Board of Education* had already invalidated. These frantic efforts were still insufficient; the poorest states in the Union (and Mississippi was the poorest) were still investing far more of their limited resources in white education than black.[18] Those pupils who managed to get to college, who managed to triumph over such adversity, were hardly anaesthetized against the painful discrimination from which they had suffered. Around 1960 enough like-minded, indignant young blacks congregated on the campus—especially at Fisk University in Nashville and in the Atlanta University system—to jump-start the moribund and limited traditions of student protest that had largely evaporated over the course of several decades.

The decision to fight against the humiliations of Jim Crow stemmed in no small measure from the feelings of guilt at having been so passive under the weight of oppression. On February 1, 1960, four students at North Carolina Agricultural and Technical College in Greensboro inaugurated the sit-ins that were to explode into the generalized protests that eventually transformed the South and the nation. One of the students, Franklin McCain, recalled: "There were many words and few deeds," so "we did a good job of making each other feel bad."[19] It is reasonable to speculate that the sensation of an incident like the Till lynching contributed to the guilt that galvanized defiance of white supremacy. There is also some evidence for this conjecture.

Joyce Ladner (née Perryman) was born in Waynesboro, Mississippi, and was eleven years old when *Brown* v. *Board of Education* was announced. She recalled: "Black parents, knowing the hazards of a segregated society, were especially protective of their sons. I never fully understood why until the summer of 1955: Emmett Till." She added: "As the search for his body went on, my older sister and I ran to the white-owned Hundson's corner grocery each day at 4:30. We wanted to be first in line to buy the *Hattiesburg American*. Each day we pored over the clippings of the lynching we kept in our scrapbook, and cried: Emmett Till was about our age; we cried for him as we would have cried for one of our four brothers. . . . When we saw the picture of his bloated body in *Jet* magazine, we asked each other. 'How could they do that to him? He's only a young boy!'"

Ladner's "sister promised that she would become a lawyer and fight to change things. I had decided to become a social worker so that I could help black people to understand their rights and so they wouldn't have to live under such terrible conditions." Along with her sister, she joined the Student Nonviolent Coordinating Committee (SNCC) in 1960 and became active in civil rights. She also graduated from Tougaloo College in Mississippi in 1964. Joyce Ladner subsequently became a professor of sociology at Hunter College and is perhaps best known for the 1973 anthology she edited, *The Death of White Sociology*.[20]

An especially rich and poignant account of the impact of the case appears in Anne Moody's autobiography. She grew up in Centreville, Mississippi, and was coming home from her new high school when she heard about Till's death. That evening she noticed a different mood in her mother, who warned her not to talk about the case in the presence of whites. "Before Emmett Till's murder, I had known the fear of hunger, hell, and the Devil. But now there was a new fear known to me—the fear of being killed just because I was black. This was the worst of my fears. . . . I didn't know what one had to do or not do as a Negro not to be killed." After Anne Moody overheard white women mention the NAACP during a "guild meeting," she asked her teacher what the initials meant, and was told: "NAACP is a Negro organization that was established a long time ago to help Negroes gain a few basic rights. . . . They are trying to get a conviction in Emmett Till's case. You see[,] the NAACP is trying to do a lot for the Negroes and get the right to vote for Negroes in the South. I shouldn't be telling you all this. And don't you dare breathe a word of what I said. It could cost me my job if word got out I was teaching my students such."[21]

Moody recalled: "I was fifteen years old when I began to hate people. I hated the white men who murdered Emmett Till and I hated all the other whites who were responsible for the countless murders [her teacher] Mrs. Rice had told me about and those I vaguely remembered from childhood. But I also hated Negroes. I hated them for not standing up and doing something about the murders. In fact, I think I had a stronger resentment toward Negroes for letting the whites kill them than toward the whites." For Till's murder "provoked a lot of anger and excitement among whites in Centreville." That was because the community reexamined the barely concealed sexual relations between blacks and whites, particularly the affairs that white men had conducted with black women. But there was also much gossip about the reverse. "This gossip created so much tension, every Negro man in Centreville became afraid to walk the streets. . . . They had only to look at a white woman and be hanged for it," though Anne Moody herself "had never heard of a single affair in Centreville between a Negro man and a white woman."

Her autobiography recounts ugly reprisals, including the arson of one black family's home that killed the parents and children, in the wake of the tensions activated by Till's lynching. She was desperate to leave, to live away in Baton Rouge. "I had not been myself at work since the Emmett Till murder." Anne Moody was then fifteen.[22] She too became active in the civil rights movement with the Congress of Racial Equality (CORE) and SNCC, mostly with voting rights and registration and with the organization of freedom schools. Moody graduated from Tougaloo College in 1963. She helped to alter an environment in which one black mother in Greenwood felt compelled to tell her two sons: "Don't y'all look into no White woman face, cause all she got to say is dat y'all look like y'all want to rape her." Their sister recently recalled that her siblings "to this day don't know one White woman from the other by her facial features."[23]

Because Maya Angelou was older than either Joyce Ladner or Anne Moody, and because she grew up in California, she did not feel the impact of Till's death nearly so keenly. But neither was the impact of the case on her negligible. Angelou remembered that "anger was always present whenever the subject of whites entered our conversations. We discussed the treatment of Rev. Martin Luther King, Jr., the murder of Emmett Till in Mississippi, the large humiliations and the petty snubs we all knew were meant to maim our spirits."[24] Such experiences helped to forge her own sensibilities as a writer and artist.

David L. Jordan of Greenwood can never forget the day he learned of Till's death. Having graduated from high school earlier that summer, and about ready to attend Mississippi Valley State University, Jordan was strolling home from a movie with his brother and two friends when he saw an ambulance outside the Century Funeral Home on Walthall Street. At first he heard only whispers ("the boy from Chicago," "Tallahatchie River," "Emmett Till") and saw taut faces; and then he could make out the radio reports from inside houses with open windows. Jordan felt his stomach churning as the easy pleasure of that day suddenly disintegrated. By 1962 he was serving SNCC as a teacher, and three years he later became president of the Greenwood Voters League in Leflore County. Little more than a decade later, *Jordan* v. *Greenwood* was filed to compel the city to hold local elections according to district; and three decades after the Till case, Jordan became one of the first black aldermen in Greenwood since Reconstruction.[25]

Cassius Marcellus Clay was born January 17, 1942 in Louisville. In his autobiography, he records (or claims to remember) how his mother reminded him of his childhood: "When you'd hear of some injustice against blacks, you'd lay up in your bed, cry all night. . . . Then your father'd come home and dramatize what happened, make it worse." She added: "You remember when they lynched Emmett Till in Mississippi, how upset you were? Your father talked about it night and day. I told him not to upset you. You remember you were always asking ain't there something we can do to help Emmett Till? We worried about the time you in grammar school till you out of high school. If boxing hadn't come along, Lord knows what you would've got into. . . . "[26]

The teenager who grew up to become Muhammad Ali continued: "Emmett Till and I were about the same age. A week after he was murdered . . . I stood on the corner with a gang of boys, looking at pictures of him in the black newspapers and magazines. In one, he was laughing and happy. In the other, his head was swollen and bashed in, his eyes bulging out of their sockets and his mouth twisted and broken. His mother had done a bold thing. She refused to let him be buried until hundreds of thousands marched past his open casket in Chicago and looked down at his mutilated body." The future heavyweight champion "felt a deep kinship to him when I learned he was born the same year and day I was. [Till had been born a little less than six months earlier.] My father talked about it at night and dramatized the crime.

"I couldn't get Emmett out of my mind, until one evening I thought of a way to get back at white people for his death." Ali recalled throwing stones at an Uncle Sam Wants You poster and ripping up the railroad. With his closest boyhood friend, Ronnie King, young Cassius broke into the shoeshine boys' shed at the West Side railroad station and stole two iron shoe rests. They planted them on the tracks and waited. His autobiography completes the story as follows: "One of the wheels locked and sprang from the track. I remember the loud sound of ties ripping up."[27]

Cassius Marcellus Clay did not, of course, grow up to be a civil rights worker, at least not officially; but one of the pugilist's biographers amplifies Ali's own interpretation of the significance of the atrocity in the Deep South. "The impact of Till's murder on his young mind cannot be exaggerated," Robert Lipsyte has observed. "If he was to make it in the white man's world, he realized, he would have to do it by the white man's rules.

"At least until he was big enough to make his own rules.

"Boxing was the answer. Boxing kept him strong and healthy. Boxing got him out of his father's house but kept him off the streets. Boxing brought him status and privileges. Boxing imposed a moral, physical, and mental discipline that made it easier to avoid trouble and temptation."[28]

Other testaments can be cited as well. Cleveland Sellers was born in Denmark, South Carolina, in 1944; and his autobiography documents his transformation into a SNCC activist. "The atrocity that affected me the most," he recalled, "was Emmett Till's lynching." Unlike Ruby Hurley, Sellers accepted the veracity of the account that Till, unfamiliar with Southern customs, whistled at the attractive Mrs. Bryant. "Many black newspapers and magazines carried pictures of the corpse. I can still remember them. They showed terrible gashes and tears in the flesh. It gave the appearance of a ragged, rotting sponge." The acquittal of Bryant and Milam was hardly surprising, though "blacks across the country were outraged, but powerless to do anything." Sellers added: "Till was only three years older than me[,] and I identified with him. I tried to put myself in his place and imagine what he was thinking when those white men took him from his home that night. . . . I read and re-read the newspaper and magazine accounts. I couldn't get over the fact that the men who were accused of killing him had not been punished at all.

"There was something about the cold-blooded callousness of Emmett Till's lynching that touched everyone in the community [of Denmark]," Sellers added. "We had all heard atrocity accounts before, but there was something special about this one. For weeks after it happened, people continued to discuss it. It was impossible to go into a barber shop or corner grocery without hearing someone deplore Emmett Till's lynching. We even discussed it in school. . . . That's one of the good things about an all-black school. We were free to discuss many events that would have been taboo in an integrated school."[29]

The impact of the case was to be felt by other Southern blacks who were about Till's age and who, in their twenties, were to become the pivotal figures in the civil rights movement of the 1960s. The Highlander Folk School, created by a white Tennessean named Myles Horton, provided an integrated environment in which a disproportionate number of future civil rights activists studied and expanded their social and intellectual horizons. Those who came to Highlander in the 1950s remembered how they had been taught in their hometowns to keep a necessary social distance from whites, and they recalled in particular the Till case itself. At the annual "College Workshops," the attendees included future leaders like James Bevel, Marion Barry, Diane Nash, and John Lewis. One scholar who has stressed the influence of such institutions as the Highlander Folk School, Aldon D. Morris, grew up in the Delta before becoming a sociologist at the University of Michigan: "I vividly remember the South of the 1950s ... [and] the memory of the unpunished murder of young Emmett Till in 1955 makes my blood boil even now."[30]

Other activists in the civil rights movement later testified in more general terms to the impact of the case. James Forman (1928–), who served as executive secretary of SNCC and later became minister of education of the Black Panther Party, remembered how Till's "vicious killing" had made "black people all over the country ... angry ... but also frightened." For Julius Lester (1939–), a one-time SNCC field secretary, the eruption of "black power" by the mid-1960s was evidence that too many people had died. Those who demanded an end to black vulnerability and powerlessness "hadn't forgotten 14-year old Emmett Till being thrown into the Tallahatchie River ... with a gin mill tied around his ninety-pound [sic] body. They hadn't forgotten the trees bent low with the weight of black bodies on a lynching rope." No wonder then that Amzie Moore (1912–), who grew up in Grenada and Leflore counties, served in a segregated U.S. Army in World War II, and became a local NAACP president early in 1955, called the Till case "the beginning of the civil rights movement in Mississippi. . . . From that point on, Mississippi began to move."[31]

One of the most redoubtable whites in SNCC before black power tore the organization asunder was the daughter of a minister from Ohio Wesleyan University, Mary King, whose autobiography records the "powerful and traumatic effect" of the Till case. "Like many of my generation," she has written, "my first graphic confrontation with" the "social evil" of racial injustice came with this particular murder. "Following this event, I spoke to my social studies class," drawing upon *Life* magazine for evidence. Her voice broke as she addressed her classmates, who were then, like herself, fifteen years old. "This was my first speech about an issue of justice[,] and it may have represented a pre-decision leading to my working in the movement," most importantly in SNCC headquarters in Atlanta, with Ella Baker and Julian Bond, as well as in Jackson during the Mississippi Summer Project of 1964, with Amzie Moore. Later, in the administration of President Jimmy Carter, King became a deputy director of ACTION, the agency that included VISTA and the Peace Corps—a capstone to a life that in some sense began with "the sickening assault on my consciousness of Emmett Till's death."[32]

A Boston film producer, Henry Hampton of Blackside production company, may well merit consideration as the most influential popular historian of the civil rights movement because of the documentary series first aired on public television in 1987, *Eyes on the Prize.* Early in the first of six shows is an extensive segment on the Till case, and this editorial decision undoubtedly had autobiographical origins. "It ties to my [own] history," Hampton explained after working almost nine years to create the series. "So I guess that's as good an anchor as any. The first thing I remember was Emmett Till. He was my age and the fact that somebody could come and take him away and kill him. It just seared me. It was one thing my parents couldn't protect me from."[33] Hampton's was a common black reaction, which his combination of remembrance and creativity could transform into televised history of exceptional immediacy and poignancy.*

Though Hampton chronologically began the series in 1954, he would readily concede that history rarely reveals complete novelties or sudden breaks in continuity. As early as the mid-1950s, the journalist Carl Rowan had noticed that "even in Mississippi the Negro is finding second-class, voteless, powerless citizenship too heavy a burden to bear."[34] Rowan had already detected the faint glimmerings of change, the fortification of the faculty of will with which Southern blacks were gaining the moral courage to alter the circum-

---

*Molly Levinson, the ten-year-old daughter of friends of the author, watched the first episode at their home in Greensboro, North Carolina, and was awakened by nightmares for about two weeks thereafter. The audience sample presented here is hardly scientific, but her response suggests the haunting impact of the case on at least one member of yet another generation.

stances of their lives. From his perch at the *Delta Democrat-Times,* Hodding Carter observed in 1960 that young Southern blacks were "more than anything else . . . embittered by the absence of color blindness in Southern courtrooms, by the failure of too many white juries to indict or convict white murderers [and] lynchers. . . . "[35]

What Gunnar Myrdal had called the American dilemma was what civil rights workers would directly challenge, an inconsistency that may ultimately be as unbearable in the moral life as it is prohibited by the rules of logic. The American republic was slow to make a serious attempt to eliminate white supremacy, and erratic in the effort to reconcile race relations with the creed of liberal progress. But the imperative to make enlightened ideals operable could not be permanently contradicted. The murder of Emmett Till was undoubtedly one of the flares that illumined the often tragic incongruity between profession and practice.

The case helped activate a protest movement that was intended to bridge such gaps between promise and fulfillment. Just as in the late eighteenth century, when blacks in Massachusetts demanded the suffrage by echoing the slogan of "No taxation without representation," and just as black abolitionists and their allies in the nineteenth century summoned the rhetoric of the Declaration of Independence and the Bill of Rights, so, too, traditional democratic ideals were proclaimed in the civil rights movement in the 1960s.[36] "The Declaration of Independence," Herman Melville had proclaimed, "makes a difference." This was a trump that even the most vilified and miserable of American minorities could use. That blacks did so with at least some effectiveness is a historical argument that need not be belabored.

But consider in particular the momentum signified by the Albany protests in 1962. The city fathers had managed to secure an injunction from a federal district judge, J. Robert Elliott, a segregationist whom John F. Kennedy had only recently appointed to the bench. The injunction prohibited "unlawful picketing, congregating or marching in the streets . . . [or] any [other] act designed to provoke breaches of the peace." Because this was a federal injunction, it posed problems for Dr. King, who had (among others) been specifically enjoined from further protest activity. At the Shiloh Baptist Church, however, Rev. Benjamin Welles told the assembly: "I've heard about an injunction but I haven't seen one. I've heard a few names but my name hasn't been called. But I do know where my name is being called. My name is being called on the road to freedom. I can hear the blood of Emmett Till as it calls from the ground. . . . When shall we go? Not tomorrow! Not at high noon! Now!" Such martyrdom had given the movement some traction, stirring it to action as a group of 160 marched from the church toward the Albany City Hall. More than one hundred of the protesters were under the age of eighteen. They were arrested and put in cells designed to hold about a sixth of their number.[37]

The civil rights movement in which youngsters took such risks constituted a subculture that bestowed a privileged position upon folk music and spirituals. Probably the most important troubadour of the movement in the early 1960s was Bob Dylan, who had performed on sites where "black is the color and none is the number." Born in the same year as his fellow Midwesterner Till, Dylan was to transcribe his sense of the horror in the Delta in an early song, "The Death of Emmett Till." Told in the first person, Dylan recounted the story, describing the beating in the barn but omitting any mention of the episode in the store that had presumably provoked the murder. The fourth stanza gets a couple of facts wrong, because Dylan referred to the confessions as though Bryant and Milam had admitted the murder even before the trial took place; and "The Death of Emmett Till" also claims that the jury included members who were accomplices of the half-brothers. The trial in Sumner was indeed in many respects a sham, as Dylan noted. But the defendants confessed only to Huie, and not in a courtroom; nor was a conspiracy among some jurors who might have participated in the crime ever suggested. The song ends with Dylan reading the newspapers but finding himself unable to bear the sight of the grinning countenances of the killers descending the steps of the courthouse. He then exhorts other Americans to denounce such atrocities.[38]

Though its lyrics were mawkish, the ballad was a precocious attempt to continue the tradition of the folk protest song. "The Death of Emmett Till" prefigured Dylan's condemnation of callousness to suffering that also characterized "Blowin' in the Wind," a civil rights anthem that asked how long other Americans would need before they would realize that "too many people have died."

The chief moral that Dylan seemed to derive from the lynching was its inherent injustice, which a heightened ethical sensitivity might remedy. Others drew lessons that highlighted the powerlessness of blacks in the South. Shelby Steele, who became an English professor at San Jose State University, recalls a college game that he played with others in the black middle class, in which the participants tried to top one another with tales of victimization. Till's mutilation and murder "sat atop the pinnacle. . . . We probed his story, finding in his youth and Northern upbringing the quintessential embodiment of black innocence, brought down by a white evil so portentous and apocalyptic, so gnarled and hideous, that it left us with a feeling not far from awe." In recounting his story, Steele realized, "we came to *feel* the immutability of our victimization, its utter indigenousness."[39]

For those who became directly involved in the civil rights struggle, the episode was shockingly symbolic of the precariousness of black life and rights in the region, a culmination of decades of the most abject subordination. The widow of Medgar Evers expressed this interpretation perhaps most poignantly. The Till case, Myrlie Evers commented, "was the story in microcosm of every Negro in Mississippi. For it was the proof that even youth was no defense against the ultimate terror, that lynching was still the final means by which white supremacy would be upheld, that whites could still murder Negroes with impunity. . . . It was the proof that . . . no Negro's life was really safe." The case proved, she concluded, "if proof were needed, that there would be no real change in Mississippi until the rest of the country decided that change there must be and then forced it."[40] Only sensitized outsiders, in other words, could compel whites in the state to approximate national standards of race relations.

A quite different emphasis, however, appears in Oscar Handlin's history of civil rights, *Fire-Bell in the Night*. Taking the long view, the Harvard scholar noted the sharp increase by the 1960s in the "sense of personal security" among Southern blacks. Black victims of crime, whether by whites or by other blacks, were more frequently to find redress in the courts than they had in the past, and white policemen and jailers were less likely to torture and murder blacks in their custody. "Communally organized murders declined steadily," Professor Handlin argued in 1964, so that "this technique of terror has not been available to those who wished to keep the blacks in their place." Even though (or perhaps because) blacks were no longer as submissive as they had been earlier, "the rope and faggot have gone out of use. Sensitivity to national opinion, the reluctance to invite federal intervention, better police methods and years of education" accounted for the change.[41]

Handlin was certainly correct in tabulating the overall reduction of racist violence, particularly if the period is compared to 1885–1907, when more lynchings than *legal* executions occured in the United States. But he offered a misleading description of the conditions of physical safety under which rural blacks lived in the South. As early as 1940, the Association of Southern Women for the Prevention of Lynching noted in a pamphlet entitled *Lynching Goes Underground* that the unprosecuted murders of blacks were replacing mob pursuits and public violence. And in 1951 the executive director of the Southern Regional Council asserted: "The plain fact is that the dwindling number of traditional lynchings is no longer a reliable index to injustice, racial or otherwise. . . . The lawless spirit of the lynch mob is still with us, but the pattern of violence has changed."[42] Much of it was under cover of law, which was as severe in the imposition of certain penalties as the posses and vigilantes had been earlier in the century. A black attorney, Haywood Burns, observed in 1970: "Of the nineteen jurisdictions that have executed men for rape since 1930, almost one-third of them—six states—have executed *only* blacks. There have been some years in which everyone who was executed for rape in this country was black."[43] Thomas Nelson Page was wrong when he predicted in 1904 that, until blacks stopped assaulting white women, "the crime of lynching will never be extirpated."[44] But the power of the myth behind Page's error cannot be overstated.

The frequency of substitutes for the classic lynchings that were perpetrated earlier in the century cannot fully be ascertained, but certainly dozens of racially motivated murders and executions occurred even in the decade after the invalidation of *Plessy* v. *Ferguson* in 1954. Black lives came cheap, as did those of civil rights workers generally. In the period between 1954 and 1968, at least forty-four blacks and whites were murdered in pursuit of civil rights.[45] Perhaps the three most notorious killings—of James Chaney, Michael Schwerner, and Andrew Goodman—were committed in the summer of the year in which *Fire-Bell in the Night* was published. In Jackson, Medgar and Myrlie Evers had prohibited their three young children from playing outside after dark, and from playing in the street or in vacant lots at all. They were taught to jump into the bathtub if they ever heard shooting. Myrlie Evers had arranged the furniture in their home so that no one ever sat facing a window, and the children had to watch television from the floor. Still, Medgar Evers did not survive—perhaps because, returning home exhausted from the NAACP office, he forgot his precaution to get out of the car only from the right side. Such crimes provoked little outrage in the white community and were sometimes even sanctioned, as when ex-Governor Ross Barnett of Mississippi made a point of warmly greeting defendant Byron Beckwith during his trial for the Evers assassination in 1964.[46] Barnett's gesture constituted a sort of de facto recognition of violence as a legitimate response to black aspirations for dignity.

A historian whose surveillance was conducted on the scene concluded that "the crimes against humanity committed in Mississippi in the summer of 1964 will never be recorded in full."[47] Even that doleful prediction did not take into account other summers, other years. Indeed, it is impossible to refute the charge of one black Communist that, "if Emmett Till had been a Mississippi farm boy instead of a Chicago lad on vacation in Mississippi, the world would probably never have known his fate." It is worth noting the limited outside interest in the fate of local adults like George Metcalf, president of the Natchez chapter of the NAACP, critically injured by a bomb in his automobile in 1965; Vernon Dahmer, an NAACP official in Hattiesburg, killed by a firebomb in 1966; or Wharlest Jackson, former treasurer of the Natchez branch, murdered by another such bomb in his automobile in 1967.[48]

Nor were murders the only expression of racist rage. A thirty-four-year-old black veteran named Edward Aaron was a complete stranger to the six Klansmen who picked him up in 1957 while he was walking on the road in Birmingham. As part of their ritual, Aaron was humiliated and castrated, after which turpentine was poured into the wound.[49] Many other forms of intimidation were still powerful, for the civil rights movement that was the subject of Handlin's book sparked a resistance that continued to beat and maim those who felt obliged to suppress their enthusiasm for white supremacy. Nor did Handlin take into account the residual effects of the fear that the earlier and more vicious expressions of racism continued to generate. Luck and quick wits were still required for civil rights activists and blacks in the rural South to survive amid the virulent racism of trigger-happy, violence-prone whites.

For all their bluster and florid paeans to martyrdom, however,

Southern white supremacists were far less willing to die for their beliefs than were blacks, who were themselves usually unarmed and committed to passive resistance. The civil rights movement has been justly admired for its injection of moral ideals into ordinary politics, for enlarging the scope and cleansing the purpose of self-government into the United States. But the introduction of such idealism in any nation's history can perhaps be only episodic and infrequent. For the essence of politics is not only Harold Lasswell's definition of "who gets what" but—more brutally—Lenin's *kto kogo*, or "who-whom," that is, who does what to whom, or ultimately who kills whom. At its most fundamental level, the civil rights movement succeeded because its partisans were willing to be jailed for their beliefs, while those who were champions of interposition and massive resistance had acquired very little taste for self-sacrifice.

Civil rights activists were willing to risk their lives, while even violent white supremacists were not (though under conditions of secrecy and conspiracy, they were willing to engage in criminal and sadistic acts). Martyrdom was a price those closest to the struggle knew they might have to pay. King himself was undoubtedly the most explicit and self-conscious on this question, from his initial realization, posted as a warning to segregationists ("We will soon wear you down by our capacity to suffer") to his final speech in Memphis ("It really doesn't matter to me now. Because I've been to the mountain top, I won't mind. Like anybody else, I would like to live a long life. Longevity has its place. But I'm not concerned about that now. I just want to do God's will. And He's allowed me to go up to the mountain. . . . ").[50] One achievement of the cause that King so decisively shaped was the sense of purpose to which such mortal risks could be directed.

The danger of death always lurked within the movement, and those who committed themselves to its goals were well aware of the peril that "the revolt of the rednecks" presented. James Meredith's Air Force squadron commander, a white Mississippi "aristocrat," could tell him in the year of the Till case that the state's whites were ready to kill all blacks if necessary to maintain white supremacy. That prediction still did not stop Meredith from daring to enroll at Ole Miss seven years later.[51] Such tenacity and courage—without which the promises of constitutional law would have remained empty—shattered the prognosis that Senator Eastland had made on the day that Mrs. Parks refused to surrender her seat. "The next few years will be the golden hour of Southern history," the senator had confidently told the Citizens' Councils. For he expected the foes of "full social equality and amalgamation" to be "worthy of our heritage."[52] But when faced with activists willing to risk their own mortality, the Citizens' Councils and their allies—after all the damage that they inflicted—backed down.

By the mid-1960s much of the civil rights movement abandoned a principled opposition to the use of violence in self-defense. It was perhaps one measure of Malcolm X's estrangement from the earlier civil rights movement, and a sign of his growing influence by the time of his own assassination, that he refused to sanction this spirit of sacrifice, particularly if it enabled white violence to be unleashed with impunity. Speaking to the Militant Labor Forum in New York, he refused in a question-and-answer period to acknowledge seriously the contributions of white activists: "Lumumba was murdered, Medgar Evers was murdered, Mack Parker was murdered, Emmett Till was murdered, my own father was murdered. You tell that stuff to someone else. It's time some white people starting dying in this thing." In alluding to his own father, a Garveyite preacher whose outspokenness had led to Klan threats to his life, which was abruptly ended under mysterious circumstances in Omaha, Malcolm X was perhaps inadvertently touching on some curious crosshatchings with the issues that the Till case itself raised. For Malcolm Little was not only the nephew of a victim of a white lynch mob; he had also, at the end of his career as a burglar, gotten a much stiffer sentence (ten years) in a Massachusetts criminal court because an accomplice was a white woman with whom "Detroit Red" enjoyed a liaison. "You had no business with white girls!" his own defense attorney, flushed with anger, had informed the twenty-year-old hustler.[53]

His autobiographical account of his transfiguration in prison and rebirth as a Black Muslim is justifiably famous. But what is relevant in the context of this chapter is that Malcolm X joined a sect that used the Till case for education and propaganda. The leading scholarly authority on the Nation of Islam, C. Eric Lincoln, conjectured in 1962 that its growth in the late 1950s may well have stemmed— in small part—from the Till lynching and the acquittal of the two killers. In any event, "the Muslims very often use the Till case in their arguments against the white man's sense of justice. To the Muslims, Emmett Till had become a symbol of the depravity of the 'white devils' and of the helplessness of the Federal government to provide protection for all of its citizens, or to bring whites who are guilty of crimes against Negroes, to justice."[54]

Martyrdom was not a role that Emmett Till had sought or a destiny that he felt compelled to enact. To have included him in the category of "sacred martyrs" for democracy therefore strained the argument of Dr. King, who acknowledged in a speech in Florida in 1958 that, "as a mere boy," Till was "unqualified to vote." He was nevertheless "used as a victim to terrorize Negro citizens and keep them from the polls"—a farfetched accusation for which King had little warrant.[55] It is also odd that, in the dedication to Juan Williams's splendid companion volume to the Public Broadcasting System series on the civil rights movement, *Eyes on the Prize*, Till's name is included among those—black and white—who died in quest of equal justice under the law. His death was surely less self-conscious—less a willed act of resignation—than that; and mortality alone, however premature, should not be converted into a synonym for martyrdom. But what happened to Till helped spur others who became committed to social justice to put that death into a context of suffering that could be redeemed, if at all, by ending such conditions of vulnerability and victimization. George Lee and Lamar Smith, two Mississippi blacks who fancied themselves American citizens exercising their most fundamental rights, had been murdered that same summer. They may well have fathomed the peril that they faced in trying to vote. But their names are forgotten; while Till, whose youth had probably deprived him of such understanding, was rescued from an arbitrary fate, from the nimbus of oblivion, because he was a minor.

Retrospect also permits the placement of his murder exactly between two landmarks. As the decade of the 1950s began, it was possible for David L. Cohn to perpetrate the following non sequitur in the *New York Times* about his hometown of Greenville: "Segregation of the races is strictly enforced. But otherwise race relations are, on the whole, excellent."[56] The decade had opened with growing Southern white resistance, thanks to the Sweatt and McLaurin cases, in which the Supreme Court had unanimously affirmed in June 1950 the efforts of Negro petitioners to puncture the myth of "separate but equal" status, at least in higher education. In these cases the Vinson Court concluded that the state of Texas had not provided Hemon Sweatt with equal protection of the laws merely by opening a new law school for blacks only, preventing him on grounds of color alone from satisfying his preference to attend the University of Texas Law School. Nor were the constitutional rights of G. W. McLaurin secured when, though admitted to a graduate program at the University of Oklahoma, he was assigned to sit only in a designated area of classrooms and the library and was initially required to eat in the cafeteria in a special spot and at a different time from other students—as though McLaurin suffered from a communicable disease. But what a difference a decade made. In 1960 the sit-in movement exploded, beginning in Greensboro, North Carolina, as black resistance to racial injustice took a dramatic new turn. Within the span of a decade, the impetus had passed from white supremacists to black activists, and it had been lifted out of the courts and into the streets. What had seemed at best the harbinger of a remote equality had within a decade become charged with ethical urgency.

Some younger blacks now refused to follow the tempo that the Supreme Court had mandated, of "all deliberate speed." When they were children growing up, the officials whom blacks had no responsibility or voice in choosing were firmly predicting horrible carnage, if the federal government were to attempt to realize the utterly impossible prospect of desegregation. The same officials were also invoking the bravery against impossible odds of their gallant Confederate ancestors. But those same black children grew up into civil rights activists whose courage—both physical and moral—was far more awesome than that of those Southern whites whose violence consisted of forming mobs to beat up schoolchildren and whose bravery consisted of burning down churches and shooting other citizens in the back. Southern leaders who had vowed uncompromising resistance invariably preferred in the end to surrender rather than suffer contempt of court, fines, and jail terms. Such politicians and community leaders dropped their Rebel flags in the dust as the momentum shifted to a presumably inferior race. In 1955 the Deep South had yelled, "Never!" A decade later the first president since Zachary Taylor to be elected from Dixie had promised a joint session of Congress that "we shall overcome"; and the Deep South soon began switching to, "Well, if you insist."

Among the achievements of the resurgent civil rights movement was acceleration of Congressional passage of the Civil Rights Act of 1968, which finally incorporated a federal antilynching provision.

Thus, the aim of the last Negro to serve in Congress in the post-Reconstruction era was at last fulfilled, for before George H. White of North Carolina retired in 1901, he had introduced the first such bill. The 1968 law came at least half a century too late to have deterred the worst outbreaks of this crime, and the irony came too late for such gallant activists as Du Bois, Ida B. Wells-Barnett and Walter White to appreciate. The statute was also something of an anachronism in a decade of riots in black ghettos. But violence was outlawed if committed "by one or more persons, part of an assemblage of three or more persons which act or act [that] . . . shall result in . . . injury . . . to the person of any other individual."[57] Such language, which would not even have been applicable to the facts of the Till case, might sound antiquated in an era replete with assassins armed with rifles with telescopic sights. But the history of lynchings was not yet over. In 1981, Klansmen randomly abducted and murdered a nineteen-year-old black named Michael Donald in Mobile, stringing his body up to a tree. Two Klansmen were convicted on criminal charges; and the victim's mother, Mrs. Beulah Mae Donald, won a $7 million lawsuit against the United Klans of America. She may be able to realize only about $150,000 of that sum, but Mrs. Donald's victory may eventually put the largest of the Klan organizations out of business. The Mobile jury was all white.[58]

The Till affair alone, of course, did not accomplish the revolution in civil rights in the South. But his murder deserves recognition as an overlooked and obscured factor in catalyzing resistance. For history should be more than the slate that records what happens to people. It should also be an account of how they *respond* to what happens to them, how they fashion from their distinctive heritage as well as their circumstances the instruments to achieve at least some glimpses of their own emancipation. That is the historical significance of the black perception of the Till slaying as a logical terminus of Jim Crow. What two half-brothers committed with impunity did help to fortify what Faulkner in Stockholm had called "a spirit capable of compassion and sacrifice and endurance."

S E V E N

Race and Sex

The story of this death in the Delta extended well past its impact on the burgeoning civil rights movement, for it also helped to expose the tangled relationship between sex and race in America. Because Till's wallet—if not his whistle—had at least implicitly threatened the elaborate code that regulated racial and sexual relations, the case has resonated in surprising ways in an era marked by dramatically evolving, far more open attitudes toward sexuality.

Less than a decade after that implicit challenge in Money, a remarkable transformation in sexual attitudes and behavior would alter the very texture of national life, signaling a discernible shift from puritanism to permissiveness. In the 1950s the leading best-seller was the Reverend Norman Vincent Peale's *The Power of Positive Thinking*. Its successor as the most popular new book in the United States over the course of a decade addressed not spirituality but carnality: Dr. Alex Comfort's *The Joy of Sex*. Whether in the more extensive practice of premarital and extramarital sex or in the wider availability of pornography; whether in the constitutional validation of the right to "reproductive freedom" or the general claim for the legitimacy of any sexual practice between or among consenting adults; whether in the explicitness of public discourse, or the artistic presentation of intercourse, or the establishment of abortion clinics and sex therapy clinics, a radically different atmosphere was bound to alter perspectives on the immediate past. Among the ideals that were to be questioned was the need of males to protect females from the dark temptations of sexuality outside the sanctity of matrimony. Nor were the myths and mysteries associated with interracial sex immune from revision.

In *Caste and Class in a Southern Town* (first published in 1937), John Dollard had reported on the Delta town of Indianola, where the Citizens' Councils were later born; and the Yale social scientist noted the delicacy and predictability with which black subordination to white beliefs and fantasies about blacks were perfected. It was the sort of code that a Chicago teenager might not have been able to decipher quickly enough to save his own life. Books like Lillian Smith's *Killers of the Dream* (1949), Calvin Hernton's *Sex and Racism in America* (1965), and Charles Herbert Stember's *Sexual Racism* (1976) also merit attention for their speculation on the complicated psychological charges emitted by the commingling of race and sex, especially in the South.

The ambivalence and the allure, the temptation and the terror, the resentment and the resistance were all felt by Eldridge Cleaver, whose *Soul on Ice* confirmed some of the most remarkable effects of the case on an individual. Cleaver was eighteen years old in 1954 when he entered Folsom state prison in California for getting caught with "a shopping bag full of marijuana." The following year, the Till incident "turned me inside out," he wrote from his cell; Cleaver "was, of course, angry over the whole bit." But then came a stunning moment of candor: "One day I saw in a magazine a picture of the white woman with whom Emmett Till was said to have flirted. While looking at the picture, I felt that little tension in the center of my chest I experience when a woman appeals to me. I was disgusted and angry with myself. . . . " The prisoner admitted: "I looked at the picture again and again, and in spite of everything and against my will and the hate I felt for the woman [for having caused Till's murder] and all that she represented, she appealed to me. I flew into a rage" is how Cleaver described his reaction to the woman *L'Aurore* called "a crossroads Marilyn Monroe."[1]

Two days afterward, Cleaver experienced "a 'nervous breakdown.' For several days I ranted and raved against the white race, against white women in particular, against white America in general. When I came to myself, I was locked in a padded cell with not even the vaguest memory of how I got there." The analysis of the prison psychiatrist underestimated the racial element at the heart of the breakdown, and Cleaver was released "back into the general inmate population just as if nothing had happened." But he "continued to brood over these events and over the dynamics of race relations in America."

Reading the works of Russian radicals, the prisoner fancied himself an "outlaw," and after his parole Cleaver assumed a new identity: "I became a rapist. . . . I crossed the tracks and sought out white prey. I did this consciously, deliberately, willfully, methodically. . . . Rape was an insurrectionary act. It delighted me that I was defying and trampling upon the white man's law, upon his system of values, and that I was defiling his women. . . . I felt I was getting revenge." The whiteness of his victims, he wrote in a poem, their femaleness, had become "symbol of the rope and hanging tree,/ Of the burning cross."[2] *Soul on Ice* contains no meditation on what he did to the women he violated and victimized. But it was one sign of the author's capacity eventually to transcend his pathology that he dedicated his book to his white attorney, Beverly Axelrod, with whom he shared "the ultimate of love."[3] Cleaver's ugly antisocial impulses were channeled into politics through the Black Panthers and his vocation as a writer, and he became an ideologue who championed virtually everything that nearly a century of white racism had forbidden. Much later, of course, Cleaver abandoned political radicalism and became a born-again Christian.

The starkness of the contrast between good and evil in the Till case, the natural and instinctive horror that is evoked by the murder of a child (killed because of the color of his skin), would seem to preclude much redistribution of sympathies. But a kind of historical revisionism about the affair has nevertheless emerged, especially in Susan Brownmiller's sulfurous tract against the crime of rape, *Against Our Will*. From the perspective of radical feminism, Brownmiller argued in 1975 that the boastfulness of the fourteen-year-old Till was symptomatic of the common male assumption that all females were available for possession. After recounting the incident in the store at Money and the subsequent murder, Brownmiller commented: "We are rightly aghast that a whistle should be cause for murder[,] but we must also accept that Emmett Till and J. W. Millam [*sic*] shared something in common. *They both understood* [italics in original] that the whistle was no small tweet of hubba-hubba or melodious approval for a well-turned ankle. . . . [Instead] it was a deliberate insult just short of physical assault, a last reminder to Carolyn Bryant that this black boy, Till, had in mind to possess her. . . . " Brownmiller added that she had come "to understand the

insult implicit in Emmett Till's whistle, the depersonalized challenge of 'I can have you[,]' with or without the racial aspect. Today
a sexual remark on the street causes within me a fleeting but mur-
derous rage."[4]

A former civil rights worker in Mississippi, Brownmiller was
hardly claiming that Till had been justly punished, and she drew
back from implying that such advances and suggestiveness merited
some form of revenge. Brownmiller made clear in response to Till's
murder that "nothing in recent times can match it for sheer outra-
geousness, for indefensible overkill with community support." And
she acknowledged that Till was not even the last victim of the myth
of the savage black rapist and of what W. J. Cash called Southern
white "gynealotry." In 1959 twenty-three-year-old Mack Charles
Parker was scheduled to stand trial for rape, based on the testimony
of a white woman who picked him out of a lineup of twenty blacks,
though she later admitted: "I told these police that I wasn't positive
it was him but it looked like him." June Walters added: "I can't be
positive because I was scared to death and there wasn't much light.
I believe he's the one." Two days before the designated trial, a mob
of masked men pulled Parker from a Poplarville jail cell and shot
him; and though townspeople knew who the killers were, the mayor
saw no point in prosecution: "You couldn't convict the guilty parties
if you had a sound film of the lynching."[5]

Susan Brownmiller was nevertheless right to conclude that the
breaking point was not Parker's death but Till's four years earlier.
The civil rights movement was to drive the white South to defend
racial supremacy "on grounds apart from the white woman's body.
. . . It was the landmark case of white male retaliation for black male
transgression. In a sense, it broke the mold."[6] But Brownmiller's inclination to blur the moral lines was nevertheless disorienting, as
Jean Stafford averred in a review of *Against Our Will*: "There is a
story in this book so satanically ugly and the author's reaction to it
so bloodcurdling that I wish I could forget it[,] and I know that I
never can." Stafford added: "I am very much afraid that Miss
Brownmiller is saying that Till's murder, if not altogether justified
under the law, was wholly understandable in larger (i.e., feminist)
terms. The want of mercy is a serious drawback in personality."[7]

Stafford's reading was unduly tendentious and unfair, for what
the author of *Against Our Will* was grappling with and seeking to
understand was that neither patriarchal stereotyping nor contempt

for women was confined to one race alone, and that even racism can be grasped as symptomatic of the larger phenomenon of dehumanization. White men did not have a monopoly on the urge to circumscribe the liberties and opportunities of women. On the contrary, a special issue of *Ebony* in 1966 featured a full-page editorial that insisted that the black father should dominate his family, and recommended that the black woman emulate the Jewish mother "who pushed her husband to success, educated her male children first and engineered good marriages for her daughters."[8] Black militancy was hardly more sensitive than Southern gallantry to women's rights or to mounting a challenge to the prerogatives of patriarchy. "We Must Protect Our Most Valuable Property[,] Our Women" was a banner unfurled above the female gallery at rallies of the Nation of Islam.[9]

Brownmiller apparently did not realize that Till had probably done more than merely whistle at Carolyn Bryant. But the molestation nevertheless constituted a prank, a joke that would soon, in the evolution of American culture, come to be seen as sexist and therefore nastily unfunny. Brownmiller's analysis was hardly "bloodcurdling." But she failed to consider and to underscore the insincerity—the playacting—of Till's advances. It is not likely that the Chicago lad really believed, as she put it, that he "was going to show his black buddies that he, and by inference, *they* could get a white woman and Carolyn Bryant was the nearest convenient object" (italics in original).[10] It is possible in retrospect to note the repugnant assumptions behind such masculine "humor" in front of the grocery store and still minimize the actual peril that his particular bravado posed to the woman behind the counter.

Any reconsideration of the Till case from a feminist angle risked generating a tension with racial apologetics that blacks might not readily reconcile. Minority militancy had to be enlisted in defense against the friendly fire coming from predominantly white women activists. That is why Angela Davis felt compelled, while praising *Against Our Will* as "a pioneering scholar contribution to the contemporary literature on rape," to condemn the book for helping to resuscitate "the old racist myth of the Black rapist." Brownmiller's account is "pervaded with racist ideas" because her "provocative distortion" depicted Till "as a guilty sexist—almost as guilty as his white racist murderers. After all, she argues, both Till and his murderers were exclusively concerned about their rights of possession over women." However much Till's actual fate may be deplored in *Against Our Will*, Davis argued, Brownmiller "succumb[ed] to the old racist sophistry of blaming the victim."[11]

The Communist writer and political candidate herself has missed the point, which was to insist that women must also be seen as victims of widespread assumptions about their own availability, that a wolf whistle can have an overtone so sinister that the category of victimization ought to be enlarged. Brownmiller could scarcely have been clearer in her effort to reinterpret the meaning of the incident at the Bryant store, without depreciating the awful horror of the lynching. *Against Our Will* cannot reasonably be read as taking satisfaction with any sort of punishment—even short of homicide—that might have been meted out to Emmett Till. Davis's book is so anxious to eradicate the myth of the black rapist, however, and to absolve black men of fraudulent and exaggerated charges of rape, that she cannot appreciate the ambiguities of the Till case that Brownmiller was trying to elucidate. According to Davis's analysis, Brownmiller "clearly invites us to infer that if this fourteen-year-old boy had not been shot in the head and dumped into the Tallahatchie River after he whistled at one white woman, he would probably have succeeded in raping another white woman."[12] Against such preposterous and perverse readings, such deliberate intentions at misunderstanding, it is unlikely that any author could fashion much of a riposte.

The emergence of feminism in the 1960s is related to the dramatic decline of racism, which could not be effectively combated until the sexual myths and obsessions could be exorcised. However subtle, a connection existed between the collapse of Jim Crow and the extinction of the notion that some women required unusual protection ("weaker vessels"), while others were available for possession. Obedience and subordination were part of the price that the system of patriarchy extracted for the protection of the lady. The concept of women as autonomous agents, including a sense of themselves as sexual beings, had to be more fully cultivated before the most tenacious forms of white supremacy could be challenged. What Cash called the mind of the South—historians would now say *mentalité*—had to be altered before the weight of both kinds of repression could be lifted. The civil rights advocate Virginia Foster Durr, who was born in Alabama in 1903, remembered being warned as a girl of the danger of rape. She was also "told that black men

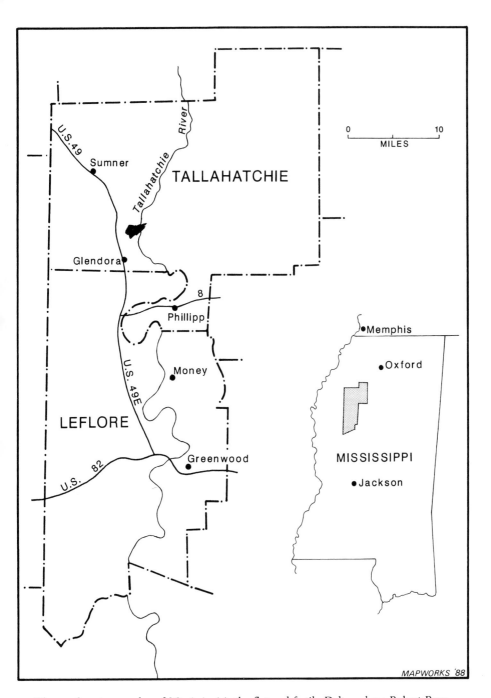

The northwestern wedge of Mississippi is the flat and fertile Delta, where Robert Penn Warren, among others, observed a "sad and baleful beauty." The Delta has historically had the state's highest ratio of blacks to whites. In August 1955, Emmett Till walked fatefully into a store in Money; he was killed a week later near Glendora. Till's corpse was recovered near Phillipp. Less than a month later, the accused killers were tried in Sumner, the county seat of Tallahatchie County. *(Herb Heidt, Mapworks)*

Emmett Louis Till was born near Chicago in 1941, and had finished the seventh grade on the South Side of that city when he visited cousins and other relatives in the Mississippi Delta in the late summer of 1955. His parents were divorced in 1943, two years before his father's death. There were no other children. *(UPI/Bettmann NewsPhotos)*

(Above) The population of Money, Mississippi, was a couple of hundred residents having the use of one paved road. Among the three stores in the town was one that specialized in selling to black field hands. It was owned and operated by Roy Bryant, 24, and his wife Carolyn, 21. Except for her sister-in-law, Mrs. Bryant was alone in this general store when Till entered it on the evening of August 24. *(Ed Clark, Life Magazine © 1955 Time Inc.)* (Right) The killers of the brash young visitor from Chicago needed an object heavy enough to keep the corpse weighted at the bottom of the Tallahatchie River. Near the town of Boyle, they selected this cotton gin fan. Tallahatchie County Sheriff Harold Clarence Strider, who helped recover Till's body but who later testified for the defense, is shown next to the gin fan that had been tied to the victim's neck. *(Ed Clark, Life Magazine © 1955 Time Inc.)*

(Opposite page: Above) Though Sheriff Strider had ordered an immediate burial in the vicinity of the killing, Emmett Till's mother, Mrs. Mamie Bradley, insisted that the casket be sent back to Chicago, where she received it in the Illinois Central terminal from which her son had left for his vacation two weeks earlier. After crying, "Lord, take my soul," Mrs. Bradley collapsed. Thousands of Chicago blacks filed past the open casket at the funeral home soon thereafter. *(UPI/Bettmann NewsPhotos)* (Below) Three relatives gather at the trial of the two accused murderers. It was from the shack of Moses "Preacher" Wright *(on the left)* that Till was abducted, despite his great-uncle's plea that the young man, born and raised in the North, was ignorant of the etiquette of white supremacy in the Delta. Till's mother testified at the Sumner, Mississippi, trial, insisting that the corpse recovered from the river was her son. One of Till's local cousins, 16-year-old Maurice Wright, was later suspected of having reported to Roy Bryant that Till had insulted Mrs. Bryant. *(Ed Clark,* Life *Magazine © 1955 Time Inc.)*

(Above) In 1955 neither blacks nor women were permitted to serve on Mississippi juries, and the panel in Sumner was no exception. These twelve peers of Roy Bryant and his half-brother, J. W. Milam, included nine farmers, two carpenters, and an insurance agent. All five attorneys in Sumner worked *pro bono* for the defense. Their strategy was to appeal to the state's "Anglo-Saxon" traditions and plant doubt in the minds of the jurors that the corpse had been correctly identified. *(UPI/Bettman NewsPhotos)*

(Opposite page: Above) This moment was an epiphany in the eclipse of Jim Crow in the Deep South. Testifying for the state, Moses Wright pointed out the two defendants in the Sumner courthouse as the abductors of Emmett Till. When the district attorney asked for identification, the 64-year-old sharecropper first acknowledged J. W. Milam and said, "Thar he," and then pointed to Roy Bryant. During the trial Wright was in hiding; afterwards he fled the state. But his testimony signified that the intimidation of Delta blacks was no longer as effective as in the past. (UPI/Bettman NewsPhotos) While Roy Bryant (below left) was making a delivery of shrimp in Texas, the Chicago teenager entered Bryant's Grocery and Meat Market and engaged in the improper prank and advance toward Mrs. Bryant that later provoked the outraged husband to help murder Till. Roy and Carolyn Bryant were later divorced. He still lives in the Mississippi Delta, though incognito. (Ed Clark, Life Magazine © 1955 Time Inc.) J. W. Milam, 36 (below right), was the half-brother of Roy Bryant and—like him—a former soldier and the father of two sons. He rented mechanical cotton pickers for plantations in the Delta. Milam was pivotal to the abduction and the killing, and later spoke on the record most unashamedly of how and why the two men murdered Emmett Till. Milam died of cancer in 1981. (Ed Clark, Life Magazine © 1955 Time Inc.)

(Above) The Sumner jury deliberated for little more than an hour before acquitting the two defendants, and would have announced its verdict even earlier had the jurors not passed the time drinking Coca-Cola, one later reported. Since Bryant and Milam could not be tried again for the same offense, they celebrated the verdict with their wives in the presence of supporters and photographers. Shown from left are Roy Bryant, Carolyn Bryant, Juanita Milam, and J. W. Milam. (UPI/Bettman NewsPhotos)

In 1976 this sculpture of Martin Luther King, Jr., and Emmett Till was erected and dedicated in Denver's City Park. The statue suggests the link between the highly publicized atrocity in Mississippi and the civil rights movement, which was inaugurated with the Montgomery bus boycott less than three months after Till's death. The grief and outrage among blacks were eventually to be translated into political and civic action in the South, and some civil rights activists later bore witness to the impact that Till's death exerted on their desire to overcome the legacy of black powerlessness. (*Aaron Tomlinson*)

like to rape white women" but was insulated against a description of what rape actually was: "I was rather confused over what to guard against." Having matured into a personification of "the Cult of Pure, White Southern Womanhood," Mrs. Durr only gradually came to realize that her own struggle for liberation required freedom for blacks as well.[13] The antilynching activist Jessie Daniel Ames offered a more orotund protest: "The crown of chivalry . . . has been pressed like a crown of thorns on our heads," suggesting at least a vision of sexual as well as racial emancipation.[14]

When twenty-six white women from six Southern states formed the Association of Southern Women for the Prevention of Lynching in 1930, they began to alter quite decisively the prevailing assumptions about women—at least as much as they were politically effective in eradicating the barbarism that officially sparked their movement. "The lady insurrectionists," Lillian Smith explained, "said calmly that they were not afraid of being raped; as for their sacredness, they could take care of it themselves; they did not need the chivalry of a lynching to protect them and did not want it." In the 1930s such women defined themselves as citizens as well as moral agents, and not as fragile targets cowering before the specter of "the nameless horror," "the unspeakable crime." They asked only for the civilized protection of the rule of law, not for the sadistic vestiges of gallantry with which the white South had so desperately defined manliness.[15]

Another generation of white women would, beginning in the civil rights movement in the 1960s, defy the traditions of sexual politics even more radically by asserting the right to sleep with whomever they chose—including black men. In its explicitness and directness, this new formulation of an entitlement would torpedo whatever still lingered of the older rationale for lynching and interracial murder— as succinctly proclaimed by an Alabama judge in one of the Scottsboro trials: "There is a very strong presumption under the law," William W. Callahan observed in 1933, that a white woman "would not and did not yield voluntarily to intercourse with the defendant, a Negro. . . . " That is true, the jurist added, "whatever the station in life the prosecutrix may occupy, whether she be the most despised, ignorant and abandoned woman of the community, or the spotless virgin and daughter of a prominent home of luxury and learning."[16]

In 1951 the chief justice of Mississippi's state supreme court was, if anything, even more entrapped in this presumption that a Southern white woman could not possibly wish to engage voluntarily in sexual relations with a black man. Considering the desperate appeal of Willie McGee, who had been convicted of raping Mrs. Willamette Hawkins two years earlier, Judge Harvey McGehee found the defense attorneys' claim that the liaison might have been consensual a "revolting insinuation." In the presence of the governor and attorney general of Mississippi, the chief justice fumed to the attorneys from the Civil Rights Congress: "You not only do not know what you are talking about, but you are insulting us, the whole South." Against the sovereign myth of the black rapist, all admissible evidence had to be subordinated; the most elemental and disinterested quest for justice could not prevail against that archetype. Despite the introduction of affidavits stating that Mrs. Hawkins had initiated the relationship at least nine years earlier, the chief justice was adamant: "We could not entertain such a proposition . . . we could not even consider it in court." One of the doomed Willie McGee's attorneys was future Congresswoman Bella Abzug.[17] The racist presumptions that she confronted in 1951 began to wither little more than a decade later, and the synchronous rebirth of feminism was not merely a coincidence.

In attempting to explain sexual feelings across the racial divide, the candid ruminations of Cleaver and Brownmiller contributed, ultimately, to the exposure of false consciousness and to the demystification of both race and sex. These authors helped to corroborate the "one clear and certain truth" that the NAACP's James Weldon Johnson had learned: "In the core of the heart of the American race problem[,] the sex factor is rooted. . . . Other factors are obvious and are the ones we dare to deal with," he asserted in 1933, "but regardless of how we deal with these, the race situation will continue to be acute as long as the sex factor persists."[18]

That linkage may explain, among other instances of disproportionate punishment, the way that the legal system has treated convicted rapists. Since 1930, 455 men have been executed for that particular crime. Of them, 405 were black, and virtually all the victimized women were white.[19] The state of Mississippi had executed only blacks for the crime of rape.[20] The sentencing courts of military justice treated convicted rapists according to the same pattern, a decade after James Weldon Johnson's remarks were published. In Europe during World War II, ninety-five soldiers were hanged for the crimes of rape or murder of unarmed civilians. Statistically improbable as it may seen, eighty-seven of those executed were black.

Even more in defiance of the odds, it was a terrible and grotesque coincidence that one of the soldiers was the father of Emmett Till. Private Louis Till was convicted of raping two Italian women, Benni Lucrezia and Frieda Mari, and of killing a third, Anna Nanchi. These crimes were perpetrated in Civitavecchia, in June 1944. Private Till, who was then twenty-two years old, pleaded not guilty. He was nevertheless court-martialed for violating Article of War #92 in February 1945, and was hanged at Aversa, Italy, on July 2. From the lapse of over a year between the capital crimes and the execution, the *Memphis Commercial Appeal* inferred that "the case was given extended consideration by Army authorities." When the *Jackson Daily News* confronted Mrs. Bradley with the Department of Defense records in mid-October, she claimed that the War Department had informed her only that the cause of her husband's death had been "willfull misconduct"; and she added that her efforts to probe further had been bureaucratically stymied. Her attorney, William Henry Huff of Chicago, acknowledged that such reports of Private Till's execution "may be true, but it has no bearing on the case pending."[21]

Of course, Emmett Till had never known his father, whose crimes were utterly irrelevant and immaterial to the charges against the defendants in the courtroom in the Delta in 1955. They would nevertheless have been acquitted even sooner had such information been revealed; and when it was disclosed, the sense of vindication among some white Mississippians was palpable. One newspaper noted that "the offices of Mississippi's two Senators, James O. Eastland and John Stennis, assisted reporters by obtaining most of the important facts from the Army and urging the release of additional details." Since the Sumner jury had doubted that the corpse was that of Emmett Till, it was strange that the effort to find the lad, or to identify the corpse properly, elicited so little interest compared to the quest to discover the facts surrounding the death of Till's father a decade earlier. The *Jackson Daily News* put the story on the front page, below a huge, lurid headline ("Till's Dad Raped 2 Women, Murdered a Third in Italy"), next to an editorial that noted that "fabulous sums of money" were raised for the NAACP's "war chest to be used against Mississippi," based in part on the claim that

Private Till had died a martyr to patriotism. The editorial sanctimoniously urged "the Negro organizations . . . to stop peddling manufactured stories to the nation about Mississippi and about their own people." Such vigorous journalism impelled J. J. Breland, one of the Sumner defense attorneys, to write a letter of congratulations to the editor of the *Daily News*: "This is the first time that I have noticed any Southern paper who [*sic*] has made a serious attempt to combat the NAACP propoganda [*sic*] against the South."[22] Among others, Robert Patterson of the Citizens' Councils complained that publicity about the crimes of the father never matched the "tear-jerking article" that *Life* published about Emmett Till.[23]

Actually, the weekly magazine had asserted in the form of an editorial, that "no man can condone a brutal murder. Those in Sumner, and elsewhere, who do condone it, are in far worse danger than Emmett Till ever was." *Life* then explained: "He had only his life to lose, and many others have done that, including his soldier-father who was killed in France fighting for the American proposition that all men are equal. Those who condone a deed so foul as this are in danger of losing their souls."[24] The dean of the Cathedral Church of St. John the Divine in New York City, the Very Reverend James A. Pike, read the entire editorial to his congregation the following Sunday. But the publication soon apologized for its error, admitting that recently released War Department records indicated that Private Till had been executed for rape-murder.[25]

The failure of *Life* to check the facts especially annoyed Faulkner, heightening his anxiety that his own desegregationist views were discrediting him among his xenophobic neighbors. One of the reasons that the novelist did not want his essay "On Fear" submitted to *Life* was its "blooper" about how Emmett Till's father had died a hero in Europe—"a statement which I would have thought any $50.00 leg man or typist would have gone to the trouble to verify first." Another foe of the Citizens' Councils told Robert Penn Warren that such errors were readily interpreted as signs of Northern press bias that could somehow be twisted to vindicate the Southern case for segregation. "*Life* magazine's editorial on the Till case, that sure fixed it," Warren was told. "If Till's father had died a hero's death fighting for liberty, as *Life* said, that would have been as irrelevant as the actual fact that he was executed by the American army for rape-murder. It sure makes it hard."[26] The NAACP's Wilkins also conceded that he too "almost got caught in that Louis

Till trap. I had written a speech in which I referred to the soldier-father's dying for the American proposition—all that stuff in *Life.* But before I delivered it, my intuition warned me. I cut it out—and am I glad I did!"[27]

Brownmiller's book makes no mention of Private Till's crime. But the guilt of the father casts a tiny but eerie shadow on a case already sufficiently weighted with evidence of the sinister bend of the human heart, a case so refractory that it might even heighten sensitivity to victimization due to sex as well as race.

One of Alice Walker's short stories, "Advancing Luna—and Ida B. Wells," entangles those two categories even further. A black woman recalls her friendship with one of her contemporaries, a white woman named Luna, who had worked with her in the civil rights movement. The narrator has also briefly met another black activist, named Freddie Pye, who "was coarse and spoke of black women as 'our' women" and who had first shouted the Black Power slogan later attributed to Stokely Carmichael. What helps evoke the memory of the two women's friendship is that Pye had raped Luna.

"Why didn't you scream?" the narrator asked Luna.

"You know why," was her response.

"I did," the narrator realizes. "I had seen a photograph of Emmett Till's body just after he was pulled from the river. . . . I knew why, all right." Because of Luna's ordeal—and her scruples—her companion is led to dream of "a society in which Luna's word alone on rape can never be used to intimidate an entire people, and in which an innocent black man's protestation of innocence of rape is unprejudicially heard." In this instance the narrator believes the white woman's word, but realizes that "historical fear and the threat of violence" not only will poison the relations between black men and white women but will compromise any "solidarity among black and white women."[28]

A feminist perspective also permeates *Dreaming Emmett* (1986), the first (and to date only) play written by the best-selling novelist Toni Morrison, later a winner of the Pulitzer Prize. She had conceived of the play about two years earlier: "I wanted to see a collision of three or four levels of time through the eyes of one person who could come back to life and seek vengeance. Emmett Till became that person." He is the only character in the play who has remained his age as of 1955, a device that invites consideration of the social changes of the past three decades. Insofar as the drama presents historical evidence, it is accurate; for Morrison has read the indispensible William Bradford Huie. Set in an abandoned cotton mill, Dreaming Emmett is not however a "docudrama," or a dramatization of a historical episode in which narrowly empirical research does the work of the artistic imagination. It is instead a dream play, which dips deeply into the memory bank as well. Morrison thus solved the artistic problem once propounded by the drama critic Robert Brustein: "Any work inspired by the Emmett Till case is almost automatically destined to be melodrama."[29] But since the eponymous protagonist is condemned to be a spirit that has not dissipated, that cannot grow or suffer genuine pain, it is possible to suggest that the emotions of the audience cannot be as fully engaged as in a realistic drama that forcefully attempts to represent anguish and injustice.

Perhaps Morrison's most original contribution to the ramifications of the case was the introduction of an imaginary feminist, Tamara, a character who emerges from the audience in the final scenes to condemn "Emmett Till" for his attraction to white women and for his indifference to black women. Without forsaking in any way the grievance against the pressures of white racism, a voice that compels recognition as Morrison's own pierces the indifference of black men—or at least of one of them—to the circumstances of their sisters. Morrison herself had been nagged by "the contradictions of black people, the relationships between black men and women, between blacks and whites, the differences between 1955 and 1985." Echoing Brownmiller's own analysis, Morrison commented that the wolf whistle "was a male rite of passage that all men understand," a matter of "such importance" that Milam and Bryant had to kill Till rather than risk losing their lordly status among the blacks who were their customers and neighbors.[30]

The world premiere was staged in Albany, where Morrison was serving as Albert Schweitzer Professor of the Humanities at the State University of New York, in early January 1986. It coincided with the first celebration of Martin Luther King's birthday as a national holiday. Dreaming Emmett was directed by Gilbert Moses, who directed Imamu Amiri Baraka's Slave Ship and two segments of the television dramatization of Alex Haley's Roots. The Albany novelist William Kennedy praised the play: "Toni has been able to take one of the toughest themes, child murder, and make it the subject of a retrospective history. It puts Till's death in a totally different context."[31] Though *Dreaming Emmett* met with mixed notices and is undoubtedly too stylized to offer an illuminatingly new insight into American race relations, its composition and production testify to the enduring interest that that slaying can still elicit.

Morrison's play was certainly her fullest but by no means the first effort to extract meaning from Till's murder. In her novel *Song of Solomon*, which won the National Book Critics Circle Award, a group of blacks in a Midwestern barbershop hear over the radio the news that "a young Negro boy had been found stomped to death in Sunflower County, Mississippi. There were no questions about who stomped him—his murderers had boasted freely—and there were no questions about the motive. The boy had whistled at some white woman, refused to deny he had slept with others, and was a Northerner visiting the South. His name was Till." Morrison can be granted novelistic license here, since the confessions were publicized half a year after the murder was reported; and far from refusing to deny his sexual experience, Till apparently boasted of it.

But *Song of Solomon* is intriguing for its gauge of the reactions—with some men "exploding, shouting angry epithets all over the room," one man predicting that the incident would not be at all newsworthy, and another certain that the white community would treat the perpetrators as heroes. The most important response, however, is sexual, for the characters are suddenly forced to grapple with the definition of black manhood. A character named Freddie wonders how Till could have been "acting [so] big down in Bilbo country. Who the hell he think he is?"

Railroad Tommy replies: "Thought he was a man, that's what."

"Well, he thought wrong," Freddie responds. "Ain't no black men in Bilbo country."

Guitar chimes in: "The hell they ain't." But the only example he can cite is dead: Emmett Till.

The tension rises in the barbershop, with accusations of cowardice traded until tales of humiliation are swapped and then converted into humor directed at themselves: "They laughed then, unroariously, about the speed with which they had run, the pose they had assumed, the ruse they had invented to escape or decrease some threat to their manliness, their humanness.[32] For them the news of a murder in Mississippi has become an occasion to confront, to evade, and to sublimate the indignities to their manhood that white America has imposed on them.

Morrison's was not even the first play inspired by this death in the Delta. At the urging of Elia Kazan, James Baldwin wrote his first work for the theater, which ANTA staged in 1964: *Blues for Mr. Charlie*.[33] The preface to the published version acknowledges that the play was "based, very distantly indeed, on the case of Emmett Till. . . . I do not know why the case pressed on my mind so hard—but it would not let me go." Baldwin sought to provide an artistic solution to a moral problem—how to account for the motives and rationalizations of murder. For *Blues for Mr. Charlie* is an attempt to portray a killer, "this wretched man," who must realize that "what he is doing is evil; but in order to accept the knowledge the man would have to change. What is ghastly and really almost hopeless in our racial situation now is that the crimes we have committed are so great and so unspeakable that the acceptance of this knowledge would lead, literally, to madness." Conjecturing that such murderers cannot see themselves as villains, the novice playwright sought to trace a descent into "spiritual darkness" stemming from the denial of self-knowledge.[34]

Blues for Mr. Charlie is set somewhere in the Deep South early in the 1960s, during the full force of the civil rights movement—and, indeed, when rumors abound that local blacks have begun to arm themselves in desperation. Its villain (Lyle Britten) is a poor-white racist storekeeper whose wife Josephine is working behind the counter when she is insulted by a leering young black (Richard Henry). His formative experiences were in the North, where he has known white women whose photographs are supposedly in his wallet. He is, in Judge Tom Brady's words, that "supercilious, glib young negro, who has sojourned in . . . New York, and who considers the counsel of his elders archaic." Britten murders an unrepentant Richard Henry not long after the incident in the store, dumping his body in the weeds and, while journalists with national and international credentials arrive to cover the trial, a jury acquits him.

The play does not appear to have been designed to cast new light on the incident in Money in 1955, though one commentator clumsily interpreted Baldwin's work as somehow having shown that, "far from being an innocent child, Till himself was a sexually mature teenager."[35] Whatever is supposed to have happened in the Delta served primarily as a stimulus for the presentation of some of Baldwin's characteristic motifs. *Blues for Mr. Charlie* addresses, for example, the terrible stunting and waste of the lives of young blacks in a society pervaded by blind bigotry, the sexual allure and superiority of blacks and the dangerous repressiveness and frustration of white sexuality (for Britten had earlier murdered the husband of the black woman with whom he had had a liaison), the powerful influence—mostly for evil—that Christianity has exerted in the black community (for Richard Henry is the son of a local preacher), and the precarious and audacious dream of human solidarity and love. The impotence and bad faith of white liberalism are embodied in a major character—a wealthy and well-heeled newspaper editor named Parnell James—even though his counterparts were rarely to be found in actual Deep South communities like Sumner, Mississippi.

The playwright was involved in stormy conflicts with the Actors Studio at least as dramatic as anything occurring onstage, and the production was not well received. The portrayal of Southern whites drew some reactions of disbelief, though Baldwin responded that "nothing in my *text* [is] nearly as vindictive and *horrible* as things I've seen, and nothing as *grotesque* and *outrageous*." He later insisted that his presentation of the central character had been utterly misunderstood. "It was very important for *me*, you know, to have Richard Henry as *offensive* and *brash* *and* stupid as he *is*. Sure, he had no right to talk to *anybody* like that." But then Baldwin cut close to the heart of the Till case itself: "But do you have the right to *shoot* him? *That's* the question" (italics in original). One critic who stressed the theme of sexual fear and envy in the play was forced to resign as drama critic of the *Reporter*. The editor of the magazine, Max Ascoli, denounced the review as "objectionable" and "rabble-rousing,"[36] though white jealousy of black virility had been expressed on stage as far back as that most repugnant of all villains, Iago, who soliloquizes in *Othello*: "I hate the Moor,/ And it is thought abroad that 'twixt my sheets/ He has done my office. . . . I do suspect the lusty Moor hath leaped into my seat" (I, iii, 392–394; II, i, 307–308).

Almost two decades after *Blues for Mr. Charlie* was produced, Baldwin visited Atlanta in the wake of the disappearances and deaths of black children. The Georgia capital certainly could not live up to its own billing as "the city too busy to hate," but it was noteworthy that the mayor—himself a former lieutenant of Dr. King—and the police chief of the city were both black. Baldwin, an expatriate living in the south of France, nevertheless wrote as though Atlanta (and he himself) were still completely locked into the oppression of its past, in some sort of time warp. When Clifford Jones, the thirteenth child, was found strangled in 1980, the novelist claimed that official interest was stirred by the victim's Northern origins. "Jones, like Emmett Till, in 1955—a comparison I wish neither to force nor avoid—was an out-of-state visitor," Baldwin speculated. "Had he been a 'Mississippi boy,' his bones might yet be irrecoverable at the bottom of the river."[37]

But as Nathan Glazer pointed out in a cogent review of Baldwin's book about the crimes in Atlanta, the author left unexplained why a black mayor and a black police chief would become concerned— would become aware of the sensational pattern of killings—only when a black child from outside their community is murdered.[38] The accused murderer, Wayne Williams, turned out to be black and was found guilty and imprisoned; and though he was formally convicted of only the last two of the twenty-eight homicides, the killings did stop with his arrest. Nevertheless, the almost instinctive retrieval of the Till case served—at least for James Baldwin—as a historical index of black vulnerability.

Another notorious episode in the annals of American crime deserves mention, however, in revealing not only the grip that interracial sex in the South continued to maintain on the national imagination but also the emerging differences from the pattern of criminal justice in Leflore and Tallahatchie counties in 1955. In the case that a headline in the *Washington Star* defined as the "Biggest Civil Rights Trial of [the] '70s,"[39] the alleged male sexual aggressor was white and the female victim black; and it was she who killed him and was put on trial for her life. A convicted burglar named Joan Little, twenty-one years old, was incarcerated in the Beaufort County Jail in North Carolina on August 27, 1974, when one of the jailers entered her tiny cell. Under oath she later claimed that Clarence Alligood had attempted to rape her; to defend herself, Ms. Little grabbed an ice pick from him, stabbed him to death, and fled. Slightly less than a year later, a jury in Raleigh found her not guilty, after a rambunctious and searing trial that attracted the attention and support of the women's movement, civil rights organizations, prisoners' rights groups, and opponents of capital punishment.

Apart from its reversal of the racial identities that were characteristic of Southern rape trials, the Joan Little case exhibited a number

of striking features. Unlike nearly all earlier Southern black defendants, she was hardly alone. An estimated $350,000 was raised for
her defense, and counsel included two highly energetic and dedicated white attorneys plus other lawyers, who utilized over a hundred assistants and even a psychic.[40] Though the trial did not attract
any congressmen to monitor the proceedings for signs of racial bias,
observers who attended the trial included Angela Davis and Georgia
state representative Julian Bond. William Kunstler, the nation's
most celebrated and flamboyant radical attorney, tried in vain to
represent the defendant as well.

By 1975 the struggle to eradicate the systematic exclusion of
blacks from jury rolls had been won, at least in Raleigh: half the
jurors were of Joan Little's own race. That enabled her chief attorney, Jerry Paul, to trump the state by *affirming* the cause of civil
rights. "Sometimes you have to stand up for morality," he argued
in his summation, "and sometimes God chooses people to make
points just like he chose Rosa Parks, just like he chose Joan Little."[41]
And because the defense was able to tell journalists Joan Little's
side of the story while the prosecution was forced into silence to
avoid a mistrial or failure to get unbiased jurors, the press had little
choice but to circulate only her version of what had happened in
her cell that night. The prosecution itself was lackluster and badly
outmatched, both inside and outside the courtroom, according to
the two books subsequently published about the case.

The most important irony of all highlights the contrast with the
legal outcome of the Till case. The jurors in Sumner could not have
imagined themselves voting the death penalty for Bryant and Milam
regardless of their guilt. And despite the jurors' verdict in Raleigh
exactly two decades later, it is almost as unlikely that Joan Little was
innocent. As in Mississippi, there were no living witnesses to the
murder other than the defendant. But to believe that Joan Little
acted in self-defense collided with too many implausible—and incontrovertible—facts. She claimed that Alligood had held an ice
pick in one hand, intending to commit rape, and somehow managed
to take his pants off while watching his prisoner—a feat she herself
had trouble describing. Though the jailer was physically imposing,
far larger than Joan Little, she had managed to stab him eleven
times and to emerge from their struggle unharmed, with only half
a dozen blood spots on the floor, near where the blanket was still
perfectly folded.

It is far more likely—though of course unprovable—that the defendant had lured Alligood into her cell to seduce him, kill him, and escape.[42] It is therefore no wonder that Jerry Paul foolishly boasted: "Given enough money, I can buy justice. I can win any case in this country, given enough money. I can create illusion." Even *he* privately considered his client "a nymphomaniac."[43] Neither did her criminal activities—including the stabbing of a boyfriend—come to a halt after her acquittal. This, then, was one moment in Southern history when a black female may well have made a spurious charge of rape against a *white* male. Though the melodramatic publicity surrounding the case had compared the defendant with Emmett Till,[44] this particular interracial rape trial in the South constituted an odd coda to the sharper dichotomies of good and evil that had surfaced two decades earlier.

E I G H T

No Longer White

A paradox nevertheless presents itself. The incident at a country store in Money, Mississippi, has affected and even singed artists as popular, important, and diverse as Bob Dylan, Rod Serling, Toni Morrison, and James Baldwin. But no historian has ever shown more than a passing interest in this virtually final spasm of traditional Southern white violence against blacks. And that absence of curiosity in this nearly last lethal gesture may be related to a wider indifference among scholars to the historical significance of such crimes.

"Despite the central place that lynching occupies in the southern imagination and in the idea of the South in the rest of the country." Jacquelyn Dowd Hall has observed, "historians have paid remarkably little attention to the phenomenon. [By contrast] the imagery of the lynch mob pervades black autobiography and fiction and provides a chief dramatic device for the southern novel of gothic terror."[1] Lynching—or the threat of lynching—is prominent in much Southern literature and film. The theme even appears in so harmless and charming a work as Harper Lee's *To Kill a Mockingbird* (1960), in which Tom Robinson is falsely accused of an improper advance toward a white girl and is saved from a lynching (though later killed). His defender is Atticus Finch, a valiant attorney whose kind seems to show up in works of fiction more often than in history books. Other Southern white novelists who have explored the theme of lynching include Jesse Hill Ford (*The Liberation of Lord Byron Jones*) and Madison Jones (*Cry of Absence*). In Robert Benton's film *Places in the Heart* (1984), set in Texas during the Great

Depression, a blind white man rescues an itinerant black farmer from a Klan lynch mob.

Richard Wright made this theme of racist violence integral to the fate of Chicago's Bigger Thomas in his greatest novel, *Native Son* (1940). Even in the urban North, in the home of a liberal white family, the protagonist's inadvertent presence in the bedroom of the sleeping daughter ignites shocking, lethal consequences. Writing as an expatriate in France, Wright later explained that murders, such as Emmett Till's specifically, filled him with "disgust, uneasiness [and a] sense of dread," making it impossible for him to live in the United States. Long before W.E.B. Du Bois left his native land for Ghana, he wrote movingly in his 1940 autobiography of the persistent impact of lynchings upon his consciousness.[2] Grief for the victims was expressed in one of Billie Holiday's most haunting songs, written by Lewis Allan, "Strange Fruit" (1939). It included such graphic and appalling images as corpses of blacks swaying in the wind, as though an unnatural part of the Southern landscape, and the horrid contrast between the aroma of local flowers and the stench of scorched bodies. Many other examples could be cited. Indeed, one literary critic has drawn attention to the ritualistic role that lynchings play in the fiction of virtually every significant black writer, including Wright, William Wells Brown, Jean Toomer, James Weldon Johnson, Langston Hughes, and Ralph Ellison—though in recent years only James Baldwin had given such rituals a significant place in his literary corpus.[3] The point can easily be established that Till was the victim of a peculiarly Southern crime, a murder that resounds with the deepest reverberations within Southern society and the myths through which it vindicated itself.

Nevertheless, no modern historical analysis of lynching has been published. The vacuum has hardly been filled by Ralph Ginzburg's *100 Years of Lynching*, a paperback anthology of newspaper clippings (including those from the Till case), arranged in chronological order. But its editor acknowledged that some of the press reports "have been drastically rewritten for the sake of clarity or conciseness." When newspaper accounts differed on the facts of a lynching, "the information from all sources has been synthesized into one story and attributed to the newspaper which provided most of the facts." If scholarly methods can be taught by pointing to bad examples, *100 Years of Lynching* would make a fine textbook. It is, incidentally, a curiosity that Ginzburg was prosecuted and jailed for obscenity under the jurisdiction of Attorney General Robert Kennedy, who objected to photos of a black male and white female in sexual embrace in a magazine that Ginzburg published.[4] In the introducion to a collection of documents on American violence, Richard Hofstadter noted that "descriptive and statistical books [have been written] on lynching, as well as works of moral protest; but there is no great history of the subject that assesses its place in the political culture of the South." And though lynching was essentially an American invention,[5] with no real counterparts elsewhere, the primary sources reprinted after Hofstadter's introduction recount slave rebellions and their suppression, race riots, ghetto riots—and only one lynching.

Historians still consider *The Tragedy of Lynching,* which the sociologist Arthur Raper wrote for the Interracial Commission in 1932, the standard account of the subject. Even a recent state-of-the-art survey of scholarship in black history barely mentions the topic, and does not profess to find the gap in the secondary literature urgently worthy of being filled. Lynching does not appear in the index of the two-volume history of Mississippi edited by Richard Aubrey McLemore, a 1973 work superseding previous scholarly studies of the history of the state.[6] Even in recent editions of his textbook on the heritage of the Magnolia State, *Mississippi Yesterday and Today,* John K. Bettersworth, a professor at Mississippi State University, manages to omit mention of the Till case itself, though the affair was hardly unpublicized, nor is it irrelevant to an understanding of the state's legacy.

Though the extent of scholarly indifference can be overstated, its persistence merits not only redress but explanation. The absence of jury records, the need of at least some lynchers to conceal their own responsibility for what after all constituted murder, the refusal of townspeople to cooperate with outside investigators and journalists, and the inclination of local officers of the law to make innocuous reports to their superiors help account for the paucity of documentary evidence—the primary sources on which historical researchers depend. Such lacunae go far to account for the neglect of the topic in the American historical scholarship, but Hall has offered a further explanation. She has emphasized the commitment that many historians have given to the categories of consensus and pluralism, leading them to ignore the function of coercion in maintaining the status quo: "The practice of lynching represents a notorious contradiction to such norms."[7]

One of the few historical analysts of lynching, or more precisely of the struggle against it, has been Robert L. Zangrando, who has written that "the lynching of young Emmett Till in 1955 and a wave of civil rights activism over the next ten years quickened my interest in the problem of twentieth-century interracial violence and the social dynamics surrounding it."[8] Unlike Zangrando's fellow historians, however, sociologists have at least contributed to "a considerable body of literature on the subject," in Hall's summation. "Studies have related the incidence of lynching to seasonal rhythms, the structure and autonomy of southern county governments, economic fluctuations, the isolation of southern rural life, inadequate legal institutions, frontier conditions of rapid in-migration, revivalism, and the proportion of blacks in the population. Social psychologists have suggested that lynch mobs were made up of frustrated poor whites using blacks as scapegoats for displaced aggression and have delineated an 'authoritarian personality' typical of mob leaders."[9]

Lynching was an expression "of what the sociologist Emile Durkheim termed 'repressive justice,' designed not to punish or to rehabilitate the individual but to enforce social conformity. . . . " Southern whites "responded to the threat of black aggression with a communal ritual that demonstrated and reinforced white unity, intimidated blacks as a group, and ensured allegiance to caste roles on the part of both whites and blacks." Professor Hall herself is critical of the facile application of Durkheim's formulation to the early twentieth-century South, which was engaged in modernizing and was really a biracial rather than a monolithic community. Nevertheless, *The Division of Labor* can still be profitably consulted on the nature of repressive justice. For, according to Durkheim, the entire community designs ritual punishments to subordinate the individual to the collectivity, and does not delegate law enforcement to one segment of the population.[10]

A sociological perspective deserves to be tested and qualified in the light of historical evidence, which can also indicate the ways in which the Till case differed from such customary forms of "repressive justice." Beginning in the early 1930s, when Jessie Daniel Ames and her Association of Southern Women for the Prevention of

Lynching entered the struggle, their primary target was mob action designed to enforce the will of the community. Such violence was conducted with the support and activity of men of property and standing, and it was usually done openly, as an extension or fulfillment or acceleration of what a jury or the court system might have done anyway. In the classic lynchings of the postbellum South, the entire white community was openly supportive. Policemen were often actively involved, ministers were silent, and congressmen and senators who represented the region—including such valiant liberals as future Supreme Court Justice Hugo Black—opposed antilynching legislation.[11]

Such communal violence was already declining by the 1920s, however, and was marked by greater surreptitiousness, by the fear that blatant terror might produce outside pressure and even a federal antilynching law. To ensure the continuation of this means of social control, coroner's juries typically hid the identities of the known killers (often pillars of the community) by claiming that death was "at the hands of parties unknown."[12] The flimsiness of this excuse for injustice was inadvertently revealed after the last of the pre–civil rights lynchings, when the Mississippi judge who was to have presided in the rape trial of Mack Charles Parker was asked in Connecticut whether the Poplarville slayers would ever be caught. This less-than-brilliant member of the State Sovereignty Commission expressed his doubt, which he buttressed with the comment that in the meantime three members of the mob "are already dead."[13]

The distinction between such classic lynchings and the case of Emmett Till should therefore be noted. Though socially sanctioned after the fact, his murder was neither a community ritual nor a community activity; and though the killers were acquitted, they were hardly transformed into heroes. Indeed, the very fact that they were prosecuted marked a change from the concealment of their identities as "parties unknown." It might even be argued that, in the traditional sense, Till's death was not a lynching at all, just as Governor Hugh White had insisted at the time. For the "jungle fury" of a mob had not descended on the alleged perpetrator of an outrage that had inflamed local whites. Even though Bryant and Milam probably did not act alone, they felt obliged to conceal the existence of their accomplices, knowing that their fellow conspirators were in jeopardy of prosecution.

But if it was not a communal rite, however weakened and infrequent, how could the motives of the murderers otherwise be explained? It strains credulity to interpret the hardworking and upstanding Milam and Bryant as malcontents, and certainly none of their relatives or neighbors would have recognized them as psychopaths. Though the two men and their accomplices did not have recourse to self-defense in rationalizing their murder of a minor, neither Milam nor Bryant could be considered in any clinical sense a degenerate. For a few terrible hours, they acted in ways that their particular culture and environment—that the very traditions of their milieu—had stimulated or suggested and had for decades legitimated. The half-brothers embodied the hypothesis of the historian Sheldon Hackney that what is peculiar to the excesses of Southern violence is its adherence to a "world view that defines the social, political, and physical environment as hostile and casts the white Southerner" as besieged by "malevolent forces. . . . The sense of grievance . . . is at the heart of Southern identity." Hackney has argued that this identity was forged in the need to defend the peculiar institution from assault from without, just as the descendants of the slaveholders tried to form a *cordon sanitaire* against Carpetbaggers, socialists, Communists, trade union organizers, atheists, and eventually civil rights activists and federal voting registrars. All change—even industrialization—had come from outside, engendering "extreme sensitivity to criticism," "a feeling of persecution," and a need to lash out at the alien forces that so persistently imperil the grace of the Southern Way of Life.[14] What happened to Emmett Till therefore reflected a history of distinctive violence rooted in such anxiety and in hostility toward strangers.

But the facts that Huie in particular presented also permit the inference that the parochial world of Milam and Bryant was already crumbling under the impact of modernization. Carolyn Bryant apparently did not want her dishonor to be avenged, and seemed after the molestation neither to fear for her own physical safety nor desire the life of the reckless teenager to be taken. Nor were local blacks so certain of what her husband might do that they felt compelled to hustle Till out of the county or the state immediately. If Bryant and Milam can be believed on this point, they did not initially intend to kill the "uppity" teenager, whose foolish bravado was so novel to them and so unprecedented in the challenge to caste posed by a picture in a wallet. The half-brothers felt it necessary to hide the body. They were not immune to prosecution, and they denied committing homicide. The community where they lived did not celebrate them, even if it quickly came around to supporting them. Such behavior and such fears were quite remote from the social universe of fanatics like Pitchfork Ben Tillman and Thomas Dixon half a century earlier, or even from lynchings a generation before that the press reported in the future tense—such as Claude Neal's in 1934. "Florida to Burn Negro at Stake: Sex Criminal Seized from Brewton Jail, Will Be Mutilated, Set Afire in Extra-Legal Vengeance for Dead," read the headline in the *Dothan Eagle*, amplified nationally—again in advance of the lynching—through the wires of the Associated Press.[15]

"Modernization," Hall has observed, "is not a unilateral process, cultural forms often lag behind economic changes, and values carried over from earlier times affect the way men and women respond to new material conditions. In a deeply racist society, determined to maintain the subordination of a large black population, racial beliefs and practices persisted independently of and sometimes in conflict with social and economic exigencies." She added that "even as lynching was increasingly discredited in the eyes of the world and disavowed by southern leaders, it survived in the small towns and rural areas of the South as a communal ritual that ... helped to maintain a set of entrenched cultural preoccupations."[16] But by the 1950s lynching had ceased to fulfill even that function in such communities. For even though the white jurors of Sumner sanctioned such private violence, they showed no inclination to coalesce into a lynch mob themselves—or to perform the ritual of several generations: the appeal to arms and to vengeance, the congregation of the pursuers, the discovery or seizure of the victim, his torture and mutilation, the distribution of parts of the body as souvenirs, the display of the corpse in a public place, and its photographing as an act of remembrance.[17] Such rites had disappeared even in counties as geographically isolated and historically backward as Tallahatchie and Leflore.

Further proof that the bigotry even of Mississippi was beginning to crumble can be found amid the sordidness of the Parker case four years later. The young Army veteran maintained his innocence even as lynchers pumped bullets into his body, and the evidence against him was circumstantial at best. The woman he may have raped, June Walters, did not insist on vengeance and was willing to testify in court—even if it meant that a black defense attorney would force her to relive the trauma of sexual assault. "I would have rather they had gone through with the trial," she claimed. When Parker was captured, a state highway patrolman gave Jimmy Walters a pistol with which to shoot the man assumed to have raped his wife. But the invitation was declined: "I didn't want the man killed. . . . I wanted him to be brought to trial where people could understand what . . . we went through." Jimmy Walters refused to become part of the lynch mob that took Parker from the Poplarville jail ("I'm not a killer"), and even his own brother did not inform him that he had joined the group that stormed the jail and hastened Parker to his death. The lynchers who shot Parker at close range found the immediacy of the experience sufficiently cathartic that they did not emasculate him before dumping the corpse into the Pearl River.[18]

Indeed this lynching, which assumed more of the traditional forms than Till's murder, occurred in part because racial change was beginning to stir even in this isolated section of southern Mississippi. The headwinds of history came in the form of the *Goldsby* case, in which the U.S. Court of Appeals for the Fifth Circuit twice reversed the death sentence meted out to a black defendant who had been convicted of the shotgun slaying of a white woman in Vaiden, Mississippi, in 1954. Because no blacks served on either jury, the federal court voided the convictions of Robert Lee Goldsby. Had Parker lived long enough to come to trial, his conviction would presumably also have been overturned according to the same principle, since only those eligible to vote were included on jury rolls, and no blacks were known to have voted in Pearl River County in thirteen years. By denying blacks access to both the ballot box and the jury box, the white South was beginning to lose its power to convict blacks accused of committing crimes. White supremacy could not be enforced unless its champions were willing to abandon a criminal justice system that was itself needed to help perpetuate that supremacy. That is why the attorney general of Mississippi, Joe Patterson, told the Subcommittee on Constitutional Rights of the Senate Judiciary Committee that "the Poplarville lynching would never have occurred" if the Court of Appeals had not invalidated the jury's verdict in *Goldsby*.[19] Gunnar Myrdal proved to be right after all: Jim Crow could not ultimately be reconciled with the aspirations of democracy itself, and the Parker slaying was among the final barbaric gestures of the Deep South to traduce the ideal of color-blind law.

The authority of Myrdal can also be summoned to argue that the decline of lynching could be attributed to the end of the seclusion and isolation of rural Southern life. In the very year of Till's birth, the Greenville lawyer and poet William Alexander Percy had complained that "every black buck in the South today has gone or will go to Chicago, where it is not only possible but inexpensive to sleep with a white whore." The shattering of this taboo in the North, Percy feared, would only mean trouble back home, because "the untouchability of white women by Negro men ... is the cornerstone of friendly relations, of inter-racial peace. In the past it has been not the eleventh but the first commandment." But blacks with whom genteel Delta planters like Percy had felt so patronizingly familiar were increasingly subject to Northern and urban influences, and the results were "covert insolence" and the loss of the "most valuable weapon of defense" that the Negro possessed—"his good manners."[20]

The end of the isolation of Delta blacks not only had its effect on race relations; the South to which they returned from visits to the North was also undergoing transformation. It is true that historians can get so addicted to the notion of an era of transition that it has been compulsively applied even as far back as the expulsion from Eden, but analysts of the Deep South after World War II could not help noting the changes.

Prior to the era of the Till case, the rest of the nation had left Mississippi so alone that the last presidential candidate to bother to visit the Magnolia State was Henry Clay.[21] An anecdote widely circulated about Ross Barnett reflected this isolation. Running for governor during the foreign policy crisis over the Chinese offshore islands that the Taiwanese government insisted on defending, Barnett was asked about Quemoy and Matsu. He is supposed to have told the reporter: "They're good men, and I'm sure I can find a place for them in Fish and Game."[22] But that sort of ignorance, and indifference to the outside world, was going into eclipse as well. The xenophobia of so many whites in the Delta was itself a sign of how imminent and immediate was the peril from beyond its confines, and those unreconstructed natives who took a stand to live and die in Dixie no longer felt assured that the hallowed verities were secure.

The rural way of life itself was dissipating. Though the population of Alaska contained a higher proportion of urbanites than Mississippi, by 1950 nearly half the residents of the region were already living in cities and towns. In Mississippi itself, the proportion of the work force engaged in agriculture dropped from 58 percent in 1940 to 21 percent in 1960. The fierce attachment to the soil was fading. Anyone gazing at cotton or soybean fields thereafter would be likely to see machine operators, managers, and airplane pilots rather than field hands. A two-row picker could daily harvest as much cotton as 140 field hands, and a large tractor with the right cultivating equipment was more effective than dozens of mules and drivers.[23] Harold C. Fleming, who served as executive director of the Southern Regional Council, also observed how the Southern political ambience had changed: "Racial antagonism is a ready outlet for the fears and frustrations bred by economic and social upheaval. The old isolation has broken down, leaving the South unprotected against the influx of people and ideas alien to its once impervious way of life."[24]

That way of life was already being subjected to the strain of change more rapid and dramatic than at any previous moment in Southern history, with the possible exception of the Civil War itself.[25] The 1980 statistics revealed that Mississippi was the poorest state in the Union, so buried in last place in per capita income that it had no hope of catching up to Arkansas. But that meant that Mississippi was in first place per capita in receiving federal funds; a higher proportion of Mississippians got food stamps and Medicaid than any other state.[26] Such largess was bound to render paradoxical the classification of Washington as prepotent evil, as an alien and subversive force.

For every ten persons leaving the state of Mississippi, only one was coming in. Blacks themselves were leaving the land and their tar-paper shacks—indeed, leaving the South itself—in unprecedented numbers. In the decade prior to 1950, over 300,000 blacks emigrated from the state of Mississippi. "Your race is adapted to be a race of farmers, first, last, and for all time," President William Howard Taft had informed a group of Negro students in 1909; but this seer in the White House would have found the demography of Afro-American life unrecognizable half a century later, his confident prediction utterly shattered. For in 1950 the typical black family could earn $3,243 in a Northern city in contrast to $763 on a Southern farm, and only one out of six American Negroes was living on a Southern farm.[27] An illiterate black Alabamian named Ned Cobb explained to a Harvard graduate student that the Southern black had "once in days past made crops under the white man's administration and didn't get nothin' out of it. . . . That was his bondage and he turnin' away from it." Such sharecroppers, Cobb pithily added, were "leavin' the possession and use of the earth to the white man." The resulting migration was about as dramatic as the enclosure movement that depopulated rural England two centuries earlier.[28]

Modernization was blurring the familiar images and roles, which were aptly summarized in Judge Tom Brady's 1955 tract, *Black Monday*:

> If you had a negro mammy take care of you and keep you from eating dirt; if you played with negro boys when a boy; if you have worked with and among them, laughed at their ribald humor; if you have been stunned by their abysmal vulgarity and profanity; if you can find it in your heart to overlook their obscenity and depravity; if you can respect and love their deep religious fervor; if you can cherish their loyalty and devotion to you, then you are beginning to understand the negro.

Brady added:

> If you have had a negro man and his wife and children live and work with you on your place; if he has worked your crops, tended your cattle and performed all other obligations; if his wife has cooked you meals, cleaned your home, and watched over your children; . . . if you have bailed the husband out of jail on Monday morning after his 'crab-apple switch' [straight razor] had been active in a dice game or at some 'tunk' on Saturday night; if you have taken him to the doctor and had his wounds treated, paid his bill and fine without expecting to be or having been reimbursed; . . . if you have given him in addition to his salary, extra money at Christmas and at other times in order that he might buy some presents for the three or four illegitimate children which he acknowledges as his own, THEN you are beginning to know the negro. . . . [29]

Such racism was, however, already conflicting with other values that were beginning to complicate—and eventually nullify—a commitment to white supremacy. While the expectation of a "new South" is one of the most ancient of regional novelties, this time it was for real. Industrialization and the fuller incorporation of the South in the national economy were having their effect, and even Mississippi was eventually to pick Henry Grady over Tom Brady after all. The intricate intermingling of tradition, race, poverty, and caste was at last entering a phase of decomposition.

Within a decade of the Till case, a writer from Yazoo City interviewed a Texan who explained why the school in his town was integrated without difficulty. "Well, we only had a coupla colored families, and the kids went to a one-room school," Willie Morris was informed. "One of the [Negro] boys weighed 210, did the 100 in 10.1 [and] kicked 50 yards barefoot, so we integrated."[30] This might be contrasted with the fate of the basketball team of Mississippi State University, which won the Southeastern Conference championship three times. Yet it did not compete in the NCAA tournaments thereafter, which would have meant playing against integrated teams from elsewhere in the nation. "It is no safer to mix with negroes on the ball courts than in the classroom," a state legislator nervously explained; and the *Meridian Star* noted that the "after-game social affairs" associated with national tournaments would be mixed. "Dear as the athletic prestige may be," the newspaper piously proclaimed, "our Southern way of life is infinitely more precious."[31]

That would not eventually be the option that white Mississippians would choose. Less than two decades later, Morris noticed the black male cheerleader from Ole Miss holding up his white female colleague—"a moment that was actually more important than the [football] game" against Mississippi State, because nobody seemed to find such casual physical contact noteworthy. The overt signs of an ancient sexual neurosis seemed to have been erased. When the two teams played basketball, at one point all ten young men on the court were black. By 1980, Morris had concluded that the tension had gone slack and the obsession with race—the "damnable question"—was over. It was closing time in the museum of antiquities that featured what the historian Ulrich B. Phillips had highlighted as "The Central Theme of Southern History." The achievement of some measure of sanity did not mean that Mississippi had transformed itself into paradise, "but, hell," Morris insisted, "nothing under the Lord's sun is paradise."[32] Nor did it deserve to remain the alibi of a nation still dodging "the shadow of the Ethiopian." In 1984 the state with the highest percentage of children enrolled in de facto segregated schools was New York.[33] In the heart of the Black Belt in the mid-1950s, however, ideals of tolerance and social equality had not yet begun to compete effectively enough to counteract the sanction still granted to racism and the violence it elicited.

Robert Penn Warren, who was born in Guthrie, Kentucky, in 1905, was acutely aware of the impact of modernization as well. The civil rights movement, he argued, was accentuated by not only the energy but also the condescension of urban activists who infiltrated the rural South with their alien habits and mores. Indeed, Warren interpreted one particular death in the Delta as a clash of subcultures: "It would seem, in fact, that something as innocent as showing off before the country cousins was what got poor little Emmett Till into trouble. He was just showing how you did things in Chicago."[34] The incident was thus a mark of the trauma of that transition from an era when the lines were taut and unmistakable. "If a Negro wants to escape the danger of lynching," the *Atlanta Constitution* had advised in 1895, "let him keep his hands off white women." Such certitudes were fading half a century later. But the Southern subculture of private violence was still coherent enough to challenge the increasing influence of outside mores. Till "was a strange niggah," Milam had told William Bradford Huie, and "I guess he had never met a white man like me."[35] Half a century earlier the stranger would have encountered and learned to cower before such venomous white men. Because he had not been acclimated quickly enough in 1955, the stranger died.

The blacks who would come into the Deep South only a decade later would be even more alien and would far more deliberately shatter the stereotypes by which whites in the Delta had lived. Into Mississippi, a state where a third of the counties had never built a public library and where the only bookstore in the capital was religious (run by the Baptists), came Robert Moses in 1961. He was a civil rights activist whose thoughtfulness matched his courage and whose integrity equaled his tenacity. Holding a Harvard graduate degree in philosophy, Moses had been a teacher of mathematics and spent one jail term reading Camus and struggling toward a *mystique noire*. Into Lowndes County, Alabama, in 1965 came Stokely Carmichael, another SNCC organizer, who sought to deflate the fears of local blacks and to taunt the pretensions of the white sheriff by imitating his strut and by cursing him in Yiddish.[36] Into Leflore County, Mississippi, in 1963 came a black from Chicago even bolder than Till, in support of a SNCC voter registration drive. When a local cop tried to insult Dick Gregory with a racial epithet, the comedian replied: "Your momma's a nigger. Probably got more Negro blood in her than I could ever hope to have in me." The policeman backed away. One night in Greenwood, Gregory suddenly found himself facing a huge white man poking a shotgun at him and vowing "to blow your black nigger guts out." Gregory responded without cowering: "Is that all you plan to do, boy, just kill me? Pull that fucking trigger, boy, you just pull that fucking trigger." The defiance worked. The would-be assassin walked away, Gregory concluded, because "he just couldn't do anything a Negro told him to do."[37]

Such outside agitators, whether drawing on the resources of *agape* or of verbal aggression, whether appealing to Christian love or existentialist philosophy or updating the trick of begging to be thrown into the briar patch, eventually overwhelmed and outsmarted white men of Milam's class and made them look like losers. "The old ultra-violence" (to lift out of context the famous phrase of Anthony Burgess's novel *A Clockwork Orange*) was becoming less impulsive and available, and the vast majority of Southern whites abstained from participation in the brutality that became the price of maintaining segregation.[38]

That is why Bertrand Russell (who was once prevented from teaching philosophy at the City College of New York) was wrong to point to the Till case as proof of the intolerance and bigotry of American society.[39] He missed the point. The murder sent shock waves outside the South, but it needs to be understood as far more specifically a regional phenomenon. Despite the passivity of the federal government, the case exposed the aberrant nature of the Deep South and especially of the Magnolia State itself. Russell did not and could not share the bloody experience of the first SNCC organizer to operate a voter registration project in Mississippi, a state that officially celebrated the birthdays of Robert E. Lee and Jefferson Davis as well as Confederate Memorial Day (but not Lincoln's Birthday or the national Memorial Day). "When you're in Mississippi," Robert Moses concluded after risking his life there beginning in 1961, "the rest of America doesn't seem real. And when you're in the rest of America, Mississippi doesn't seem real."[40]

For all the formidable failures of the rest of the United States to fulfill the promises of equality, only the white South—and one state in particular—showed a willingness to go to such lengths, to excuse such crimes, in defense of racial supremacy. Elsewhere in the United States, there was more than enough hypocrisy and phony liberalism to disenchant even the most cynical and pessimistic blacks. But Southern deviation from even the pretenses of equality had become a luxury that American diplomacy could not afford in an era when the goodwill of the emerging independent nations of Africa and Asia was becoming so pivotal. A decent respect for the opinions of mankind in a postcolonial world required the repudiation of racism. That spurred efforts to rectify such blatant examples of violent prejudice, though not during the two terms of the Eisenhower administration itself.

Till was murdered in an era when it was no longer politically prudent for the lives of people of color to be extinguished so brutally. For in James Baldwin's lapidary words, "this world is white no longer, and it will never be white again."[41] Indeed, in that sense not even the South was ever to be white again—for political power would cease to be exclusively color-coded, and that became the condition of the Delta as well. In early January 1963, the Fifth Circuit Court of Appeals granted an injunction against the sheriff of Tallahatchie County, Ellett Dogan, who had—like his predecessors such as H. C. Strider—been preventing blacks from trying to pay the poll taxes that were a precondition of suffrage. By February of that year, the first three black residents in over half a century became voters in Tallahatchie County, though its reputation was so "tough" that civil rights activists rarely ventured there.[42] Among the blacks who subsequently registered and voted was the brother-in-law of Moses Wright, Crosby Smith, who also got the right to serve on a jury.[43] The school board has remained all white, but blacks have been serving in white-collar positions in the very courthouse in Sumner where Till's killers were acquitted three decades ago. Sheriff Strider never again ran for office, citing the consequences of the Till case, immediately after which five black families had moved off his plantation because of his cooperation with the defense.

Aaron Henry, the Clarksdale druggist who had disguised himself as a field hand to investigate the murder, has served his second term in the state legislature, to which sixteen other blacks were elected in 1979. By then over three hundred elected officials in the Magnolia State were black. It was the largest number in the United States.[44] Reuben Anderson, who in 1967 became the first black to attend the law school at Ole Miss, was appointed to the state supreme court exactly three decades after Emmett Till had arrived in the Delta for his summer vacation.[45] It was too late for Judge Anderson to savor the satisfaction of joining Tom Brady on the bench, however. The coauthor of the inscription on the Mississippi Monument at Gettysburg had died at the age of seventy in 1973. By then even Brady had become something of a moderate. Only a decade after his fierce "Black Monday" speech, he opined from the bench that "irrespective of how erroneous it may appear, or how odious it is, a decision of the United States Supreme Court is still . . . binding on the tribunals and citizens of the respective states." After having written a majority opinion that overturned the grand larceny conviction of a black defendant because blacks had been systematically omitted from jury rolls, Brady received nasty phone calls at midnight, accusing him of being a "nigger lover."[46]

The poverty that historically afflicted the Deep South remained to be licked in the Delta, and its burdens were not equitably shared. According to the 1970 census, the median income in Leflore County for whites was $6,513. For blacks it was $3,461—or a little more than half, which was also the proportion of Negro homes without at least some basic plumbing facilities.[47] Such misery was draining the willingness to remain rooted in the land, which the mechanization of agriculture was taking care of anyway. Like the general demographic hemorrhaging of the rest of the state, Tallahatchie County had also lost a fifth of its population in the decade of 1950–1960.[48]

Among the emigrants were Roy and Carolyn Bryant. In the aftermath of the 1955 trial, black customers boycotted the chain of country stores that the extended Bryant-Milam family owned in Money, Glendora, and Sharkey. In three weeks the grocery in Money could not clear one hundred dollars. And since the stores depended almost entirely on black clientele, all three were closed within fifteen months.[49] But the crime also made the half-brothers into outcasts within the white community because, as Huie explained, men who are capable of murder do not make very lovely neighbors. Even contributors to the Sumner defense fund "want[ed] those killers to get on out of the county. They'll start thinking, 'Well, my gosh, if those guys are capable of killing, they just might decide to kill me sometime.' So here are men that cain't get a job." That is why, two weeks after the acquittal, a few representatives of that amorphous collectivity known as "the good people of Mississippi" confronted Bryant in Sumner when he came to withdraw his savings account. They told the grocery store operator never to show his face in their town again. For the trouble "with encouragin' one o' these peckerwoods to kill a nigger," Huie was informed, is that "he don't know when to stop. . . . We figured we might as well be rid of 'em."[50] Ostracism was a fate that could not have been foreseen after their acquittal, when the Gaullist daily *L'Aurore*, for example, cynically assumed that "these two brutes . . . will return to their jobs to be saluted, admired and praised just as if nothing had happened."[51]

After Bryant gave up his store in Money, he had trouble finding employment, sometimes working at odd jobs for as little as seventy-five cents a day. He then moved to Inverness, Mississippi, to learn welding under the GI Bill of Rights. But facing stigma in the Delta, Bryant and his family moved out of the Magnolia State altogether, ending up in east Texas in 1957. There he worked fifteen years as a boilermaker, a job that cost him much of his eyesight. In 1972 the Bryants moved back to Mississippi to take over a grocery store that one of his brothers owned. Carolyn Bryant, for whose honor he had been willing to kill, eventually divorced him in 1979 and remarried. Bryant also remarried and now runs a general store back in Ruleville. It is a converted gas station with a wooden floor, and its clientele is predominantly black. "I don't mistreat a man because he's black any more than I do a white man," he insisted in an interview three decades after Till walked into his earlier store. "I treat a man like I want to be treated." Bryant professes not to "know what happened to Emmett Till" and denies having killed him, but believes that "if Emmett Till hadn't got out of line, it probably wouldn't have happened to him." Resisting further interviews but dependent on his disability check, Bryant has also announced that his memory could be jogged "for a bunch of money." Despite current professions of innocence, he lives in fear not only of economic retaliation but also of "a bullet some dark night"; and he has refused to be photographed or to allow the exact location of his store to be revealed.[52]

J. W. Milam became a farmer after the collapse of the chain of stores. Too poor to own land, he was unable to rent it either, when the Bank of Charleston—the most powerful in Tallahatchie County—refused him a loan in 1956. Even after Milam managed to secure crop loans, many blacks refused to work for him; and white men had to be hired at higher pay. He turned to bootlegging, was arrested but not prosecuted, and also left the state, joining the Bryants in east Texas. Milam and his wife eventually moved back to the Delta, living in Greenville, where he did construction work. They were divorced before Milam succumbed to cancer of the spine on December 31, 1981. "He was a hell of a fine fellow," Bryant recalled. "He was gentle as a lamb and helped a lot of people."[53] The sharecropper's shack from which they had abducted Till was destroyed in a tornado, and a subsequent owner of the grocery store in Money professed to be unaware of the incident that had once made the dusty hamlet so notorious.[54]

Emmett Till's mother served as a public school teacher in Chicago for twenty-four years until her retirement. Now Mrs. Mamie Mobley, she is married to a Cadillac salesman and lives in an upper-middle-class neighborhood.[55] She has established the Emmett Till Players to keep alive among black teenagers in that city the rhetoric of the civil rights struggle that her son was not destined to hear. Mrs. Mobley has also stretched her loyalty and her maternal memory past the point of credibility. In 1987, during a conference on youth leadership in Alabama, she claimed never to have heard about the allegation that her son had made a pass at Mrs. Bryant, "until I saw it on that film [that is, the PBS documentary *Eyes on the Prize*]. That was totally out of character for Emmett."[56] Exactly three decades after the case burst on the world, Mayor Harold Washington proclaimed Emmett Till Day in Chicago, a city that itself had long been scarred with racial violence usually ignited by "changing neighborhoods." Indeed, after one such riot in the suburb of Cicero shortly before Till took his fatal vacation in the Delta, Walter White found the "implacable hatred" of the white ethnics living there worse than Southern lynch mobs. Such "beneficiaries of American opportunity," the NAACP executive secretary concluded, "were as virulent as any Mississippian in their willingness to deny a place to live to a member of a race which had preceded them to America by many generations." But the local press in Chicago had generally refrained from reporting such violence.[57] A statue was dedicated in Denver, showing Martin Luther King, Jr., with his arm around Till's shoulders. Denver Councilman Bill Roberts, a key figure in the decision to erect the sculpture, explained: "We wanted to portray ... the struggle that black people had at that time for justice and freedom."[58]

Two cents' worth of bubble gum and a girl's picture in a wallet—

these were the paltry artifacts of ordinary life, the commonplace detritus that decorated the genesis of the case. But however unspectacular the *mise-en-scène*, this was one murder that has remained entrenched in memory, and the interest and publicity that it galvanized may, finally, be among its most salient features.

Amzie Moore of Cleveland, Mississippi, called it "the best advertised lynching that I had ever heard [of]," and Charles Diggs claimed that "the picture in *Jet* magazine showing Emmett Till's mutilation was probably the greatest media product in the last forty or fifty years.... That picture stimulated a lot of ... anger on the part of blacks all over the country."[59] In the retrospective view of *Eyes on the Prize*, "a generation of black people would remember the horror of that photo"; and it steeled the determination of some of them to reduce their own vulnerability.[60] John Popham, the retired *New York Times* reporter who had covered the trial in Sumner, called it "the first step of the changes that eventually came to the entire South. ... It gave us the general sense of where things would be in the future." Bill Minor of the *New Orleans Times-Picayune* also covered the trial and has asserted that the case was so significant because, "for the first time[,] you couldn't have a quiet little lynching without getting real attention."[61] The NBC reporter in Sumner, John Chancellor, had apparently been threatened himself by a menacing group of whites, who drew back only when he pointed his microphone at them and warned: "The whole world is going to see what you'll do to me."[62] In a sense this unprecedented exposure worked posthumously for Emmett Till as well.

Such coverage marked a dramatic reversal in the role of the press. For earlier in the century, sensational headlines, mischievous adjectives, and presumptions of guilt in local newspapers tended to inflame white mobs and make lynchings more likely to occur. Reporters and editors in the region sometimes did their best to advertise lynchings, contributing to the sense of communal purpose and prophylaxis, foreclosing any feelings of shame or remorse among their readers. The advance notice of such hangings and burnings that radio stations and newspaper columns sometimes gave were likely to incite lynchers rather than warn them. Half a century before the Till case, the impact of publicity on the spirit of the lynch mob was more to encourage its crimes than to discredit them.

But the customary fate of black victims of Southern white mobs was oblivion and anonymity; it was scarcely newsworthy, and national memory faded quickly. Justice Oliver Wendell Holmes once professed a failure to understand the fuss over the Sacco and Vanzetti trial, when "a thousand-fold worse cases of Negroes come up from time to time, but the world does not worry about them."[63] Innumerable blacks had been the victims of arbitrary acts of vengeance and perversity, without attracting much notice in the national and international press. Walter White's *Rope and Faggot* (1928), an indispensable chronicle of such crimes against blacks, records the deaths of many other blacks whose cases hardly merited a footnote. The Scottsboro affair—with its lurid charge of gang rape committed on two Southern white women—may be the only exception to the claim that no other episode of Southern racism aroused more international concern, horror, and indignation than the corpse that was discovered in the Tallahatchie River.

The racist killing of an "uppity" black, the acquittal of the presumed murderers by an all-white jury—these phenomena were hardly deemed newsworthy in an earlier era, when frenzied mobs could torture, mutilate, and kill even pregnant women. But the publicity that was focused upon the Delta meant that the deadly logic of white supremacy could be exposed before the world, and this was exceptional. Journalists therefore represented the "outside agitators" whom Southern racists had shrewdly recognized as the most immediate harbingers of social and political change. In 1975, for instance, the founder of the Citizens' Councils identified the moment when the civil rights movement began. "It all started probably with a case of a young Negro boy named Emmett Till getting killed for offending some white woman . . . that made every newspaper on the face of the earth. And following that," Robert Patterson recalled, "whenever something happened to a Negro in the South, it was made a national issue against the South."[64]

A trial in Sumner was indeed the first big racial story after the Supreme Court overturned *Plessy* v. *Ferguson*; but it would be wrong to interpret press behavior as spliced between North and South, as a prejudiced assault on those who chose to uphold the ancient verities. Even a radio station in Clarksdale broke the customs of caste by identifying the mother of the victim as *Mrs.* Bradley,[65] and the hour of protest calls that were provoked are in retrospect less significant than the decision not to use "Mamie." The newspaper that was located closest to the scene of the trial, the *Mississippi Sun* in Charleston, did report in an unbiased manner the arrests of Bryant and Milam and the arrival of out-of-state journalists. But the *Sun* did not provide any news coverage whatsoever of the trial itself or its aftermath. This is puzzling, since it was front-page news in *Le Monde* if not in Tallahatchie County. Perhaps the silence was due to shame and embarrassment, perhaps to anger at excessive publicity elsewhere, perhaps to the assumption that all its readers would have learned the news before the weekly edition could be published. But what is most significant is that such muteness contrasted with the incendiary coverage that such rural newspapers gave to lynchings earlier in Southern history.

Not long after the case itself, a sociologist from Sophie Newcomb College in New Orleans examined eleven newspapers (North and South, urban and rural, black and white) for signs of divergence from a norm of objectivity. All considered the Till case big news; the two Mississippi papers devoted sixty-seven and sixty-five stories to it. Though differences emerged in Negro and white press coverage, and though a Delta newspaper (none was named in the study) was aberrant in its claims that Till had attempted to rape Carolyn Bryant (which not even the defense counsel alleged), another Delta newspaper located sixty miles away was free of such inflammatory bias. Indeed, the most striking conclusion to emerge from the content analysis was how little editorial difference separated Southern and Northern newspapers, a small index of the eclipse of the regional commitment to racial discrimination.[66] Though the velocity of change affecting "our colored" was barely noticeable, the walls of segregation were already showing signs of crumbling.

When Emmett Till hopped off that Illinois Central train, no civil rights activists were yet patrolling the Delta. Nor had voter registration campaigns been mounted by then; no Freedom Schools had been established either. But all these depth charges set off against Jim Crow in the 1960s were made possible in some measure when the magnitude and the intensity of the Southern commitment to preserve its "way of life" was exposed. The brutality of Roy Bryant and J. W. Milam and the communal support that they commanded helped to erode the very arrangement of race relations that they believed themselves to be reinforcing. The memory of their young victim came back to haunt the culture that stamped them—and, in a larger sense, nicked part of the national imagination itself. Their crime was embedded in paradox. It made sense only in terms of a caste system that they took for granted, and yet the murder was especially shocking because that system was already beginning to collapse. A death in the Delta intersected the antinomies of black and white, male and female, urban and rural, north and south, old and new, and native and stranger. And the very turpitude of the deed committed one Sabbath morning posed anew the ineluctable query of Dostoevsky's Grand Inquisitor: how is it possible to explain the death of a single child?

Notes

Preface

1. Tom P. Brady, *Black Monday* (Winona, Miss.: Association of Citizens' Councils, 1955), 12, 63–64; James G. Cook, *The Segregationists* (New York: Appleton-Century-Crofts, 1962), 13–33; George Thayer, *The Farther Shores of Politics* (New York: Simon & Schuster, 1967), 109–111; James W. Silver, *Mississippi: The Closed Society* (New York: Harcourt, Brace & World, 1966), 25.

2. David Herbert Donald, review of *A History of Mississippi*, ed. Richard Aubrey McLemore, *American Historical Review* 78 (December 1973): 1524.

3. George W. Cable, *The Grandissimes: A Story of Creole Life* (New York: Charles Scribner's Sons, 1880), 200.

Chapter 1. The Ideology of Lynching

1. Carl N. Degler, *Place Over Time: The Continuity of Southern Distinctiveness* (Baton Rouge: Louisiana State University Press, 1977), 13.

2. Jonathan M. Wiener, "The 'Black Beast Rapist': White Racial Attitudes in the Postwar South," *Reviews in American History* 13 (June 1985): 224; George M. Fredrickson, *The Black Image in the White Mind: The Debate on Afro-American Character and Destiny, 1817–1914* (New York: Harper & Row, 1971), 272–282.

3. Mary Frances Berry and John Blassingame, *Long Memory: The Black Experience in America* (New York: Oxford University Press, 1982), 122; Philip Alexander Bruce, *The Plantation Negro*, pp. 83–84, quoted in Jacquelyn Dowd Hall, *Revolt Against Chivalry: Jessie Daniel Ames and the Women's Campaign Against Lynching* (New York: Columbia University Press, 1979), 146.

4. Miss. Code Ann., 2000, 2002, 2339, cited in Hugh Stephen Whitaker,

"A Case Study in Southern Justice: The Emmett Till Case" (M. A. thesis, Florida State University, 1963), 9.

5. Thomas Nelson Page, *The Negro: The Southerner's Problem* (New York: Charles Scribner's Sons, 1904; reprint New York: Johnson Reprint, 1970), 112–113; Walter Lord, *The Past That Would Not Die* (New York: Harper & Row, 1965), 30; Lawrence J. Friedman, *The White Savage: Racial Fantasies in the Postbellum South* (Englewood Cliffs, N.J.: Prentice-Hall, 1970), 62–76; I. A. Newby, *Jim Crow's Defense: Anti-Negro Thought in America, 1900–1930* (Baton Rouge: Louisiana State University Press, 1965), 135–140.

6. Louise Westling, *Sacred Groves and Ravaged Gardens: The Fiction of Eudora Welty, Carson McCullers and Flannery O'Connor* (Athens: University of Georgia Press, 1985), 13–14; Leslie A. Fiedler, *The Inadvertent Epic: From Uncle Tom's Cabin to Roots* (New York: Simon & Schuster, 1979), 43–57; Willie Lee Rose, "Race and Region in American Historical Fiction: Four Episodes in Popular Culture," in *Region, Race, and Reconstruction: Essays in Honor of C. Vann Woodward*, ed. J. Morgan Kousser and James M. McPherson (New York: Oxford University Press, 1982), 113–139.

7. Tillman, quoted in Joel Williamson, *The Crucible of Race: Black-White Relations in the American South since Emancipation* (New York: Oxford University Press, 1984), 133.

8. Ibid., 133–139.

9. Tillman, quoted in Martin Duberman, *In White America* (New York: Signet, 1964), 62–63.

10. Friedman, *The White Savage*, 56, 172.

11. Davis, quoted in Raymond Arsenault, *The Wild Ass of the Ozarks: Jeff Davis and the Social Bases of Southern Politics* (Philadelphia: Temple University Press, 1984), 205–206.

12. Howard Smead, *Blood Justice: The Lynching of Mack Charles Parker* (New York: Oxford University Press, 1986), xi.

13. John Shelton Reed, "'To Live—and Die—in Dixie': Southern Violence," in *The Enduring South: Subcultural Persistence in Mass Society* (Chapel Hill: University of North Carolina Press, 1974), 46.

14. Degler, *Place Over Time*, 24–25; Edward L. Ayers, *Vengeance and Justice: Crime and Punishment in the 19th-Century American South* (New York: Oxford University Press, 1984), 12–13, 16, 17–18.

15. Peter Berger, Brigitte Berger, and Hansfried Kellner, *The Homeless Mind: Modernization and Consciousness* (New York: Random House, 1973), 83–84, 88–89; Ayers, *Vengeance and Justice*, 19–20.

16. Robert L. Zangrando, *The NAACP Crusade Against Lynching, 1909–1950* (Philadelphia: Temple University Press, 1980), 4; Berry and Blassingame, *Long Memory*, 123; "Lynchings by State and Race," in *The Negro in the Twentieth Century*, ed. John Hope Franklin and Isidore Starr (New York: Vintage, 1967), 186.

17. Wilbur J. Cash, *The Mind of the South* (New York: Knopf, 1941), 116–120; Daniel T. Williams, ed., "The Lynching Records at Tuskegee Institute," in *Eight Negro Bibliographies* (New York: Kraus Reprint, 1970), n. 7, p. 2.

18. David L. Cohn, *Where I was Born and Raised* (South Bend, Ind.: University of Notre Dame Press, 1967 [1935, 1947], 66–67.

19. Hall, *Revolt Against Chivalry*, 151, 156; Pete Daniel, *Standing at the Crossroads: Southern Life since 1900* (New York: Hill and Wang, 1986), 56–58.

20. Ayers, *Vengeance and Justice*, 244.

21. Hall, *Revolt Against Chivalry*, 133; Berry and Blassingame, *Long Memory*, 125.

22. James Weldon Johnson, *Along This Way* (New York: Viking, 1933), 165–170; Trudier Harris, *Exorcising Blackness: Historical and Literary Lynching and Burning Rituals* (Bloomington: Indiana University Press, 1984), 190; Berry and Blassingame, *Long Memory*, 124.

23. John Dollard, *Caste and Class in a Southern Town* (Garden City, N.Y.: Doubleday, Anchor Books, 1949 [1937]), 331; Charles S. Johnson, *Growing Up in the Black Belt: Negro Youth in the Rural South* (New York: Schocken, 1967), 316–318.

24. Richard Wright, *Black Boy* (New York: Harper & Row, 1966 [1945]), 63, 83–84, 190.

25. Dollard, *Caste and Class*, 48; Numan V. Bartley, *The Rise of Massive Resistance: Race and Politics in the South During the 1950's* (Baton Rouge: Louisiana State University Press, 1969), 194.

26. Gunnar Myrdal, *An American Dilemma: The Negro Problem and American Democracy* (New York: Harper & Brothers, 1944), 60–61; Cohn, *Where I Was Born and Raised*, 282–286.

27. Herman Talmadge, *You and Segregation*, 42, quoted in Bartley, *The Rise of Massive Resistance*, 238; Cook, *Segregationists*, 291.

28. Perez, quoted in Reese Cleghorn, "The Segs," in *Smiling Through the Apocalypse: Esquire's History of the Sixties*, ed. Harold Hayes (New York: McCall, 1969), 656.

29. Thomas Waring, C. P. Liter, Frederick Sullens, et al., "Interviews with

Southern Editors: Race Trouble to Grow in South; No Mixed Schools Yet," *U.S. News & World Report* 40 (February 24, 1956): 134, 135, 138; *Jackson Daily News*, May 18, 1954, p. 1; Whitaker, "Case Study in Southern Justice," 64–65.

30. *New York Times*, May 24, 1954, p. 19; Whitaker, "Case Study in Southern Justice," 67.

31. Beth Day, *Sexual Life Between Blacks and Whites: The Roots of Racism* (New York: World, 1972), 9–11, 13–14.

32. Brady, *Black Monday*, v, 45, 89; Cook, *Segregationists*, 23; Lerone Bennett, Jr., *Before the Mayflower: A History of the Negro in America, 1619–1964* (Baltimore: Penguin, 1966), 312.

33. "Down the Memory Hole," *New Republic* 193 (July 1, 1985): 9.

34. "Why the South Must Prevail," *National Review* 4 (August 24, 1957): 149; George H. Nash, *The Conservative Intellectual Movement in America: Since 1945* (New York: Basic Books, 1976), 200, 202, 207, 396.

35. Myrdal, *An American Dilemma*, 586–592; Bartley, *The Rise of Massive Resistance*, 236; Gerald Mast, *The Movies in Our Midst* (Chicago: University of Chicago Press, 1982), 333.

36. Calvin C. Hernton, *Sex and Racism in America* (New York: Grove Press, 1966), 64.

37. John Howard Griffin, *Black Like Me* (New York: Signet, 1963), 60.

38. Cohn, *Where I Was Born and Raised*, 12; Willie Morris, *Terrains of the Heart and Other Essays on Home* (Oxford, Miss.: Yoknapatawpha Press, 1981), 8, 71.

39. John K. Bettersworth, *Mississippi: A History* (Austin, Tex.: Steck, 1959), 11–13; Johnson, *Growing Up in the Black Belt*, 305; Jack Temple Kirby, *Rural Worlds Lost: The American South, 1920–1960* (Baton Rouge: Louisiana State University Press, 1987), 246–247.

40. Neil R. McMillen, *The Citizens' Council: Organized Resistance to the Second Reconstruction, 1954–64* (Urbana: University of Illinois Press, 1971), 26.

41. Robert Penn Warren, *Segregation: The Inner Conflict of the South* (New York: Random House, 1956), 5–6.

42. Price Caldwell, quoted in Dorothy Abbott, ed., *Mississippi Writers: Reflections of Childhood and Youth*, vol. 1 (Jackson: University Press of Mississippi, 1985), 758; Mike Thelwell, "Bright an' Mownin' Star," and "Fish are Jumping an' the Cotton is High: Notes from the Mississippi Delta," in *Black and White in American Culture: An Anthology from The Massachusetts Review*, ed. Jules Chametzky and Sidney Kaplan (Amherst: University of Massachusetts Press, 1969), 3, 38, 39.

Chapter 2. Chicago Boy

1. *Jackson Clarion-Ledger,* August 25, 1985, sec. H, p. 1; Arnold R. Hirsch, *Making the Second Ghetto: Race and Housing in Chicago, 1940–1960* (Cambridge: Cambridge University Press, 1983), 16–17; Robert Palmer, *Deep Blues* (New York: Penguin, 1982), 11–12.

2. *Jackson Clarion-Ledger,* August 25, 1985, sec. H, p. 1; *Huntsville (Alabama) Times,* July 19, 1987, sec. B, p. 1; Juan Williams, *Eyes on the Prize: America's Civil Rights Years, 1954–1965* (New York: Viking, 1987), 39.

3. "Trial by Jury," *Time* 66 (October 3, 1955): 18; William Bradford Huie, *Wolf Whistle and Other Stories* (New York: Signet, 1959), 19.

4. Jones, interviewed in *Eyes on the Prize: America's Civil Rights Years* (PBS Video, 1986), Episode 1: "Awakenings (1954–56)."

5. Huie, *Wolf Whistle,* 17–19, and "The Shocking Story of Approved Killing in Mississippi," *Look* 20 (January 24, 1956): 46; *Jackson Daily News,* September 22, 1955, p. 11.

6. Jones, interviewed in *Eyes on the Prize.*

7. Huie, "Shocking Story of Approved Killing," 46, and *Wolf Whistle,* 20–21; *Jackson Daily News,* September 23, 1955, p. 9; *Memphis Commercial Appeal,* September 23, 1955, pp. 1, 2; Jones, interviewed in *Eyes on the Prize.*

8. *Jackson Clarion-Ledger,* August 25, 1985, sec. H, p. 1.

9. *Huntsville Times,* July 19, 1987, sec. B, p. 1.

10. *Jackson Daily News,* September 2, 1955, p. 8.

11. Richard Bardolph, ed., *The Civil Rights Record: Black Americans and the Law, 1849–1970* (New York: Thomas Y. Crowell, 1970), 478–479.

12. *Greenwood Commonwealth,* August 31, 1955, p. 1.

13. William Roger Witherspoon, *Martin Luther King, Jr.: To the Mountaintop* (Garden City, N.Y.: Doubleday, 1985), 21; William H. Chafe, *The Unfinished Journey: America Since World War II* (New York: Oxford University Press, 1986), 147.

14. *Greenwood Commonwealth,* September 1, 1955, p. 1; *Memphis Commercial Appeal.* September 1, 1955, p. 4; *Jackson Clarion-Ledger,* September 2, 1955, p. 1.

15. "Nation Horrified by Murder of Kidnapped Chicago Youth," *Jet* 8 (September 15, 1955): 8; *Chicago Defender,* September 10, 1955, p. 1.

16. *Jackson Clarion-Ledger,* August 25, 1955, sec. H, p. 1; "A Boy Goes Home," *Newsweek* 46 (September 12, 1955): 32.

17. Huie, "Shocking Story of Approved Killing," *Look:* 47, and *Wolf Whis-*

tle, 20–21; Whitaker, "Case Study in Southern Justice," 103–106; Williams, *Eyes on the Prize,* 41–42.

18. David A. Shostak, "Crosby Smith: Forgotten Witness to a Mississippi Nightmare," *Negro History Bulletin* 38 (December 1974): 321.

19. Huie, "Shocking Story of Approved Killing," *Look:* 47, and *Wolf Whistle,* 22–23; Williams, *Eyes on the Prize,* 42.

20. Huie, "Shocking Story of Approved Killing," *Look:* 48, and *Wolf Whistle,* 24–25; Whitaker, "Case Study in Southern Justice," 109–111; Williams, *Eyes on the Prize,* 42.

21. Huie, "Shocking Story of Approved Killing," *Look:* 49, and *Wolf Whistle,* 34–35; Huie interview in *Eyes on the Prize,* Episode 1.

22. *M is for Mississippi and Murder* (New York: NAACP, 1955), 3–4, 6, in NAACP Folder, Box 5 of Race Relations Collection, 1954–1970, University of Mississippi.

23. Testimony of George Smith, *Official Transcript,* 120–127, quoted in Whitaker, "Case Study in Southern Justice," 119; Shostak, "Crosby Smith," 322.

24. Shostak, "Crosby Smith," 320, 322; Huie, *Wolf Whistle,* 25–26; *Memphis Commercial Appeal,* September 1, 1955, p. 4; Williams, *Eyes on the Prize,* 43; Hodding Carter III, *The South Strikes Back* (Garden City, N.Y.: Doubleday, 1959), 119–120.

25. Williams, *Eyes on the Prize,* 43–44; *Chicago Defender,* September 10, 1955, p. 1.

26. Mamie Bradley, quoted in *Greenwood Commonwealth,* September 1, 1955, p. 1; *Jackson Daily News,* September 1, 1955, p.1.

27. Williams, *Eyes on the Prize,* 44; *New York Times,* September 4, 1955, sec. 5, p. 9 and September 7, 1955, p. 19; "Chicago Boy," *Nation* 181 (September 17, 1955): 235; "Boy Goes Home," *Newsweek:* 32; "The Accused," *Newsweek* 46 (September 19, 1955): 38.

28. William M. Simpson, "Reflections on a Murder: The Emmett Till Case," in *Southern Miscellany: Essays in History in Honor of Glover Moore,* ed. Frank Allen Dennis (Jackson: University Press of Mississippi, 1981), 183.

29. Whitaker, "Case Study in Southern Justice," 18–19, 20; Thomas D. Clark, *The Emerging South* (New York: Oxford University Press, 1961), 193.

30. Simpson, "Reflections," 184–185; *New York Times,* September 7, 1955, pp. 19, 30.

31. *Jackson Clarion-Ledger,* September 2, 1955, p. 1; *Memphis Commercial*

Appeal, September 2, 1955, p. 1; *New York Times*, September 2, 1955, p. 37.

32. Smead, *Blood Justice*, 68–69, 76, 167; Clark, *Emerging South*, 274.

33. Williams, "The Lynching Records at Tuskegee Institute," 1, 2, 4.

34. Cash, *Mind of the South*, 44–45.

35. Whitaker, "Case Study in Southern Justice," 121; Cothran, quoted in "Boy Goes Home," *Newsweek*: 32.

36. *Memphis Commercial Appeal*, September 2, 1955, p. 7.

37. *Jackson Daily News*, September 1, 1955, p. 1, and September 2, 1955, p. 8.

38. *Memphis Commercial Appeal*, September 4, 1955, p. 1, quoted in Whitaker, "Case Study in Southern Justice," 120–121; Shepherd, quoted in "Nation Horrified by Murder," *Jet*: 6.

39. Simpson, "Reflections," 180–181; Patterson and Brady, quoted in Cook, *Segregationists*, 19, 55; McMillen, *Citizens' Council*, 17–18, 216–217.

40. Turner Catledge, *My Life and The Times* (New York: Harper & Row, 1971), 219; *New York Times*, September 18, 1955, sec. 4, p. 7; Warren, *Segregation*, 87.

41. Degler, *Place Over Time*, 22.

42. Lewis M. Killian, *White Southerners*, rev. ed. (Amherst: University of Massachusetts Press, 1985), 5, 33, 38, 40–41, 55.

43. Lillie Neely Henry and Jean Conger May, *A History of Tallahatchie County* (Charleston, Miss.: The *Mississippi Sun*, 1960), 12.

44. "Mississippi Barbarism," *The Crisis* 62 (October, 1955): 481.

45. *New York Times*, September 8, 1955, p. 10; Wilkins, quoted in *Memphis Commercial Appeal*, September 1, 1955, pp. 1, 4; *Jackson Daily News*, September 2, 1955, p. 8.

46. "The Place of Acquittal," *Newsweek* 46 (October 3, 1955): 29.

47. Simpson, "Reflections," 180–181; *Memphis Commercial Appeal*, September 4, 1955, p. 2.

48. *New York Times*, September 18, 1955, sec. 4, p. 7, and October 30, 1955, p. 86; *Memphis Commercial Appeal*, September 7, 1955, p. 6; Westbrook Pegler to J. J. Breland and John Whitten, September 10, 1955, copy in William Bradford Huie Papers, in possession of Martha Hunt Huie, Memphis, Tenn.; *Greenwood Commonwealth*, September 2, 1955, p. 1; Whitaker, "Case Study in Southern Justice," 123.

49. Simpson, "Reflections," 181–182; Whitaker, "Case Study in Southern

Justice," 123; McMillen, *Citizens' Council*, 254–255; Hodding Carter, *First Person Rural* (Garden City, N.Y.: Doubleday, 1963), 211.

50. Florence Mars, with Lynn Eden, *Witness in Philadelphia* (Baton Rouge: Louisiana State University Press, 1977), 65.

51. Huie, *Wolf Whistle*, 27–28; Huie in Howell Raines, *My Soul is Rested: Movement Days in the Deep South Remembered* (New York: Bantam, 1978), 432; Whitaker, "Case Study in Southern Justice," 126–127.

52. Whitaker, "Case Study in Southern Justice," 119, 125; *Memphis Commercial Appeal*, September 1, 1955, p. 4, September 4, 1955, sec. 1, p. 1, and September 7, 1955, p. 3.

53. *Chicago Defender*, September 10, 1955, p. 1.

54. Carter, *The South Strikes Back*, 120; Williams, *Eyes on the Prize*, 45; *Memphis Commercial Appeal*, September 10, 1955, p. 1; Simpson, "Reflections," 186; Whitaker, "Case Study in Southern Justice," 131.

55. "Will Mississippi Whitewash the Emmett Till Slaying?" *Jet* 8 (September 22, 1955): 8.

Chapter 3. Trial by Jury

1. Greenville *Delta Democrat-Times*, September 22, 1955, pp. 11, 17.

2. Charleston *Mississippi Sun*, September 22, 1955, p. 1; *New York Times*, September 18, 1955, sec. 4, p. 7.

3. "Place of Acquittal," *Newsweek*: 29; *Memphis Commercial Appeal*, September 20, 1955, p. 17, and September 23, 1955, p. 35.

4. Dan Wakefield, *Between the Lines: A Reporter's Personal Journey Through Public Events* (New York: New American Library, 1966), 140, 144–145.

5. Dan Wakefield, "Justice in Sumner," *Nation* 181 (October 1, 1955): 284, reprinted in *Revolt in the South* (New York: Grove Press, 1960), 32–33; idem, *Between the Lines*, 148.

6. Greenville *Delta Democrat-Times*, September 22, 1955, pg. 11.

7. Whitaker, "Case Study in Southern Justice," 18, 24, 46; *New York Times*, September 19, 1955, p. 50.

8. "Trial by Jury," *Time*: 19; *Memphis Commercial Appeal*, September 21, 1955, p. 8; Whitaker, "Case Study in Southern Justice," 141, 143, 144.

9. Eastland, quoted in Carl T. Rowan, *Go South to Sorrow* (New York: Random House, 1957), 38–39, and in Robert Sherrill, *Gothic Politics in the Deep South: Stars of the New Confederacy* (New York: Ballantine, 1969), 229.

10. Quoted in Rowan, *Go South*, 42–43, and in *M is for Mississippi and*

Murder (New York: NAACP, 1955), 3–4; Ira B. Harkey, Jr., *The Smell of Burning Crosses: An Autobiography of a Mississippi Newspaperman* (Jacksonville, Ill.: Harris-Wolfe, 1967), 106–107; *Washington Afro-American*, January 3, 1956, p. 8.

11. Harkey, *The Smell of Burning Crosses*, 109; Wakefield, *Between the Lines*, 146.

12. *Jackson Daily News*, September 21, 1955, p. 14.

13. Williams, *Eyes on the Prize*, 44; Wakefield, *Between the Lines*, 142, 147, 149, and *Revolt in the South*, 34.

14. I. F. Stone, "The Murder of Emmett Till," October 3, 1955, reprinted in *The Haunted Fifties* (New York: Vintage, 1969), 107, and in *I. F. Stone's Weekly Reader*, ed. Neil Middleton (New York: Vintage, 1974), 103–105; Cloyte Murdock Larsson, "Land of the Till Murder Revisited," *Ebony* 41 (March 1986): 54.

15. Williams, *Eyes on the Prize*, 45, 48, 50–51.

16. *New York Times*, September 25, 1955, sec. 4, p. 8; David Halberstam, "Tallahatchie County Acquits a Peckerwood," *Reporter* 14 (April 19, 1956): 27.

17. "An Interview with James Hicks" and "An Interview with Congressman Charles Diggs," in Williams, *Eyes on the Prize*, 49, 50.

18. *Jackson Clarion-Ledger*, September 25, 1955, p. 8; *Jackson Daily News*, September 22, 1955, p. 12, and September 24, 1955, p. 6.

19. *New York Times*, September 20, 1955, p. 32; "Place of Acquittal," *Newsweek*: 29.

20. Shostak, "Crosby Smith," 323.

21. Williams, *Eyes on the Prize*, 47–48; *New York Times*, September 22, 1955, p. 64.

22. Murray Kempton, "He Went All the Way," in *America Comes of Middle Age: Columns, 1950–1962* (Boston: Little, Brown, 1962), 135–136; Williams, *Eyes on the Prize*, 48, 51.

23. Stone, *Haunted Fifties*, 107; "An Interview with Congressman Charles Diggs," in Williams, *Eyes on the Prize*, 49; Wakefield, *Revolt in the South*, 34, 40; "Emmett Till's Day in Court," *Life* 39 (October 3, 1955): 37; Kempton, *America Comes of Middle Age*, 137.

24. *Memphis Commercial Appeal*, September 21, 1955, p. 8, and September 23, 1955, p. 2; Stone, *Haunted Fifties*, 107.

25. *New York Times*, September 23, 1955, p. 15; *Memphis Commercial Appeal*, September 23, 1955, p. 2; Williams, *Eyes on the Prize*, 48.

26. Shostak, "Crosby Smith," 322; "Trial by Jury," *Time*: 18–19.

27. Williams, *Eyes on the Prize*, 45.

28. *New York Times,* September 23, 1955, p. 15; *Memphis Commercial Appeal,* September 23, 1955, pp. 1, 2.

29. Wakefield, *Revolt in the South,* 35–36, 37; Rowan, *Go South to Sorrow,* 43–44; Stone, *Haunted Fifties,* 107; *New York Times,* September 11, 1955, sec. 4, p. 2, September 23, 1955, p. 15, and September 24, 1955, p. 38; *Jackson Daily News,* September 23, 1955, p. 1; "Emmett Till's Day in Court," *Life:* 37.

30. Williams, *Eyes on the Prize,* 52; "Trial by Jury," *Time:* 19; Huie, *Wolf Whistle,* 31.

31. *Memphis Commercial Appeal,* September 24, 1955, p. 2.

32. Whitaker, "Case Study in Southern Justice," 154–155.

33. *New York Times,* September 24, 1955, pp. 1, 38; *Memphis Commercial Appeal,* September 24, 1955, p. 4.

34. *Memphis Commercial Appeal,* September 24, 1955, p. 2; Whitaker, "Case Study in Southern Justice," 151–152.

35. Whitaker, "Case Study in Southern Justice," 155.

36. *Delta Democrat-Times,* September 6, 1955, p. 4; Whitaker, "Case Study in Southern Justice," 136.

37. Stone, *Haunted Fifties,* 107; Simpson, "Reflections," 193; Rowan, *Go South to Sorrow,* 47–48.

38. *New York Times,* September 24, 1955, p. 38; *Jackson Advocate,* September 24, 1955, p. 4.

39. Mars, *Witness in Philadelphia,* 67–68; Smead, *Blood Justice,* 30.

40. *Jackson Clarion-Ledger,* September 25, 1955, sec. 1, p. 10.

41. Malcolm B. Parsons, "Violence and Caste in Southern Justice," *South Atlantic Quarterly* 60 (Autumn 1961): 459.

42. Whitaker, "Case Study in Southern Justice," 145–146.

43. *New York Times,* September 24, 1955, p. 38, and September 25, 1955, sec. 4, p. 1; *Jackson Daily News,* September 21, 1955, p. 14.

44. Diggs, quoted in *Greenwood Commonwealth,* September 26, 1955, p. 1; *Jackson Clarion-Ledger,* September 25, 1955, sec. 1, p. 10.

45. Wakefield, *Between the Lines,* 145–146, 154; James W. Silver, "Faulkner and the Teaching of History" (1972), in *Running Scared: Silver in Mississippi* (Jackson: University Press of Mississippi, 1984), 212.

46. "Editorials: Till Protest Meeting," *The Crisis* 62 (November 1955): 546.

47. "Double Murder in Mississippi," *Christian Century* 72 (October 5, 1955): 1132; Whitaker, "Case Study in Southern Justice," 157.

48. "Death in Mississippi," *Commonweal* 62 (September 23, 1955): 604.

49. Ibid., 603.

50. Quoted in "Editorials: French Reaction to the Till Trial," *The Crisis* 62 (November 1955): 547.

51. "L'affaire Till in the French Press," *The Crisis* 62 (December 1955): 596–597; *New York Times,* October 18, 1955, p. 33, and October 22, 1955, p. 40.

52. European Headquarters of American Jewish Committee, "Survey of Public Opinion in France, Italy, Belgium, Switzerland, Germany, Tunisia on the Emmett Till Case" (October 1955), Archives of the American Jewish Committee (copy in possession of author).

53. "Double Murder in Mississippi," *Christian Century:* 1132.

54. Memphis *Commercial Appeal,* September 24, 1955, p. 6.

55. Simpson, "Reflections," 194–196; *Greenwood Commonwealth,* September 24, 1955, p. 4.

56. *Jackson Clarion-Ledger,* September 25, 1955, sec. 1, p. 8.

57. *Delta Democrat-Times,* September 25, 1955, p. 4.

58. "Climate of Fear," *Commonweal* 63 (October 14, 1955): 29.

59. *New York Times,* September 7, 1955, p. 19, September 22, 1955, p. 64, and October 1, 1955, p. 40.

60. "Ill-Chosen Symbol," *Time* 66 (November 21, 1955): 21; *Delta Democrat-Times,* September 6, 1955, p. 2; *New York Times,* November 10, 1955, p. 10; Simpson, "Reflections," 189, 196–197.

61. Halberstam, "Tallahatchie County Acquits a Peckerwood," 26–29; Evers, *For Us, the Living,* 180–183.

62. Williams, *Eyes on the Prize,* 57, 288; *Jackson Advocate,* October 1, 1955, p. 1.

63. *Jackson Daily News,* October 11, 1955, p. 3.

64. *Chicago Defender,* October 1, 1955, p. 2, cited in Whitaker, "Case Study in Southern Justice," 166; Shostak, "Crosby Smith," 324.

Chapter 4. The Shock of Exoneration

1. *New York Times,* November 24, 1986, p. D14; Letters to the Editor, *Look* 20 (March 6, 1956): 112; Garland Reeves, "Huie's Middle, Early Writings Will Endure," *Birmingham News,* November 30, 1986, sec. F, pp. 1, 10; Bob Ward, "William Bradford Huie Paid for Their Sins," *Writer's Digest* 54 (September 1974): 16–17; William F. Buckley, "William Bradford Huie, RIP," *National Review* 38 (December 19, 1986): 20–21.

2. Simpson, "Reflections," 197.

3. Huie, quoted in Franklin and Starr, *The Negro in 20th Century America*, 193–194; Ward, "William Bradford Huie Paid for Their Sins," 21.

4. William Bradford Huie to Lee Hills, October 18, 1955, p. 2, copy in Huie Papers.

5. Huie in Raines, *My Soul is Rested*, 426–428; Huie to Dan Mich, October 17, 1955, pp. 2, 3, and to Lee Hills, October 18, 1955, p. 8, copies in Huie Papers.

6. Huie in Raines, *My Soul is Rested*, 433–434; Ward, "William Bradford Huie Paid for Their Sins," 21–22; Huie, "What's Happened to the Emmett Till Killers?", *Look* 21 (January 22, 1957): 64.

7. Ward, "William Bradford Huie Paid for Their Sins," 18.

8. *Jackson Clarion-Ledger*, August 25, 1955, sec. H, p. 1; Hernton, *Sex and Racism in America*, 59.

9. Huie to Dan Mich, October 21, 1955, p. 3, copy in Huie Papers; Whitaker, "Case Study in Southern Justice," 102n.

10. Coleman, quoted in Rowan, *Go South to Sorrow*, 53, 54–55; Huie, "What's Happened to the Emmett Till Killers?", 68.

11. Huie to Dan Mich, October 17, 1955, p. 1, copy in Huie Papers; Breland, quoted in Huie to Lee Hills, October 18, 1955, pp. 2, 3, copy in Huie Papers.

12. Breland, quoted in Huie Papers, pp. 3, 4.

13. Simpson, "Reflections," 179, 184, 189, 190–191, 198–199; *Chicago Defender*, September 10, 1955, p. 1.

14. Williams, *Eyes on the Prize*, 48; *Jackson Advocate*, September 24, 1955, p. 4.

15. Whitaker, "Case Study in Southern Justice," 149–150; Simpson, "Reflections," 191n.

16. *Greenwood Commonwealth*, August 29, 1955, p. 1, and August 31, 1955, p. 1.

17. Whitaker, "Case Study in Southern Justice," 111.

18. William Bradford Huie to Roy Wilkins, October 12, 1955, p. 2, to Dan Mich, October 17, 1955, pp. 1, 4, and to Lee Hills, October 18, 1955, p. 6, copies in Huie Papers.

19. Huie, *Wolf Whistle*, 24, 36.

20. Hurley in Raines, *My Soul is Rested*, 141–143; "An Interview with Myrlie Evers," in Williams, *Eyes on the Prize*, 46–47; Mrs. Medgar [Myrlie B.] Evers, with William Peters, *For Us, the Living* (Garden City, N.Y.: Doubleday, 1967), 170–176.

21. Hurley in Raines, *My Soul is Rested*, 141–143.

22. Endesha Ida Mae Holland, "Memories of the Mississippi Delta," *Michigan Quarterly Review* 26 (Winter 1987): 246.

23. Simpson, "Reflections," 178, 184n–185n; John Dittmer, "The Politics of the Mississippi Movement, 1954–1964," in *The Civil Rights Movement in America*, ed. Charles W. Eagles (Jackson: University Press of Mississippi, 1986), 68–70.

24. Evers, *For Us, the Living*, 170–176; "An Interview with Myrlie Evers," in Williams, *Eyes on the Prize*, 46.

25. J. J. Breland to W. W. Malone, September 26, 1955, copy in Huie Papers; Williams, *Eyes on the Prize*, 52, 57; "The Till Case," *New South* 10 (September 1955): 1.

26. Williams, *Eyes on the Prize*, 52; Carter, *The South Strikes Back*, 120.

27. Bartley, *The Rise of Massive Resistance*, 82; Stone, *Haunted Fifties*, 108; Clark, *Emerging South*, 193–195.

28. Earl Black, *Southern Governors and Civil Rights: Racial Segregation as a Campaign Issue in the Second Reconstruction* (Cambridge: Harvard University Press, 1976), 60.

29. Bartley, *The Rise of Massive Resistance*, 136; Coleman, quoted in "Don't Stone Her Until You Hear Her Side" (pamphlet of State Sovereignty Commission), in Racial Problems (Commentary), 1954–1959 Folder, Box 6 of Race Relations Collection, 1954–1970.

30. William E. Leuchtenburg, "The White House and Black America: From Eisenhower to Carter," in *Have We Overcome?: Race Relations Since Brown*, ed. Michael V. Namorato (Jackson: University Press of Mississippi, 1979), 126; Jack M. Bloom, *Class, Race, and the Civil Rights Movement* (Bloomington: Indiana University Press, 1987), 101; Robert Fredrick Burk, *The Eisenhower Administration and Black Civil Rights* (Knoxville: University of Tennessee Press, 1984), 206.

31. Judge Sebe Dale's Charge to the Pearl River County Grand Jury, Appendix B of Smead, *Blood Justice*, 210.

32. Lord, *The Past That Would Not Die*, 75; David R. Goldfield, *Promised Land: The South Since 1945* (Arlington Heights, Ill.: Harlan Davidson, 1987), 68–69.

33. *New York Times*, November 6, 1955, p. 82.

34. *Jackson Daily News*, September 25, 1955, sec. 1, p. 9.

35. Bartley, *Rise of Massive Resistance*, 180–181.

36. C. Vann Woodward, *The Strange Career of Jim Crow* (New York: Oxford University Press, 1966), 173–174; Benjamin Muse, *Ten Years of Prelude: The Story of Integration Since the Supreme Court's 1954 Decision* (New York: Viking, 1964), 244.

37. *Delta Democrat-Times*, September 30, 1955, p. 1; Kempton, *America Comes of Middle Age*, 137–141; Cook, *Segregationists*, 39–40; Anthony P. Dunbar, *Against the Grain: Southern Radicals and Prophets, 1929–1959* (Charlottesville: University Press of Virginia, 1981), 242–245.

38. Quoted in Carter, *The South Strikes Back*, 136–137; McMillen, *Citizens' Council*, 36–40, 237; Robert B. Patterson to Paul R. Davis, January 29, 1957, in Citizens' Councils Folder, Part I, Box 7, E-5, Race Relations Collection, John Davis Williams Library, University of Mississippi.

39. W. J. Weatherby, *Breaking the Silence* (Harmondsworth, England: Penguin, 1965), 168.

40. William Faulkner to Else Jonsson, June 12, 1955, quoted in Joseph Blotner, *Faulkner: A Biography* (New York: Random House, 1974), 2:1539.

41. William Faulkner, "Press Dispatch Written in Rome, Italy, for the United Press, on the Emmett Till Case," in *Essays, Speeches and Public Letters*, ed. James B. Meriwether (New York: Random House, 1965), 222–223; Blotner, *Faulkner: A Biography*, 2: 1570–1571, and idem, *Faulkner: A Biography* (one-volume ed., 1984), 609–610.

42. Faulkner, *Essays*, 223.

43. Charles D. Peavy, *Go Slow Now: Faulkner and the Race Question* (Eugene: University of Oregon Books, 1971), 65–68.

44. Marianne Weber, *Max Weber: A Biography*, translated by Harry Zohn (New York: John Wiley & Sons, 1975), 295.

45. Faulkner, "Statement to the Press on the Willie McGee Case," *Essays*, 211–212.

46. Bell I. Wiley, Foreword to William Faulkner et al., *Three Views of the Segregation Decisions* (Atlanta: Southern Regional Council, 1956), 5; Faulkner, "American Segregation and the World Crisis," in ibid., 9, reprinted in *Essays*, ed. Meriwether, 146; Silver, *Running Scared*, 60; Blotner, *Faulkner*, 2: 1582, 1584–1585, and 614 (one vol. ed.).

47. Interview with William Faulkner in *Writers at Work: The Paris Review Interviews*, First Series, ed. Malcolm Cowley (New York: Viking, 1959), 140, reprinted in *Lion in the Garden: Interviews with William Faulkner*, ed. James B. Meriwether and Michael Millgate (New York: Random House, 1968), 254–255; Faulkner, "American Segregation and the World Crisis," 12.

48. Faulkner, "On Fear: Deep South in Labor: Mississippi," *Essays*, 100–101.

49. Faulkner, "Letter to a Northern Editor," in ibid., 90.

Chapter 5. Washington, D.C.

1. Leuchtenburg, "The White House and Black America," in *Have We Overcome?*, 121.

2. Dwight D. Eisenhower, *White House Years: Mandate for Change, 1953–1956* (Garden City, N.Y.: Doubleday, 1963), 229–230; Earl Warren, *The Memoirs of Earl Warren* (Garden City, N.Y.: Doubleday, 1977), 291–292.

3. Leuchtenburg, "The White House and Black America," in *Have We Overcome?*, 123, 125; Bartley, *The Rise of Massive Resistance*, 62–63; Herbert Parmet, *Eisenhower and the American Crusades* (New York: Macmillan, 1972), 438–439.

4. McKinley, quoted in Zangrando, *The NAACP Crusade Against Lynching*, 15; Michal R. Belknap, *Federal Law and Southern Order: Racial Violence and Constitutional Conflict in the Post-Brown South* (Athens: University of Georgia Press, 1987), 33–34, 39.

5. Roy Wilkins, with Tom Mathews, *Standing Fast* (New York: Viking, 1982), 222.

6. Bartley, *Rise of Massive Resistance*, 47–49, 50.

7. Smead, *Blood Justice*, 172; Lord, *The Past That Would Not Die*, 76–77.

8. Leuchtenburg, "The White House and Black America," in *Have We Overcome?*, 123: Parmet, *Eisenhower and the American Crusades*, 446; Stephen E. Ambrose, *Eisenhower: The President* (New York: Simon and Schuster, 1984), volume 2, pp. 306, 308.

9. Parmet, *Eisenhower and the American Crusades*, 444–446.

10. Burk, *Eisenhower Administration and Black Civil Rights*, 207; Leuchtenburg, "The White House and Black America," in *Have We Overcome?*, 122; Fred P. Graham, "'Jim Crow Justice' on Trial in South," *New York Times*, October 31, 1965, reprinted in *The Negro in 20th Century America*, 406; "No Remedy in Law," *New Republic* 133 (November 21, 1955): 5.

11. *New York Times*, November 21, 1955, p. 33, and January 5, 1956, p. 22.

12. E. Frederic Morrow, *Black Man in the White House: A Diary of the Eisenhower Years* (New York: Coward-McCann, 1963), 28–30, 46; Ambrose, *Eisenhower*, 2:304–305; Belknap, *Federal Law and Southern Order*, 37; Chafe, *Unfinished Journey*, 153–156.

13. Belknap, *Federal Law*, 37, 40.

14. *New York Times*, November 11, 1955, p. 17, and December 7, 1955, p. 30.

15. Parmet, *Eisenhower and the American Crusades*, 444–446; Burk, *Eisenhower Administration and Black Civil Rights*, 208–209.

16. Steven F. Lawson, *Black Ballots: Voting Rights in the South, 1944–1969* (New York: Columbia University Press, 1976), 146–151; Belknap, *Federal Law and Southern Order,* 40–44.

17. Eastland, quoted in Arthur M. Schlesinger, Jr., *Robert Kennedy and His Times* (Boston: Houghton Mifflin, 1978), 234.

18. Herbert Shapiro, *White Violence and Black Response: From Reconstruction to Montgomery* (Amherst: University of Massachusetts Press, 1988), 353–354; Rowan, *Go South to Sorrow,* 49.

19. Belknap, *Federal Law,* 36–37.

20. Richard Gid Powers, *Secrecy and Power: The Life of J. Edgar Hoover* (New York: Free Press, 1987), 328–329; Don Whitehead, *The FBI Story: A Report to the People* (New York: Random House, 1956), 257–258.

21. Jack Greenberg, *Race Relations and American Law* (New York: Columbia University Press, 1959), 313, 322; Belknap, *Federal Law,* 32.

22. David J. Garrow, *The FBI and Martin Luther King, Jr.: From "Solo" to Memphis* (New York: W. W. Norton, 1981), 152–153; Sanford J. Ungar, *FBI* (Boston: Little, Brown, 1976), 255–256, 328, 408–409, 410.

23. Hoover, quoted in ibid., 408.

24. William Manchester, *The Glory and the Dream: A Narrative History of America, 1932–1972* (Boston: Little, Brown, 1974), 738.

25. Richard J. Daley, quoted in *Greenwood Commonwealth,* September 2, 1955, p. 1.

26. John T. Elliff, "Aspects of Federal Civil Rights Enforcement: The Justice Department and the F.B.I., 1939–1964," in *Law in American History,* ed. Donald Fleming and Bernard Bailyn (Boston: Little, Brown, 1971), 644–647; Burk, *Eisenhower Administration and Black Civil Rights,* 213; Mary Frances Berry, *Black Resistance/White Law: A History of Constitutional Racism in America* (New York: Appleton-Century-Crofts, 1971), 180; *New York Times,* September 4, 1955, sec. 5, p. 9.

27. Carter, *First Person Rural,* 62.

28. Harold R. Isaacs, *The New World of Negro Americans* (London: Phoenix House, 1963), 6–7.

29. Hall, *Revolt Against Chivalry,* 163, 196.

30. Stevenson, quoted in *New York Times,* February 13, 1956, p. 15; Wilkins, *Standing Fast,* 231–232.

31. Ambrose, *Eisenhower,* 2:306, 307.

32. *New York Times,* September 26, 1955, p. 10, September 30, 1955, p. 18, and October 25, 1955, p. 27.

33. Harry Barnard, Letter to the Editor, *Nation* 181 (September 24, 1955): 252.

34. "Strengthen Justice Department's Civil Rights Powers," October 22, 1955, press release, Archives of the American Jewish Committee; *New York Times*, October 22, 1955, p. 40.

35. Belknap, *Federal Law*, 40.

36. Jamie L. Whitten to John Whitten, n.d., and to John Whitten et al., September 27, 1955, copies in Huie Papers.

37. Testimony of Representative Jamie L. Whitten before House of Representatives Subcommittee No. 5 of Judiciary Committee, February 14, 1957, in Racial Problems (Commentary) Folder, Box 6 of Race Relations Collection, 1954–1959, 5–6.

38. Burk, *Eisenhower Administration and Black Civil Rights*, 212–226; Whitaker, "Case Study in Southern Justice," 183–185; *Congressional Record*, 84th Congress, 2nd Session, 1957, CII, part 10, pp. 13182, 13338; part 7, pp. 8644, 8705, 9194, 9211, 9189; part 8, p. 10998, cited in ibid., 184–185.

39. Val Washington, quoted in Burk, *Eisenhower Administration*, 225.

40. Robert Alan Aurthur, Rod Serling, et al., *The Relation of the Writer to Television* (Santa Barbara, Calif.: Center for the Study of Democratic Institutions, 1960), 10–12; Erik Barnouw, *The Image Empire*, vol. 3 of *A History of Broadcasting in the United States* (New York: Oxford University Press, 1970), 35–36.

Chapter 6. Revolution

1. "Till Protest Meeting," *The Crisis* 62 (November 1955): 546; Williams, *Eyes on the Prize*, 52.

2. *New York Times*, September 25, 1955, p. 33, and October 12, 1955, p. 62.

3. *New York Times*, September 30, 1955, p. 18.

4. *Jackson Daily News*, October 15, 1955, p. 1.

5. Ibid; *Greenwood Commonwealth*, September 26, 1955, p. 1; *Jackson Clarion-Ledger*, September 25, 1955, sec. 1, p. 10; *Jackson Daily News*, October 11, 1955, p. 3.

6. *New York Times*, April 16, 1956, p. 8; Gerald Horne, *Black and Red: W. E. B. Du Bois and the Afro-American Response to the Cold War, 1944–1963* (Albany: State University of New York Press, 1986), 233.

7. W. E. B. Du Bois, "The American Negro and Communism" (1958), in *Against Racism: Unpublished Essays, Papers, Addresses, 1887–1961*, ed.

Herbert Aptheker (Amherst: University of Massachusetts Press, 1985), 295.

8. Stone, *Haunted Fifties,* 107–109.

9. James O. Eastland, *We've Reached the Era of Judicial Tyranny* (Winona: Citizens' Councils of Mississippi, 1956), 3, 4, 5; Lord, *The Past That Would Not Die,* 68; Goldfield, *Promised Land,* 86–87.

10. Williams, *Eyes on the Prize,* 57.

11. Aldon D. Morris, *The Origins of the Civil Rights Movement: Black Communities Organizing for Change* (New York: Free Press, 1984), 51; Parks, quoted in *Jackson Clarion-Ledger,* August 25, 1985, sec. A., p. 1.

12. William Bradford Huie to Martin Luther King, Jr., April 10, 1959, and King to Huie, April 21, 1959, in File Drawer IV, 4 of Papers of Martin Luther King, Jr., at Boston University.

13. Harvard Sitkoff, *The Struggle for Black Equality, 1954–1980* (New York: Hill and Wang, 1981), 48–49.

14. Lerone Bennett, Jr., *What Manner of Man: A Biography of Martin Luther King, Jr.* (Chicago: Johnson Publishing, 1964), 58; J. Mills Thornton to author, September 16, 1985; Martin Luther King, Jr., *Stride Toward Freedom: The Montgomery Story* (New York: Harper Perennial, 1964), 156–157.

15. Mamie T. Bradley, quoted in Williams, *Eyes on the Prize,* 57; Milton Viorst, *Fire in the Streets: America in the 1960's* (New York: Simon & Schuster, 1979), 99.

16. "1963 Seen as Deadline for Racial Settlement," *Memphis Press-Scimitar,* May 18, 1959, n. p., in Box 5 of Race Relations Collection, 1954–1970, University of Mississippi.

17. Simpson, "Reflections," 199–200; Williams, *Eyes on the Prize,* 57.

18. Lord, *The Past That Would Not Die,* 91–93.

19. Clayborne Carson, *In Struggle: SNCC and the Black Awakening of the 1960s* (Cambridge: Harvard University Press, 1981), 15, 18.

20. Joyce Ladner, "The South: Old-New Land," *New York Times,* May 17, 1979, p. 23; George A. Sewell and Margaret L. Dwight, *Mississippi Black History Makers* (Jackson: University Press of Mississippi, 1984), 246.

21. Anne Moody, *Coming of Age in Mississippi* (New York: Dell, 1968), 121–127.

22. Ibid., 129–138; Bloom, *Class, Race, and the Civil Rights Movement,* 134–135.

23. Holland, "Memories of the Mississippi Delta," 246.

24. Maya Angelou, *The Heart of a Woman* (New York: Random House, 1981), 32.

25. Margaret Edds, *Free at Last: What Really Happened When Civil Rights Came to Southern Politics* (Bethesda, Md.: Adler and Adler, 1987), 1–2, 4–5; *Jackson Clarion-Ledger,* August 25, 1955, sec. A, p. 4.

26. Muhammad Ali, with Richard Durham, *The Greatest: My Own Story* (New York: Random House, 1975), 34.

27. Ibid., 34–35.

28. Robert Lipsyte, *Free to be Muhammad Ali* (New York: Harper & Row, 1978), 19–21.

29. Cleveland Sellers, with Robert Terrell, *The River of No Return* (New York: William Morrow, 1973), 14–15.

30. Morris, *Origins of the Civil Rights Movement,* v, 141–147.

31. James Forman, *The Making of Black Revolutionaries: A Personal Account* (New York: Macmillan, 1972), 93; Julius Lester, *Look Out, Whitey! Black Power's Gon' Get Your Mama!* (New York: Grove Press, 1969), 97; Amzie Moore in Raines, *My Soul is Rested,* 253–254.

32. Mary King, *Freedom Song: A Personal Story of the 1960s Civil Rights Movement* (New York: William Morrow, 1987), 251, 254.

33. Hampton, quoted in "Casting Their 'Eyes,'" *Boston Phoenix,* January 13, 1987, sec. 3, p. 21.

34. Rowan, *Go South to Sorrow,* 59.

35. Carter, *First Person Rural,* 98.

36. James Oliver Horton, "Comment," in *The State of Afro-American History: Past, Present, and Future,* ed. Darlene Clark Hine (Baton Rouge: Louisiana State University Press, 1986), 134–135.

37. Thomas R. Brooks, *Walls Come Tumbling Down: A History of the Civil Rights Movement, 1940–1970* (Englewood Cliffs, N.J.: Prentice-Hall, 1974), 181–182.

38. Bob Dylan, "The Death of Emmett Till," in *Writings and Drawings* (New York: Knopf, 1973), 19.

39. Shelby Steele, "On Being Black and Middle Class," *Commentary* 85 (January 1988): 45.

40. Myrlie Evers, *For Us, the Living,* 173–174.

41. Oscar Handlin, *Fire-Bell in the Night: The Crisis in Civil Rights* (Boston: Little, Brown, 1964), 8–9; Arnold M. Rose, "The American Negro Problem in the Context of Social Change," in *Roots of Rebellion: The Evolution of Black Politics and Protest Since World War II,* ed. Richard P. Young (New York: Harper & Row, 1970), 62.

42. Harold C. Fleming, "The Law Gains Ground," *New South* 6 (January 1951): 8; Smead, *Blood Justice*, 104n.

43. Myrdal, *An American Dilemma*, 566; Parsons, "Violence and Caste in Southern Justice," 463–464; Burns, quoted in Berry and Blassingame, *Long Memory*, 125.

44. Page, *The Negro: The Southerner's Problem*, 115.

45. Richard Maxwell Brown, "Southern Violence vs. the Civil Rights Movement," in *Perspectives on the American South*, ed. Merle Black and John Shelton Reed (New York: Gordon and Breach Science Publishers, 1981), 1:52.

46. Evers, *For Us, the Living*, 279–280, 287, 367–368.

47. James R. McGovern, *Anatomy of a Lynching: The Killing of Claude Neal* (Baton Rouge: Louisiana State University Press, 1982), 141n; Silver, *Mississippi: The Closed Society*, 253.

48. Louis Burnham, *Behind the Lynching of Emmett Louis Till* (New York: Freedom Associates, 1955), 5; Evers, *For Us, the Living*, 372.

49. William Bradford Huie, *Three Lives for Mississippi* (New York: WCC Books, 1965), 18–31.

50. King, *Stride Toward Freedom*, 194; King, quoted in Coretta Scott King, *My Life with Martin Luther King, Jr.* (New York: Holt, Rinehart & Winston, 1970), 328.

51. James Meredith, *Three Years in Mississippi* (Bloomington: Indiana University Press, 1966), 323.

52. Eastland, *We've Reached the Era of Judicial Tyranny*, 7.

53. Malcolm X, quoted in Peter Goldman, *The Death and Life of Malcolm X* (New York: Harper Perennial, 1974), 176; Alex Haley, *The Autobiography of Malcolm X* (New York: Grove Press, 1965), 1–2, 10–11, 150.

54. C. Eric Lincoln to Hugh Stephen Whitaker, October 5, 1962, quoted in Whitaker, "Case Study in Southern Justice," 182.

55. Martin Luther King, Jr., "Who Speaks for the South?", *Liberation* 2 (March 1958): 13–14, reprinted in *A Testament of Hope: The Essential Writings of Martin Luther King, Jr.*, ed. James Melvin Washington (New York: Harper & Row, 1986), 92.

56. David L. Cohn, "Greenville Filibusters Against Father Time," *New York Times*, March 20, 1949, sec. 6, p. 64.

57. Rayford W. Logan, *The Betrayal of the Negro: From Rutherford B. Hayes to Woodrow Wilson* (New York: Collier, 1965), 195; United States Statutes at Large, 1968, 82:76, quoted in McGovern, *Anatomy of a Lynching*, 147.

58. *New York Times*, March 8, 1987, p. 24, and February 21, 1988, p. 45.

Chapter 7. Race and Sex

1. Eldridge Cleaver, *Soul on Ice* (New York: Dell, 1968), 3–4, 10–11; "L'af-faire Till in the French Press," *The Crisis:* 601.

2. Cleaver, *Soul on Ice,* 11–14.

3. Ibid., vi; Michele Wallace, *Black Macho and the Myth of the Super-woman* (New York: Dial, 1979), 27–28.

4. Susan Brownmiller, *Against Our Will: Men, Women and Rape* (New York: Simon & Schuster, 1975), 247–248.

5. Sara Davidson, "Foremothers," *Esquire* 80 (July 1973): 159; Weatherby, *Breaking the Silence,* 18; Smead, *Blood Justice,* 13–14, 91, 178, 186–187.

6. Brownmiller, *Against Our Will,* 245.

7. Jean Stafford, "Brownmiller on Rape: A Scare Worse than Death," *Esquire* 84 (November 1975): 52.

8. Quoted in Pauli Murray, "The Liberation of Black Women," in *Voices of the New Feminism,* ed. Mary Lou Thompson (Boston: Beacon, 1970), 92.

9. Goldman, *Malcolm X,* 180.

10. Brownmiller, *Against Our Will,* 247.

11. Angela Y. Davis, *Women, Race and Class* (New York: Random House, 1981), 178–182.

12. Ibid., 197.

13. Virginia Foster Durr, "The Emancipation of Pure, White, Southern Womanhood," *New South* 26 (Winter 1971): 51–52, 54.

14. Ames, quoted in Jacquelyn Dowd Hall, "'The Mind That Burns in Each Body': Women, Rape, and Racial Violence," in *Powers of Desire: The Politics of Sexuality,* ed. Ann Snitow, Christine Stansell, and Sharon Thompson (New York: Monthly Review Press, 1983), 340.

15. Lillian Smith, *Killers of the Dream* (Garden City, N.Y.: Doubleday, Anchor, 1963 [1949]), 126–127; Hall, *Revolt Against Chivalry,* 337–340.

16. Hall, *Revolt Against Chivalry,* 340; Sara Evans, *Personal Politics: The Roots of Women's Liberation in the Civil Rights Movement and the New Left* (New York: Knopf, 1979), 78–80, 88, 98–99; Callahan, quoted in Dan T. Carter, *Scottsboro: A Tragedy of the American South* (New York: Oxford University Press, 1971), 297.

17. Shapiro, *White Violence and Black Response,* 395–396, 397, 513 n. 1.

18. Johnson, *Along This Way,* 170; William Peters, *The Southern Temper* (Garden City, N.Y.: Doubleday, 1959), 190–205.

19. Hall, "The Mind That Burns in Each Body," 343.

20. Shapiro, *White Violence and Black Response*, 397.

21. *New York Times*, October 30, 1955, p. 86; Lt. Col. James G. Chesnutt, Office of the Chief of Information, Department of the Army, letter to William Bradford Huie, in Huie Papers; Huie, *Wolf Whistle*, 47–50; *Memphis Commercial Appeal*, October 16, 1955, sec. 1, p. 4; *Jackson Daily News*, October 15, 1955, p. 1.

22. *Jackson Daily News*, October 15, 1955, p. 1; *Memphis Commercial Appeal*, October 16, 1955, sec. 1, p. 4; Whitaker, "Case Study in Southern Justice," 158; Simpson, "Reflections," 190n; J. J. Breland to Fred Sullins, October 18, 1955, copy in Huie Papers.

23. Patterson in Raines, *My Soul is Rested*, 328.

24. "In Memoriam, Emmett Till," *Life* 39 (October 10, 1955): 48; Huie, *Wolf Whistle*, 47.

25. Letters to the Editor, *Life* 39 (October 31, 1955): 17–18.

26. William Faulkner to Harold Ober, January 18, 1956, in *Selected Letters of William Faulkner*, ed. Joseph Blotner (New York: Random House, 1977), 392–393; Warren, *Segregation*, 25.

27. Wilkins, quoted in Huie, *Wolf Whistle*, 49.

28. Alice Walker, "Advancing Luna—and Ida B. Wells," in *You Can't Keep A Good Woman Down* (San Diego: Harcourt Brace Jovanovich, 1981); 92–93, 102.

29. Morrison, quoted in Margaret Croyden, "Toni Morrison Tries Her Hand at Playwriting," *New York Times*, December 29, 1985, sec. 2, pp. 6, 18; Harlow Robinson, "Dreams of a Prophetic Past," *American Theatre* 2 (January 1986): 18–19; Robert Brustein, "Everybody's Protest Play," in *Seasons of Discontent: Dramatic Opinions, 1959–1965* (New York: Simon & Schuster, 1965), 162.

30. Morrison, quoted in Croyden, "Toni Morrison Tries Her Hand at Playwriting," p. 6.

31. Kennedy, quoted in Croyden, *New York Times*, p. 16; Robinson, "Dreams of a Prophetic Past," *American Theatre*, 18–19.

32. Toni Morrison, *Song of Solomon* (New York: Knopf, 1977), 80–82.

33. Fern Marja Eckman, *The Furious Passage of James Baldwin* (New York: Popular Library, 1966), 202–206.

34. James Baldwin, "Notes for *Blues*," in *Blues for Mr. Charlie* (New York: Laurel, 1976), 5–6.

35. Day, *Sexual Life Between Blacks and Whites*, 2.

36. Baldwin, quoted in Eckman, *Furious Passage of James Baldwin*, 195–203; Day, *Sexual Life*, 2; Tom F. Driver, "Barking Off Cue, or Mr. Charlie's Dilemma," *Village Voice*, June 4, 1964, pp. 16–17.

37. James Baldwin, *The Evidence of Things Not Seen* (New York: Holt, Rinehart & Winston, 1985), 40.

38. Nathan Glazer, "The Fire This Time," *New Republic* 193 (December 30, 1985): 42–44.

39. Quoted in Fred Harwell, *A True Deliverance* (New York: Knopf, 1980), 200.

40. James Reston, Jr., *The Innocence of Joan Little: A Southern Mystery* (New York: Times Books, 1977), xii; Harwell, *A True Deliverance*, 278.

41. Paul, quoted in Reston, *The Innocence of Joan Little*, 321.

42. Harwell, *A True Deliverance*, 280; Reston, *The Innocence of Joan Little*, 278–279.

43. Paul, quoted in Reston, *The Innocence of Joan Little*, 328, and in Harwell, *A True Deliverance*, 245, 279.

44. Harwell, *A True Deliverance*, 281.

Chapter 8. No Longer White

1. Hall, *Revolt Against Chivalry*, 137.

2. Wright, quoted in Addison Gayle, *Richard Wright: Ordeal of a Native Son* (Garden City, N.Y.: Doubleday, Anchor, 1980), 262; W. E. B. Du Bois, *Dusk of Dawn: An Essay Toward an Autobiography of a Race Concept* (New York: Schocken, 1968), 29, 55–56, 67, 223, 241, 251, 264–266.

3. Harris, *Exorcising Blackness*, 35, 69–71, 72–76, 80–81, 83–84, 95, 104–128, 129, 184, passim.

4. Ralph Ginzburg, *100 Years of Lynching* (New York: Lancer, 1962), pp. 5–6, 240–243; Victor S. Navasky, *Kennedy Justice* (New York: Atheneum, 1971), 391; Charles Herbert Stember, *Sexual Racism: The Emotional Barrier to an Integrated Society* (New York: Elsevier, 1976), 10.

5. Richard Hofstadter, "Reflections on Violence in the United States," in *American Violence: A Documentary History*, ed. Hofstadter and Michael Wallace (New York: Knopf, 1970), 4, 20.

6. Darlene Clark Hine, "Lifting the Veil, Shattering the Silence: Black Women's History in Slavery and Freedom," in *The State of Afro-American History*, ed. Hine, 241–242; Donald, review of McLemore in *American Historical Review*, 1524.

7. Hall, *Revolt Against Chivalry*, 137; McGovern, *Anatomy of a Lynching*, 3.

8. Zangrando, *The NAACP Crusade Against Lynching*, vii.

9. Hall, *Revolt Against Chivalry*, 137.

10. Ibid., 139, 302 n. 34; Emile Durkheim, *The Division of Labor* (Glencoe, Ill.: Free Press, 1947), 70–133.

11. Hall, *Revolt Against Chivalry*, 139.

12. Zangrando, *The NAACP Crusade Against Lynching*, 4, 8, 9.

13. Silver, *Mississippi: The Closed Society*, 8n; Smead, *Blood Justice*, 201.

14. Sheldon Hackney, "Southern Violence," *American Historical Review* 74 (February 1969): 924–925.

15. McGovern, *Anatomy of a Lynching*, 74.

16. Hall, *Revolt Against Chivalry*, 144–145.

17. McGovern, *Anatomy of a Lynching*, 140.

18. Smead, *Blood Justice*, 13, 39, 56, 91–92, 202.

19. Ibid., pp. 22, 32, 102, 167.

20. Myrdal, *An American Dilemma*, 565; William Alexander Percy, *Lanterns on the Levee: Recollections of a Planter's Son* (Baton Rouge: Louisiana State University Press, 1973 [1941]), 306–309.

21. Lord, *The Past That Would Not Die*, 33.

22. Barnett, quoted in Sherrill, *Gothic Politics in the Deep South*, 200.

23. Lord, *The Past That Would Not Die*, 33; Bartley, *Rise of Massive Resistance*, 10; Silver, *Mississippi: The Closed Society*, 72; William L. Giles, "The Agricultural Revolution in the Delta," *Journal of Mississippi History* 31 (May 1969): 86–87.

24. Fleming, quoted in Bartley, *Rise of Massive Resistance*, 17; Peters, *Southern Temper*, 41–42.

25. C. Vann Woodward, *Thinking Back: The Perils of Writing History* (Baton Rouge: Louisiana State University Press, 1986), 68; Clark, *Emerging South*, x–xiii, 8–9.

26. Morris, *Terrains of the Heart*, 10.

27. Lord, *The Past That Would Not Die*, 32, 33, 41, 48, 49.

28. Cobb, quoted in Theodore Rosengarten, *All God's Dangers: The Life of Nate Shaw* (New York: Knopf, 1974), 537; Kirby, *Rural Worlds Lost*, xiv, xv.

29. Brady, *Black Monday*, 47–48.

30. Willie Morris, *North Toward Home* (Boston: Houghton Mifflin, 1967), 246.

31. Silver, *Mississippi: The Closed Society*, 62; Stember, *Sexual Racism*, 25.

32. Interview with Willie Morris in *Mississippi Writers Talking*, vol. 2, ed. John Griffin Jones (Jackson: University Press of Mississippi, 1983), 101, 104; Morris, *Terrains of the Heart*, 29.

33. *New York Times*, July 26, 1987, pp. 1, 24.

34. Robert Penn Warren, *Who Speaks for the Negro?* (New York: Random House, 1966), 30.

35. Quoted in Logan, *Betrayal of the Negro*, 288; Milam, quoted in Huie, *Wolf Whistle*, 37–38.

36. Williams, *Eyes on the Prize*, 208; Warren, *Who Speaks for the Negro?*, 49, 95, 97; Jack Newfield, *A Prophetic Minority* (New York: Signet, 1967), 50–51, 78.

37. Dick Gregory, with Robert Lipsyte, *Nigger: An Autobiography* (New York: Pocket Books, 1965), 167–176.

38. Brown, "Southern Violence vs. the Civil Rights Movement," 51–53, 64–65.

39. Barry Feinberg and Ronald Kasrils, ed., *Bertrand Russell's America, 1945–1970* (Boston: South End Press, 1983), 221–222.

40. Newfield, *Prophetic Minority*, 48.

41. James Baldwin, *Notes of a Native Son* (New York: Bantam, 1964), 149.

42. *United States v. Dogan, et al.*, 314 F. 2d. 267 (1963), cited in Whitaker, "Case Study in Southern Justice," 174–175; Charles Miller, ed., "The Mississippi Summer Project Remembered: The Stephen Mitchell Bingham Letter," *Journal of Mississippi History* 47 (November 1985): 306.

43. Shostak, "Crosby Smith," 325.

44. Larsson, "Land of the Till Murder Revisited," 57; Whitaker, "Case Study in Southern Justice," 163–165; Sewell and Dwight, *Mississippi Black History Makers*, 4–5; Morris, *Terrains of the Heart*, 14.

45. Edds, *Free at Last*, 9.

46. McMillen, *Citizens' Council*, 265–266.

47. Shostak, "Crosby Smith," 324.

48. Whitaker, "Case Study in Southern Justice," 175.

49. Larsson, "Land of the Till Murder Revisited," 4–5; Huie, "What's Happened to the Emmett Till Killers?", 65.

50. Huie in Raines, *My Soul is Rested*, 432; Shostak "Crosby Smith," 324; Huie, "What's Happened to the Emmett Till Killers?", 67–68.

51. Quoted in "L'affaire Till in the French Press," *The Crisis*: 599–600.

52. *Jackson Clarion-Ledger*, August 25, 1985, sec. H, pp. 1, 3.

53. Williams, *Eyes on the Prize*, 288; Whitaker, "Case Study in Southern Justice," 160–162; Huie, "What's Happened to the Emmett Till Killers?", 67; *Jackson Clarion-Ledger*, August 25, 1985, sec. H, pp. 1, 3.

54. Shostak, "Crosby Smith," 325.

55. *Jackson Clarion-Ledger*, August 25, 1955, sec. H, p. 1.

56. Mamie Mobley, quoted in *Huntsville Times*, July 19, 1987, sec. B, p. 1.

57. *Jackson Clarion-Ledger*, August 25, 1985, sec. A, p. 1; Hirsch, *Making the Second Ghetto*, 5, 42, 51–53, 65–66, 79–80.

58. *Jackson Clarion-Ledger*, August 25, 1985, sec. A, p. 1.

59. Moore in Raines, *My Soul is Rested*, 253–254; "An Interview with Congressman Charles Diggs," in Williams, *Eyes on the Prize*, 49; Louis E. Lomax, *The Negro Revolt* (New York: Harper & Row, 1962), 76; Smead, *Blood Justice*, 203.

60. Narration by Julian Bond and interview with Fred Shuttlesworth in *Eyes on the Prize*, Episode 1.

61. Popham and Minor, quoted in *Jackson Clarion-Ledger*, August 25, 1985, section A, p. 1.

62. Reminiscence of John Chancellor in "Covering the South: A National Symposium on the Media and the Civil Rights Movement," University of Mississippi, April 3, 1987 (telecast on C-Span).

63. Holmes, quoted in Edmund Wilson, *Patriotic Gore; Studies in the Literature of the American Civil War* (New York: Oxford University Press, 1966), 778.

64. Smead, *Blood Justice*, 30–31; Patterson in Raines, *My Soul is Rested*, 327–328.

65. Wakefield, *Between the Lines*, 150.

66. Warren Breed, "Comparative Newspaper Handling of the Emmett Till Case," *Journalism Quarterly* 35 (Summer 1958): 291–298.

Bibliography

Books

Abbott, Dorothy, ed. *Mississippi Writers: Reflections of Childhood and Youth*, vol. 1. Jackson: University Press of Mississippi, 1985.

Ali, Muhammad, with Richard Durham. *The Greatest: My Own Story*. New York: Random House, 1975.

Ambrose, Stephen E. *Eisenhower: The President*. New York: Simon & Schuster, 1984.

Angelou, Maya. *The Heart of a Woman*. New York: Random House, 1981.

Arsenault, Raymond. *The Wild Ass of the Ozarks: Jeff Davis and the Social Bases of Southern Politics*. Philadelphia: Temple University Press, 1984.

Aurthur, Robert Alan, Rod Serling, et al. *The Relation of the Writer to Television*. Santa Barbara, Calif.: Center for the Study of Democratic Institutions, 1960.

Ayers, Edward L. *Vengeance and Justice: Crime and Punishment in the 19th-Century American South*. New York: Oxford University Press, 1984.

Baldwin, James. *Blues for Mr. Charlie*. New York: Laurel, 1976.

———. *The Evidence of Things Not Seen*. New York: Holt, Rinehart and Winston, 1985.

———. *Notes of a Native Son*. New York: Bantam, 1964.

Bardolph, Richard, ed. *The Civil Rights Record: Black Americans and the Law, 1849–1970*. New York: Thomas Y. Crowell, 1970.

Barnouw, Erik. *The Image Empire*. New York: Oxford University Press, 1970.

Bartley, Numan V. *The Rise of Massive Resistance: Race and Politics in the South During the 1950's*. Baton Rouge: Louisiana State University Press, 1969.

Belknap, Michal R. *Federal Law and Southern Order: Racial Violence and Constitutional Conflict in the Post-Brown South.* Athens: University of Georgia Press, 1987.

Bennett, Lerone, Jr. *Before the Mayflower: A History of the Negro in America, 1619–1964.* Baltimore: Penguin, 1966.

———. *What Manner of Man: A Biography of Martin Luther King, Jr.* Chicago: Johnson Publishing, 1964.

Berger, Peter, Brigitte Berger, and Hansfried Kellner. *The Homeless Mind: Modernization and Consciousness.* New York: Random House, 1973.

Berry, Mary Frances. *Black Resistance/White Law: A History of Constitutional Racism in America.* New York: Appleton-Century-Crofts, 1971.

Berry, Mary Frances, and John Blassingame. *Long Memory: The Black Experience in America.* New York: Oxford University Press, 1982.

Bettersworth, John K. *Mississippi: A History.* Austin, Tex.: Steck, 1959.

Black, Earl. *Southern Governors and Civil Rights: Racial Segregation as a Campaign Issue in the Second Reconstruction.* Cambridge: Harvard University Press, 1976.

Bloom, Jack M. *Class, Race, and the Civil Rights Movement.* Bloomington: Indiana University Press, 1987.

Blotner, Joseph. *Faulkner: A Biography,* two volumes. New York: Random House, 1974. (One-volume edition [1984].)

Brady, Tom P. *Black Monday.* Winona, Miss.: Association of Citizens' Councils, 1955.

Brooks, Thomas R. *Walls Come Tumbling Down: A History of the Civil Rights Movement, 1940–1970.* Englewood Cliffs, N.J.: Prentice-Hall, 1974.

Brown, Richard Maxwell. "Southern Violence vs. the Civil Rights Movement." In *Perspectives on the American South,* edited by Merle Black and John Shelton Reed, vol. 1, 49–69. New York: Gordon and Breach Scientific Publishers, 1981.

Brownmiller, Susan. *Against Our Will: Men, Women and Rape.* New York: Simon & Schuster, 1975.

Brustein, Robert. *Seasons of Discontent: Dramatic Opinions, 1959–1965.* New York: Simon & Schuster, 1965.

Burk, Robert Fredrick. *The Eisenhower Administration and Black Civil Rights.* Knoxville: University of Tennessee Press, 1984.

Burnham, Louis. *Behind the Lynching of Emmett Louis Till.* New York: Freedom Associates, 1955.

Cable, George W. *The Grandissimes: A Story of Creole Life.* New York: Charles Scribner's Sons, 1880.

Carson, Clayborne. *In Struggle: SNCC and the Black Awakening of the 1960s.* Cambridge: Harvard University Press, 1981.

Carter, Dan T. *Scottsboro: A Tragedy of the American South.* New York: Oxford University Press, 1971.

Carter, Hodding. *First Person Rural.* Garden City, N.Y.: Doubleday, 1963.

Carter, Hodding III. *The South Strikes Back.* Garden City, N.Y.: Doubleday, 1959.

Cash, Wilbur J. *The Mind of the South.* New York: Knopf, 1941.

Catledge, Turner. *My Life and The Times.* New York: Harper & Row, 1971.

Chafe, William H. *The Unfinished Journey: America Since World War II.* New York: Oxford University Press, 1986.

Clark, Thomas D. *The Emerging South.* New York: Oxford University Press, 1961.

Cleaver, Eldridge. *Soul on Ice.* New York: Dell, 1968.

Cleghorn, Reese. "The Segs." In *Smiling Through the Apocalypse: Esquire's History of the Sixties,* edited by Harold Hayes, 651–668. New York: McCall, 1969.

Cohn, David L. *Where I Was Born and Raised.* South Bend, Ind.: University of Notre Dame Press, 1967.

Cook, James G. *The Segregationists.* New York: Appleton-Century-Crofts, 1962.

Cowley, Malcolm, ed. *Writers at Work: The Paris Review Interviews,* First Series. New York: Viking, 1959.

Daniel, Pete. *Standing at the Crossroads: Southern Life since 1900.* New York: Hill and Wang, 1986.

Davis, Angela Y. *Women, Race and Class.* New York: Random House, 1981.

Day, Beth. *Sexual Life Between Blacks and Whites: The Roots of Racism.* New York: World, 1972.

Degler, Carl N. *Place Over Time: The Continuity of Southern Distinctiveness.* Baton Rouge: Louisiana State University Press, 1977.

Dittmer, John. "The Politics of the Mississippi Movement, 1954–1964." In *The Civil Rights Movement in America,* edited by Charles W. Eagles, 65–93. Jackson: University Press of Mississippi, 1986.

Dollard, John. *Caste and Class in a Southern Town.* Garden City, N.Y.: Doubleday, 1949.

Du Bois, W. E. B. "The American Negro and Communism" (1958). In *Against Racism: Unpublished Essays, Papers, Addresses, 1887–1961,* edited by Herbert Aptheker, 294–298. Amherst: University of Massachusetts Press, 1985.

———. *Dusk of Dawn: An Essay Toward an Autobiography of a Race Concept.* New York: Schocken, 1968.

Duberman, Martin. *In White America.* New York: Signet, 1964.

Dunbar, Anthony P. *Against the Grain: Southern Radicals and Prophets, 1929–1959.* Charlottesville: University Press of Virginia, 1981.

Durkheim, Emile. *The Division of Labor.* Glencoe, Ill.: Free Press, 1947.

Dylan, Bob. *Writings and Drawings.* New York: Knopf, 1973.

Eastland, James O. *We've Reached the Era of Judicial Tyranny.* Winona: Citizens' Councils of Mississippi, 1956.

Eckman, Fern Marja. *The Furious Passage of James Baldwin.* New York: Popular Library, 1966.

Edds, Margaret. *Free at Last: What Really Happened When Civil Rights Came to Southern Politics.* Bethesda, Md.: Adler and Adler, 1987.

Eisenhower, Dwight D. *White House Years: Mandate for Change, 1953–1956.* Garden City, N.Y.: Doubleday, 1963.

Elliff, John T. "Aspects of Federal Civil Rights Enforcement: The Justice Department and the F.B.I., 1939–1964." In *Law in American History,* edited by Donald Fleming and Bernard Bailyn, 605–673. Boston: Little, Brown, 1971.

Evans, Sara. *Personal Politics: The Roots of Women's Liberation in the Civil Rights Movement and the New Left.* New York: Knopf, 1979.

Evers, Mrs. Medgar, with William Peters. *For Us, the Living.* Garden City, N.Y.: Doubleday, 1967.

Faulkner, William. *Essays, Speeches and Public Letters.* Edited by James B. Meriwether. New York: Random House, 1965.

———. *Selected Letters of William Faulkner.* Edited by Joseph Blotner. New York: Random House, 1977.

Faulkner, William, et al. *Three Views of the Segregation Decisions.* Atlanta: Southern Regional Council, 1956.

Fiedler, Leslie A. *The Inadvertent Epic: From Uncle Tom's Cabin to Roots.* New York: Simon & Schuster, 1979.

Forman, James. *The Making of Black Revolutionaries: A Personal Account.* New York: Macmillan, 1972.

Franklin, John Hope, and Isidore Starr, ed. *The Negro in 20th Century America.* New York: Vintage, 1967.

Fredrickson, George M. *The Black Image in the White Mind: The Debate on Afro-American Character and Destiny, 1817–1914.* New York: Harper & Row, 1971.

Friedman, Lawrence J. *The White Savage: Racial Fantasies in the Postbellum South*. Englewood Cliffs, N.J.: Prentice-Hall, 1970.

Garrow, David J. *The FBI and Martin Luther King, Jr.: From "Solo" to Memphis*. New York: W. W. Norton, 1981.

Gayle, Addison. *Richard Wright: Ordeal of a Native Son*. Garden City, N.Y.: Doubleday, 1980.

Ginzburg, Ralph. *100 Years of Lynching*. New York: Lancer, 1962.

Goldfield, David R. *Promised Land: The South Since 1945*. Arlington Heights, Ill.: Harlan Davidson, 1987.

Goldman, Peter. *The Death and Life of Malcolm X*. New York: Harper & Row, 1974.

Greenberg, Jack. *Race Relations and American Law*. New York: Columbia University Press, 1959.

Gregory, Dick, with Robert Lipsyte. *Nigger: An Autobiography*. New York: Pocket Books, 1965.

Griffin, John Howard. *Black Like Me*. New York: Signet, 1963.

Haley, Alex. *The Autobiography of Malcolm X*. New York: Grove Press, 1965.

Hall, Jacquelyn Dowd. "'The Mind That Burns in Each Body': Women, Rape, and Racial Violence." In *Powers of Desire: The Politics of Sexuality*, edited by Ann Snitow, Christine Stansell, and Sharon Thompson, 328–349. New York: Monthly Review Press, 1983.

———. *Revolt Against Chivalry: Jessie Daniel Ames and the Women's Campaign Against Lynching*. New York: Columbia University Press, 1979.

Handlin, Oscar. *Fire-Bell in the Night: The Crisis in Civil Rights*. Boston: Little, Brown, 1964.

Harkey, Ira B., Jr. *The Smell of Burning Crosses: An Autobiography of a Mississippi Newspaperman*. Jacksonville, Ill.: Harris-Wolfe, 1967.

Harris, Trudier. *Exorcising Blackness: Historical and Literary Lynching and Burning Rituals*. Bloomington: Indiana University Press, 1984.

Harwell, Fred. *A True Deliverance*. New York: Knopf, 1980.

Henry, Lillie Neely, and Jean Conger May. *A History of Tallahatchie County*. Charleston, Miss.: *Mississippi Sun*, 1960.

Hernton, Calvin C. *Sex and Racism in America*. New York: Grove Press, 1966.

Hine, Darlene Clark, ed. *The State of Afro-American History: Past, Present, and Future*. Baton Rouge: Louisiana State University Press, 1986.

Hirsch, Arnold R. *Making the Second Ghetto: Race and Housing in Chicago, 1940–1960*. Cambridge: Cambridge University Press, 1983.

Hofstadter, Richard. "Reflections on Violence in the United States." In *American Violence: A Documentary History,* edited by Hofstadter and Michael Wallace, 3–43. New York: Knopf, 1970.

Horne, Gerald. *Black and Red: W. E. B. Du Bois and the Afro-American Response to the Cold War, 1944–1963.* Albany: State University of New York Press, 1986.

Huie, William Bradford. *Three Lives for Mississippi.* New York: WCC Books, 1965.

———. *Wolf Whistle.* New York: Signet, 1959.

Isaacs, Harold R. *The New World of Negro Americans.* London: Phoenix House, 1963.

Johnson, Charles S. *Growing Up in the Black Belt: Negro Youth in the Rural South.* New York: Schocken, 1967.

Johnson, James Weldon. *Along This Way.* New York: Viking, 1933.

Jones, John Griffin, ed. *Mississippi Writers Talking,* vol. 2. Jackson: University Press of Mississippi, 1983.

Kempton, Murray. *America Comes of Middle Age: Columns, 1950–1962.* Boston: Little, Brown, 1962.

Killian, Lewis M. *White Southerners.* Amherst: University of Massachusetts Press, 1985.

King, Coretta Scott. *My Life with Martin Luther King, Jr.* New York: Holt, Rinehart & Winston, 1970.

King, Martin Luther, Jr. *Stride Toward Freedom: The Montgomery Story.* New York: Harper Perennial, 1964.

———. *A Testament of Hope: The Essential Writings of Martin Luther King, Jr.* Edited by James Melvin Washington. New York: Harper & Row, 1986.

King, Mary. *Freedom Song: A Personal Story of the 1960s Civil Rights Movement.* New York: William Morrow, 1987.

Kirby, Jack Temple. *Rural Worlds Lost: The American South, 1920–1960.* Baton Rouge: Louisiana State University Press, 1987.

Lawson, Steven F. *Black Ballots: Voting Rights in the South, 1944–1969.* New York: Columbia University Press, 1976.

Lester, Julius. *Look Out, Whitey! Black Power's Gon' Get Your Mama!.* New York: Grove Press, 1969.

Leuchtenburg, William E. "The White House and Black America: From Eisenhower to Carter." In *Have We Overcome?: Race Relations since Brown,* edited by Michael V. Namorato, 121–145. Jackson: University Press of Mississippi, 1979.

Lipsyte, Robert. *Free to be Muhammad Ali.* New York: Harper & Row, 1978.

Logan, Rayford W. *The Betrayal of the Negro: From Rutherford B. Hayes to Woodrow Wilson.* New York: Collier, 1965.

Lomax, Louis E. *The Negro Revolt.* New York: Harper & Row, 1962.

Lord, Walter. *The Past That Would Not Die.* New York: Harper and Row, 1965.

M is for Mississippi and Murder. New York: NAACP, 1955.

Manchester, William. *The Glory and the Dream: A Narrative History of America, 1932–1972.* Boston: Little, Brown, 1974.

Mars, Florence, with Lynn Eden. *Witness in Philadelphia.* Baton Rouge: Louisiana State University Press, 1977.

Mast, Gerald. *The Movies in Our Midst.* Chicago: University of Chicago Press, 1982.

McGovern, James R. *Anatomy of a Lynching: The Killing of Claude Neal.* Baton Rouge: Louisiana State University Press, 1982.

McMillen, Neil R. *The Citizens' Council: Organized Resistance to the Second Reconstruction, 1954–64.* Urbana: University of Illinois Press, 1971.

Meredith, James. *Three Years in Mississippi.* Bloomington: Indiana University Press, 1966.

Moody, Anne. *Coming of Age in Mississippi.* New York: Dell, 1968.

Morris, Aldon. *The Origins of the Civil Rights Movement: Black Communities Organizing for Change.* New York: Free Press, 1984.

Morris, Willie. *North Toward Home.* Boston: Houghton Mifflin, 1967.

———. *Terrains of the Heart and Other Essays on Home.* Oxford, Miss.: Yoknapatawpha Press, 1981.

Morrison, Toni. *Song of Solomon.* New York: Knopf, 1977.

Morrow, E. Frederic. *Black Man in the White House: A Diary of the Eisenhower Years.* New York: Coward-McCann, 1963.

Murray, Pauli. "The Liberation of Black Women." In *Voices of the New Feminism,* edited by Mary Lou Thompson, 87–102. Boston: Beacon, 1970.

Muse, Benjamin. *Ten Years of Prelude: The Story of Integration Since the Supreme Court's 1954 Decision.* New York: Viking, 1964.

Myrdal, Gunnar. *An American Dilemma: The Negro Problem and Modern Democracy.* New York: Harper & Brothers, 1944.

Nash, George H. *The Conservative Intellectual Movement in America: Since 1945.* New York: Basic Books, 1976.

Navasky, Victor S. *Kennedy Justice*. New York: Atheneum, 1971.

Newby, I. A. *Jim Crow's Defense: Anti-Negro Thought in America, 1900–1930*. Baton Rouge: Louisiana State University Press, 1965.

Newfield, Jack. *A Prophetic Minority*. New York: Signet, 1967.

Page, Thomas Nelson. *The Negro: The Southerner's Problem*. New York: Charles Scribner's Sons, 1904. New York: Johnson Reprint, 1970.

Palmer, Robert. *Deep Blues*. New York: Penguin, 1982.

Parmet, Herbert. *Eisenhower and the American Crusades*. New York: Macmillan, 1972.

Peavy, Charles D. *Go Slow Now: Faulkner and the Race Question*. Eugene: University of Oregon Books, 1971.

Percy, William Alexander. *Lanterns on the Levee: Recollections of a Planter's Son*. Baton Rouge: Louisiana State University Press, 1973.

Peters, William. *The Southern Temper*. Garden City, N.Y.: Doubleday, 1959.

Powers, Richard Gid. *Secrecy and Power: The Life of J. Edgar Hoover*. New York: Free Press, 1987.

Raines, Howell. *My Soul is Rested: Movement Days in the Deep South Remembered*. New York: Bantam, 1978.

Reed, John Shelton. *The Enduring South: Subcultural Persistence in Mass Society*. Chapel Hill: University of North Carolina Press, 1974.

Reston, James, Jr. *The Innocence of Joan Little: A Southern Mystery*. New York: Times Books, 1977.

Rose, Arnold. "The American Negro Problem in the Context of Social Change." In *Roots of Rebellion: The Evolution of Black Politics and Protest Since World War II*, edited by Richard P. Young, 47–68. New York: Harper & Row, 1970.

Rose, Willie Lee. "Race and Region in American Historical Fiction: Four Episodes in Popular Culture." In *Region, Race, and Reconstruction: Essays in Honor of C. Vann Woodward*, edited by J. Morgan Kousser and James M. McPherson, 113–139. New York: Oxford University Press, 1982.

Rosengarten, Theodore. *All God's Dangers: The Life of Nate Shaw*. New York: Knopf, 1974.

Rowan, Carl T. *Go South to Sorrow*. New York: Random House, 1957.

Russell, Bertrand. *Bertrand Russell's America, 1945–1970*. Edited by Barry Feinberg and Ronald Kasrils. Boston: South End Press, 1983.

Schlesinger, Arthur M., Jr. *Robert Kennedy and His Times*. Boston: Houghton Mifflin, 1978.

Sellers, Cleveland, with Robert Terrell. *The River of No Return.* New York: William Morrow, 1973.

Sewell, George A., and Margaret L. Dwight. *Mississippi Black History Makers.* Jackson: University Press of Mississippi, 1984.

Shapiro, Herbert. *White Violence and Black Response: From Reconstruction to Montgomery.* Amherst: University of Massachusetts Press, 1988.

Sherrill, Robert. *Gothic Politics in the Deep South: Stars of the New Confederacy.* New York: Ballantine, 1969.

Silver, James W. *Mississippi: The Closed Society.* New York: Harcourt, Brace, & World, 1966.

———. *Running Scared: Silver in Mississippi.* Jackson: University Press of Mississippi, 1984.

Simpson, William M. "Reflections on a Murder: The Emmett Till Case." In *Southern Miscellany: Essays in Honor of Glover Moore,* edited by Frank Allen Dennis, 177–200. Jackson: University Press of Mississippi, 1981.

Sitkoff, Harvard. *The Struggle for Black Equality, 1954–1980.* New York: Hill and Wang, 1981.

Smead, Howard. *Blood Justice: The Lynching of Mack Charles Parker.* New York: Oxford University Press, 1986.

Smith, Lillian. *Killers of the Dream.* Garden City, N.Y.: Doubleday, Anchor, 1963.

Stember, Charles Herbert. *Sexual Racism: The Emotional Barrier to an Integrated Society.* New York: Elsevier, 1976.

Stone, I. F. *The Haunted Fifties.* New York: Vintage, 1969.

Thayer, George. *The Farther Shores of Politics.* New York: Simon and Schuster, 1967.

Thelwell, Mike. "Bright an' Mownin' Star" and "Fish are Jumping an' the Cotton is High: Notes from the Mississippi Delta." In *Black and White in American Culture: An Anthology from The Massachusetts Review,* edited by Jules Chametzky and Sidney Kaplan, 3–16, 37–50. Amherst: University of Massachusetts Press, 1969.

Ungar, Sanford J. *FBI.* Boston: Little, Brown, 1976.

Wakefield, Dan. *Between the Lines: A Reporter's Personal Journey Through Public Events.* New York: New American Library, 1966.

———. *Revolt in the South.* New York: Grove Press, 1960.

Walker, Alice. "Advancing Luna—and Ida B. Wells," in *You Can't Keep A Good Woman Down,* 85–104. San Diego: Harcourt Brace Jovanovich, 1981.

Wallace, Michele. *Black Macho and the Myth of the Superwoman.* New York: Dial, 1979.

Warren, Earl. *The Memoirs of Earl Warren.* Garden City, N.Y.: Doubleday, 1977.

Warren, Robert Penn. *Segregation: The Inner Conflict of the South.* New York: Random House, 1956.

————. *Who Speaks for the Negro?* New York: Random House, 1966.

Weatherby, W. J. *Breaking the Silence.* Harmondsworth, England: Penguin, 1965.

Weber, Marianne. *Max Weber: A Biography.* Translated by Harry Zohn. New York: John Wiley & Sons, 1975.

Westling, Louise. *Sacred Groves and Ravaged Gardens: The Fiction of Eudora Welty, Carson McCullers and Flannery O'Connor.* Athens: University of Georgia Press, 1985.

Whitehead, Don. *The FBI Story: A Report to the People.* New York: Random House, 1956.

Wilkins, Roy, with Tom Mathews. *Standing Fast.* New York: Viking, 1982.

Williams, Daniel T., ed. "The Lynching Records at Tuskegee Institute." In *Eight Negro Bibliographies,* no. 7. New York: Kraus Reprint, 1970.

Williams, Juan. *Eyes on the Prize: America's Civil Rights Years, 1954–1965.* New York: Viking, 1987.

Williamson, Joel. *The Crucible of Race: Black-White Relations in the American South since Emancipation.* New York: Oxford University Press, 1984.

Wilson, Edmund. *Patriotic Gore: Studies in the Literature of the American Civil War.* New York: Oxford University Press, 1966.

Witherspoon, William Roger. *Martin Luther King, Jr.: To the Mountaintop.* Garden City, N.Y.: Doubleday, 1985.

Woodward, C. Vann. *The Strange Career of Jim Crow.* New York: Oxford University Press, 1966.

————. *Thinking Back: The Perils of Writing History.* Baton Rouge: Louisiana State University Press, 1986.

Wright, Richard. *Black Boy.* New York: Harper & Row, 1966.

Zangrando, Robert L. *The NAACP Crusade Against Lynching, 1909–1950.* Philadelphia: Temple University Press, 1980.

Articles

"The Accused." *Newsweek* 46 (September 19, 1955): 38.

Barnard, Harry. Letter to the Editor, *Nation* 181 (September 24, 1955): 252.

"A Boy Goes Home." *Newsweek* 46 (September 12, 1955): 32.

Breed, Warren. "Comparative Newspaper Handling of the Emmett Till Case," *Journalism Quarterly* 35 (Summer 1958):291–298.

Buckley, William F. "William Bradford Huie, RIP," *National Review* 38 (December 19, 1986): 20–21.

"Casting Their 'Eyes.'" *Boston Phoenix*, January 13, 1987, sec. 3, p. 21.

"Chicago Boy." *Nation* 181 (September 17, 1955): 234–235.

"Climate of Fear." *Commonweal* 63 (October 14, 1955): 28–29.

Cohn, David L. "Greenville Filibusters Against Father Time." *New York Times Magazine*, March 20, 1949, pp. 11, 64–65.

Croyden, Margaret. "Toni Morrison Tries Her Hand at Playwriting," *New York Times*, December 29, 1985, sec. 2, pp. 6, 18.

Davidson, Sara. "Foremothers," *Esquire* 80 (July 1973): 71–75 ff.

"Death in Mississippi." *Commonweal* 62 (September 23, 1955): 603–604.

Donald, David Herbert. Review of Richard Aubrey McLemore, ed., *A History of Mississippi*, *American Historical Review* 78 (December 1973): 1523–1525.

"Double Murder in Mississippi." *Christian Century* 72 (October 5, 1955): 1132.

"Down the Memory Hole." *New Republic* 193 (July 1, 1985): 9.

Driver, Tom F. "Barking Off Cue, or Mr. Charlie's Dilemma." *Village Voice*, June 4, 1964, pp. 16–17.

Durr, Virginia Foster. "The Emancipation of Pure, White, Southern Womanhood," *New South* 26 (Winter 1971): 46–54.

Editorials. *The Crisis* 62 (November 1955): 546–547.

"Emmett Till's Day in Court." *Life* 39 (October 3, 1955): 36–38.

Fleming, Harold C. "The Law Gains Ground," *New South* 6 (January 1951): 4–5, 8.

Giles, William L. "The Agricultural Revolution in the Delta," *Journal of Mississippi History* 31 (May 1969), 79–88.

Glazer, Nathan. "The Fire This Time," *New Republic* 193 (December 30, 1985): 42–44.

Hackney, Sheldon. "Southern Violence," *American Historical Review* 74 (February 1969): 906–925.

Halberstam, David. "Tallahatchie County Acquits a Peckerwood," *Reporter* 14 (April 19, 1956): 906–925.

Holland, Endesha Ida Mae. "Memories of the Mississippi Delta," *Michigan Quarterly Review* 26 (Winter 1987): 246–258.

Huie, William Bradford. "The Shocking Story of Approved Killing in Mississippi." *Look* 20 (January 24, 1956): 46–49, and in *Reader's Digest* 68 (April 1956): 57–62.

———. "What's Happened to the Emmett Till Killers?" *Look* 21 (January 22, 1957): 63–68.

"Ill-Chosen Symbol." *Time* 66 (November 21, 1955): 21.

"In Memoriam, Emmett Till." *Life* 39 (October 10, 1955): 48.

Ladner, Joyce. "The South: Old-New Land." *New York Times*, May 17, 1979, p. 23.

"L'affaire Till in the French Press." *The Crisis* 62 (December 1955): 596–601.

Larsson, Cloyte Murdock. "Land of the Till Murder Revisited," *Ebony* 41 (March 1986): 53–58.

Letters to the Editor. *Life* 39 (October 31, 1955): 17–18.

Letters to the Editor. *Look* 20 (March 6, 1956): 112.

Miller, Charles, ed. "The Mississippi Summer Project Remembered: The Stephen Mitchell Bingham Letter," *Journal of Mississippi History* 47 (November 1985): 284–307.

"Mississippi Barbarism." *The Crisis* 62 (October 1955): 480–481.

"Nation Horrified by Murder of Kidnaped Chicago Youth." *Jet* 8 (September 15, 1955): 6–9.

"No Remedy in Law." *New Republic* 133 (November 21, 1955): 5.

Parsons, Malcolm B. "Violence and Caste in Southern Justice," *South Atlantic Quarterly* 60 (Autumn 1961): 455–468.

"The Place of Acquittal." *Newsweek* 46 (October 3, 1955): 24, 29–30.

Robinson, Harlow. "Dreams of a Prophetic Past," *American Theatre* 2 (January 1986): 17–19.

Shostak, David A. "Crosby Smith: Forgotten Witness to a Mississippi Nightmare," *Negro History Bulletin* 38 (December 1974): 320–325.

Stafford, Jean. "Brownmiller on Rape: A Scare Worse than Death," *Esquire* 84 (November 1975): 50–52.

Steele, Shelby. "On Being Black and Middle Class," *Commentary* 85 (January 1988): 42–47.

"The Till Case." *New South* 10 (September 1955): 1.

"Till Protest Meeting." *The Crisis* 62 (November 1955): 546–547.

"Trial by Jury." *Time* 66 (October 3, 1955): 18.

Ward, Bob. "William Bradford Huie Paid for Their Sins," *Writer's Digest* 54 (September 1974): 16–17.

Waring, Thomas, C. P. Liter, Frederick Sullens, et al. "Interviews with Southern Editors: Race Trouble to Grow in South: No Mixed Schools Yet." *U.S. News & World Report* 40 (February 24, 1956): 44–50, 134–144.

"Why the South Must Prevail." *National Review* 4 (August 24, 1957): 148–149.

Wiener, Jonathan. "The 'Black Beast Rapist': White Attitudes in the Postwar South," *Reviews in American History* 13 (June 1985): 222–226.

"Will Mississippi Whitewash the Emmett Till Slaying?" *Jet* 8 (September 22, 1955): 8–11.

Unpublished Sources

"Covering the South: A National Symposium on the Media and the Civil Rights Movement." University of Mississippi, April 3–5, 1987 (telecast on C-Span).

Hampton, Henry (executive producer). *Eyes on the Prize: America's Civil Rights Years*. Episode 1: "Awakenings (1954–56)." New York: PBS Video, 1986.

Huie, William Bradford. Papers. In possession of Martha Hunt Huie, Memphis, Tenn.

King, Martin Luther, Jr. Papers. Mugar Library, Boston University.

Race Relations Collection. John Davis Williams Library, University of Mississippi.

"Strengthen Justice Department's Civil Rights Powers." October 22, 1955, press release. Archives of the American Jewish Committee.

"Survey of Public Opinion in France, Italy, Belgium, Switzerland, Germany, Tunisia on the Emmett Till Case." October 1955. Archives of the American Jewish Committee.

Whitaker, Hugh Stephen. "A Case Study in Southern Justice: The Emmett Till Case." Master's thesis, Florida State University, 1963.

Newspapers

Birmingham News	*Jackson Advocate*
Charleston Mississippi Sun	*Jackson Clarion-Ledger*
Chicago Defender	*Jackson Daily News*
Greenville Delta Democrat-Times	*Memphis Commercial Appeal*
Greenwood Commonwealth	*New York Times*
Huntsville Times	*Washington Afro-American*

Index

DEMCO